The WTO and the Environment

This book is a review of the development of the WTO dispute resolution procedure and the power and influence it has gained over the practices of the member countries and in relation to international treaties. The book addresses the development of environmental competency in the WTO and examines the arguments of those who oppose WTO rule making with impacts on the environment. The WTO's interactions with multilateral environmental agreements are considered and recent WTO cases including the 2011 US/Mexico tuna dispute and the US sea turtles decision are analysed in detail. In examining how an international organisation which was established with a specific purpose in mind has come to interact in fields beyond its original remit, James Watson demonstrates how the dispute resolution system at the WTO has come to work in a judicialised manner, operating with an informal system of precedent. This has led to the contracting parties placing more reliance on the decisions of the dispute panels and appeal body when considering policy options, with WTO rulings increasingly influencing the behaviour of national legislatures in regard to the environment.

The book goes on to make concrete recommendations, based on existing practice in the WTO dispute resolution procedure, which could enhance decision making in environmental cases heard by the WTO. The book argues that this could be achieved with straightforward amendments to the WTO, based on existing practices endorsed under the WTO for other policy considerations. *The WTO and the Environment* will be of particular interest to academics and students of International and Environmental law.

James K.R. Watson has been researching the international trade and environment subject for more than 15 years. Currently working in Brussels at Weber Shandwick on policy development, he previously worked for the Commonwealth Secretariat on a European Commission-funded trade policy project based in Ethiopia. He has completed an LL.M in Environmental Law and a PhD on international trade and environmental law.

Routledge Research in International Economic Law

Available:

Recognition and Regulation of Safeguard Measures Under GATT/WTO
Sheela Rai

The Interaction between WTO Law and External International Law
The Constrained Openness of WTO Law
Ronnie R.F. Yearwood

Human Rights, Natural Resource and Investment Law in a Globalised World
Shades of Grey in the Shadow of the Law
Lorenzo Cotula

The Domestic Politics of Negotiating International Trade
Intellectual Property Rights in US-Colombia and US-Peru Free Trade Agreements
Johanna von Braun

Foreign Investment and Dispute Resolution Law and Practice in Asia
Vivienne Bath and Luke Nottage (eds.)

Improving International Investment Agreements
Armand De Mestral and Céline Lévesque (eds.)

Public Health in International Investment Law and Arbitration
Valentina Vadi

The WTO and the Environment
Development of Competence beyond Trade
James Watson

Forthcoming:

Trade Remedies
A Development Perspective
Asif Qureshi

The WTO and the Environment

Development of competence beyond trade

James K.R. Watson

Routledge
Taylor & Francis Group
LONDON AND NEW YORK

First published 2013
by Routledge
2 Park Square, Milton Park, Abingdon, Oxon OX14 4RN

Simultaneously published in the USA and Canada
by Routledge
711 Third Avenue, New York, NY 10017

Routledge is an imprint of the Taylor & Francis Group, an informa business

British Library Cataloguing in Publication Data
A catalogue record for this book is available from the British Library

Library of Congress Cataloguing in Publication Data
Watson, James K. R.
The WTO and the environment : development of competence beyond trade / James K.R. Watson.
p. cm.
ISBN 978-0-415-52712-5 (hardback) – ISBN 978-0-203-09552-2 (e-book)
1. Environmental law, International. 2. World Trade Organization–Rules and practice. 3. Foreign trade regulation. 4. Dispute resolution (Law) 5. Environmental policy–International cooperation. I. Title.
K3585.W38 2012
382'.92–dc23 2012011729

ISBN 978-0-415-52712-5 (hbk)
ISBN 978-0-203-09552-2 (ebk)

Typeset in Garamond
by Cenveo Publisher Services

MIX
Paper from responsible sources
FSC www.fsc.org FSC® C004839

Printed and bound by CPI Group (UK) Ltd, Croydon, CR0 4YY

Contents

Acknowledgements

The work contained in this book represents years of research and effort, but it was not all the author's alone. It is therefore my pleasure to offer my great thanks to Professor Surya Subedi OBE, for all the support and encouragement he has provided since 2001 when we first met. It has only been possible to complete this work with his ongoing assistance and consideration. Thank you Surya for everything you have done in the past 10 years.

I dedicate this book to my parents, Dr. Michael and Margaret Watson. It would not have been possible to complete this without their time and effort. Thank you both for your ongoing encouragement, support and interest in my work. I hope that you both enjoy and appreciate the book; it is a reflection of the long discussions we have had on numerous occasions around the family table! I must also thank the rest of my family for all their support and help over the past years. Special thanks also go to Peter Hartley and his wife Linda for their generosity, kindness and interest in my work.

And to all those people who have helped me but are not named directly, thank you!

Finally I would like to show my gratitude to Kathrin Eichel, my partner and emotional safety net, for all her patience and care. This book is for you; thank you for your support.

Foreword

It is a great pleasure and an honour for me to write a few words about this intellectually stimulating book written by Dr James Watson. This book emanates from the doctoral thesis that he wrote at the University of Leeds, and I had the privilege of supervising his research.

The interaction of trade with the environment has been an area of much consideration and discussion, and the relevance of this debate has never been more salient than it is now. The relationship between global trade and environmental protection is well established, although the international legal links between the two areas can still be considered to be formative. The international legal frameworks that support the trade and environment spheres are also very different, with the World Trade Organisation (WTO) leading the regulation of international trade and a plethora of treaties addressing environmental issues at the international level with no one institution covering all the relevant environmental treaties.

This book explores the dichotomy between international trade and international environmental law and the impact this has had on the development of the legal regimes addressing both fields. The more fragmented approach under international environmental law has created certain issues in relation to effective enforcement. To the extent that the concern of many commentators has been that environmental protection enacted at the international level has been in some way subordinated to the global regulation of trade through the WTO. The fact that there is no one global environmental body dealing with all the various international environmental treaties has to a certain extent supported the interpretation of the international legal system as favouring economic concerns, given the success of the dispute resolution system of the WTO to influence national policies.

The current global situation, in terms of economic struggle and lack of serious progress in important environmental protection negotiations such as the United Nations Framework Convention on Climate Change, also feeds the view that there is a subordination of environmental rules to economic ones. This book reviews the current state of the relationship between trade and the environment and the international legal system as it stands through analysing the practice of the WTO in relation to environmental protection – primarily through an assessment of the activities of the dispute settlement system. The context of the development of the global trading system has been so different to the growth in international environmental law and the numerous treaties that cover them. This of course has implications in terms of the way states approach the two fields, but the relationship between trade and the environment is complex and requires analysis at the interface of the systems governing their administration.

The development of international trade law through the creation and operation of the WTO has led to the implementation of a robust dispute settlement system to referee the global trading regimes of 153 countries. There has been little in comparative terms in the international environmental field to match the development of the WTO covering all aspects of global environmental governance. Greater efforts in global environmental legal governance could be one way of reviewing the perceived imbalance, but there are other possibilities. In this book the practicalities of the possibilities of setting up a Global Environmental Organisation (GEO) are examined, as this has been a constant call from concerned environmentalists over the past decade and more. The questions surrounding the creation of a GEO have yet to be answered fully and indeed in the current global economic crisis, where countries are even considering reducing their contributions to the UN, the opportunity for creating a GEO seems hampered. It is thus important that practical solutions are found to enhance environmental protection in the current global legal context.

The WTO has been playing a role in international environmental law making through its dispute resolution system, since the days of the GATT. Famously the *US-Mexico Tuna Dolphin* cases in the 1990s caused headlines and stirred anti-GATT/WTO sentiment from environmental groups. Questions were raised about the suitability of the GATT/WTO system as the right forum to assess issues with environmental aspects. This situation is still the case today, as numerous trade–environment cases have come before the WTO dispute resolution panels in the last few years. Some of these cases are now infamous – such as the *US-Mexico Tuna Dolphin* dispute, which re-emerged in 2011 with another challenge from Mexico to the labelling practices of the US. This case is now subject to appeal from both parties, as Mexico contests some of the findings in terms of the discriminatory nature of the labelling. This demonstrates that finding the right balance between economic development and environmental protection will always be a challenge in the current global context, it is important to note that this could be the case in any dispute resolution forum.

Reviewing these WTO cases and the procedure applied by the WTO dispute resolution panelists and the appellate body can support an understanding of the reasoning in the law-making process at the interface of trade and environmental concerns at the WTO. As this is the forum where these decisions are taking place at the present time it is important to understand what drives the decision making. These decisions are crucial to understanding why environmentalists feel that the interests of trade are overpowering those of environmental protection; however, it is also clear that the reasoning shows proper legal consideration for the laws as they stand. The question then that should be considered is what can be done now to support improved environmental decision making when consideration is undertaken through the WTO dispute resolution system.

The competence of the WTO in the environmental field is open to interpretation. With the Committee on Trade and Environment (CTE) and the reference to sustainable development in the preamble of the WTO it is clear that the WTO members recognize the need to reconcile environmental protection with trade policy. The work of the CTE has been fitful to date and the drive for finding agreements on trade in environmental goods remains unfulfilled. There are opportunities for the WTO through the CTE to show real commitment to the trade–environmental protection paradigm, but action has not always followed the words of the WTO Secretariat – although we should recognize that much depends on the will of the contracting parties.

Nevertheless, the practice of the WTO in other areas can shed some light on the potential for how it could approach the environment. Practice exists in relation to dispute resolution procedures, for example when developing countries are involved, that show the WTO system does not operate a 'one size fits all' approach. Learning from these examples can improve the practices of the WTO in dispute resolution around environmental protection issues. This book makes recommendations that are possible and practical in the current global context.

The trade and environment debate is a crucial one for the present generation of international law and policy makers. The decisions that are made today will impact the world of the future and the environment in which future generations will live, both economically and environmentally. The work contained herein builds on the work that has gone before and now focuses on what can be achieved going forward, to best support the objectives of sustainable development through the international trade and environment legal systems.

I am pleased that Dr Watson has produced a highly commendable book on such a challenging area of international trade law and its interaction with international environmental law. He has made a major contribution to the body of knowledge on the subject and provided a great deal of food for thought for policy and decision makers. I would like to congratulate him most warmly on the publication of this book which I can happily recommend to researchers and students of international law of trade and environment as well as to those interested in issues of global governance.

Professor Surya P. Subedi, O.B.E.
DPhil (Oxford); Barrister (Middle Temple)
Professor of International Law
University of Leeds, United Kingdom
Leeds, March 2012

Table of Cases

GATT Disputes

WTO Disputes

International Court of Justice Cases

European Court of Justice Cases

United Kingdom Cases

Table of GATT Agreements, WTO Agreements and Other International Treaties

World Trade Organisation Instruments

GATT Instruments

United Nations Instruments

Regional Instruments

National Statutes

Table of Abbreviations

AB	Appellate Body
AIA	Advanced Informed Agreement
ASEAN	Association of South East Asian Nations
CBD	Convention on Biological Diversity
CCJ	COMESA Court of Justice
CITES	Convention on International Trade in Endangered Species
COMESA	Common Market for Eastern and Southern Africa
COP	Conference of the Parties
CPB	Cartagena Protocol on Biosafety
CRTA	Committee on Regional Trade Agreements
CTBT	Technical Barriers to Trade Committee
CTE	Committee on Trade and Environment
CTESS	Committee on Trade and Environment Special Sessions
DDA	Doha development agenda
DEFRA	UK Department for Environment, Food and Rural Affairs
DSB	Dispute Settlement Body
DSM	Dispute Settlement Mechanism
DSU	Understanding on rules and procedures governing the settlement of disputes (Dispute Settlement Understanding)
EC	The European Community
ECJ	The European Court of Justice
EFTA	European Free Trade Association
EGS	environmental goods and services
EKC	Environmental Kuznets Curve
EMIT	Group on Environmental Measures and International Trade
ENGO	environmental non governmental organisations
ETS	The European Union Emissions Trading System
EU	The European Union
FoE	Friends of the Earth
GATS	General Agreement on Trade in Services
GATT	General Agreement on Tariffs and Trade
GEO	Global Environmental Organisation
GMO	genetically modified organisms

ICJ	The International Court of Justice
ICTSD	International Centre for Trade and Sustainable Development
IIASA	International Institute for Applied Systems Analysis
IISD	International Institute for Sustainable Development
IMF	International Monetary Fund
INECE	International Network for Environmental Compliance and Enforcement
ITC	International Trade Centre
ITO	International Trade Organisation
LDC	least developed country
LMO	living modified organisms
MEA	Multilateral Environmental Agreement
MEP	Member of the European Parliament
MFN	Most Favoured Nation
MoP	Meeting of the Parties
NAAEC	North American Agreement for Environmental Cooperation
NAFTA	North American Free Trade Agreement
NGO	non governmental organisation
PCWTO	Preparatory Committee of the World Trade Organisation
NSA	Non State Actors
OECD	Organization for Economic Co-operation and Development
PCA	Permanent Court of Arbitration
npr PPMs	non-product-related processes and production methods
PICT	Project on International Courts and Tribunals
PPM	process and production methods
SCM	Agreement on Subsidies and Countervailing Measures
SPS	Sanitary and Phyto-Sanitary Agreement
STO	specific trade obligations
TBT	Technical Barriers to Trade
TED	turtle excluding device
TREM	Trade Related Environmental Measures
TRIPS	Trade Related Intellectual Property Rights Agreement
UN	United Nations
UNCED	United Nations Conference on Environment and Development
UNCLOS	United Nations Convention on the Law of the Sea
UNEP	United Nations Environment Programme
UNESCAP	United Nations Economic and Social Commission for Asia and the Pacific
UNFCCC	United Nations Framework Convention on Climate Change
USAID	United States Agency for International Development
USDA	United States Department of Agriculture
WHO	World Health Organisation
WSSD	World Summit on Sustainable Development
WTO	World Trade Organisation
WWF	Worldwide Fund for Nature

Introduction

The World Trade Organisation (WTO) was formed by contracting party decision in 1995, following years of discussion under the Uruguay Round of General Agreement on Tariffs and Trade (GATT) negotiations. The WTO formalised many of the practices of the GATT and ushered in a new era of international trade regulation by setting up an institutional body to oversee the GATT and its associated agreements. The WTO agreements included an Understanding on Rules and Procedures Governing the Settlement of Disputes, with the intention of formalising the practice of the GATT on resolving complaints arising from the contracting parties. This was seen as a major success at the time and the importance of this Agreement is now better understood – some 15 years after it came into existence.[1] Prior to the WTO, the GATT dispute resolution system had already gained experience of dealing with trade-related issues impacting on policies not limited to purely trade matters.[2] The WTO has continued this work, and with its enhanced dispute procedures the issues around the inter-relationship between trade and other policy areas has also been closely scrutinised.[3]

One area has been of particular interest to commentators, and that is the relationship between the rules of the WTO and the environment, particularly

1 See R. Read, 'Trade Dispute Settlement Mechanisms: the WTO Dispute Settlement Understanding in the Wake of the GATT', Lancaster University Management School Working Paper, 2005/012, 2005.

2 See D.C. Esty, *Greening the GATT: Trade, Environment and the Future*, Institute for International Economics, Washington, DC, 1994.

3 See, inter alia, E. Neumayer, 'The WTO and the Environment: Its Past Record is Better than Critics Believe, but the Future Outlook is Bleak', *Global Environmental Politics*, Vol. 4, No. 3, August 2004; C. Tisdell & R.K. Sen, *Economic Globalisation: Social Conflicts, Labour and Environmental Issues*, Edward Elgar Publishing, Cheltenham, 2004; and S.P. Subedi, 'The Road from Doha: The Issues for the Development Round of the WTO and the Future of International Trade', *ICLQ*, Vol. 52, No. 2, April 2003.

through the workings of the dispute resolution system (DSU) of the WTO.[4] Much of the attention of these commentators has been polarised between two groups of thought: one claiming that the WTO has been harmful to international and national environmental laws, and the other stating that no harm has been done to the environment through the workings of the WTO, while on the other hand going on to suggest that the global trading system is beneficial for the environment.[5] The former group seeks solutions to the problems they perceive and often call for international institutions to be established to protect the environment, whilst the latter tends to believe that such action is unwarranted.

The purpose of this study is to not only add to the well of knowledge in the debate on the role played by the WTO in the environmental field, but to suggest ways forward for the debate in the current global situation of the early 21st century. In this respect this study will look to offer achievable solutions for the international community to consider while addressing the conundrum that is the interaction between international trade and environmental law. Practical solutions are of great value at the present time when there has been so much stagnation in international trade talks and the economic crisis has had an impact on the finances of states and their ability to commit to international institutions. This study aims to suggest pragmatic solutions with regard to the interaction between the WTO and the environment.

This area has been reviewed by leading scholars, but there is a need for further research and analysis on this topic, especially when all avenues appear not to have been explored in terms of offering suggestions for enhancing the trade–environment relationship at an international level. The exploration or identification of new approaches to the debate will support the development of the discussion at an international level and could lead to new ways of addressing existing problems. The relevance of the issue is felt not just at the level of academic debate, but also throughout society on a global basis.

A recent survey of countries across the world has demonstrated that the public in developed and developing countries see it as important that environmental and labour standards are protected within the global

4 See F. MacMillan, *WTO and the Environment*, Sweet & Maxwell, London, 2001; J. Wiers, *Trade and Environment in the EC and WTO: a Legal Analysis*, Europa Law Publishing, Amsterdam, 2002; and G.P. Sampson & J. Whalley, *The WTO, Trade and the Environment*, Edward Elgar Publishing Ltd., Cheltenham, 2005.

5 The school of thought related to the protection of the environment from abuses under the WTO includes scholars such as D.C. Esty and F. MacMillan, but also non-governmental organisations (NGOs) such as Friends of the Earth and Greenpeace. The pro-WTO trade school includes scholars such as J. Bhagwati and J.H. Jackson.

trade arena.[6] A specific study on whether international trade is good or bad for the environment found that 45 per cent of Americans, 57 per cent of the Chinese and 29 per cent of the French considered that international trade was good for the environment. Conversely 49 per cent of Americans, 29 per cent of the Chinese and 66 per cent of the French considered international trade to be bad for the environment.[7] This shows that perceptions of trade and the environment vary globally, but that many populations in developed countries perceive international trade as a danger for environmental protection. This is not reflected in developing countries' responses. Therefore it is clear that the issues around trade and environment remain – and will be for the future – of great global significance.

The fact remains that the debate on trade and environment around the WTO is not black and white, as most commentators would agree. There are many shades of grey that can be analysed to offer solutions to the question of where the competence of the WTO ends and how environmental protection can be achieved at the same time as pursuing the global trade agenda. It is these shades of grey that require attention and where in fact genuine solutions may lie. An exploration of some of these 'grey' alternatives will form the intellectual guidance for this study, as well as an analysis of the reality of realising any potential suggestions for means to improve the interaction between the global trade agenda and the need for environmental protection.

To elaborate on the perceived problem it is important to note that the global trade agenda and environmental protection principles have long histories in the social and cultural activities of intellectuals and philosophers dating back hundreds of years.[8] The study here outlined considers the issues in their contemporary state at the beginning of the 21st century. The past few decades have seen an enormous growth in the interest of humanity's impact on the environment, whilst at the same time the rules of international trade have been growing more complex as more is understood of the inter-relationships

6 See 'International Publics Strongly Favor Labor and Environmental Standards in Trade Agreements', 21 March 2007, World Public Opinion.Org website, http://www.worldpublicopinion.org/pipa/articles/btglobalizationtradera/334.php?nid=&id=&pnt=334&lb=btgl (accessed 24 January 2010). The survey shows that a high number of respondents from, inter alia, the USA (91%), China (85%), India (60%), Thailand (69%), Argentina (90%) and Poland (90%) believe that the members of international trade agreements should maintain minimum levels of environmental protection standards.

7 See 'World Public Favors Globalization and Trade but Wants to Protect Environment and Jobs', 25 April 2007, World Public Opinion.Org website, http://www.worldpublicopinion.org/pipa/articles/btglobalizationtradera/349.php?lb=btgl&pnt=349&nid=&id (accessed 24 January 2010).

8 See H. Ritvo, 'Fighting for Thirlmere – The Root of Environmentalism', *Science Magazine*, Vol. 300, No. 5625, 6 June 2003; J.B. Flippen, 'A Fresh Perspective on the Roots of Environmentalism', *Reviews in American History*, Vol. 35, No. 1, Johns Hopkins Press, 1 March 2007; G.F. LaFreniere, 'Rousseau and the European Roots of Environmentalism', *Environmental History Review*, Vol. 14, No. 4, 1990.

between trade and other policy areas.[9] The coming together of these two phenomena has generated an issue of our time: can we have economic growth whilst protecting the environment and ecosystems of the world? The WTO is essentially dedicated to the preservation and furtherance of free trade principles, but pays respect to the principles of sustainable development.[10]

The concept of sustainable development is now well established in the international legal and policy order and it is important to be clear on what is meant by this term. Although the WTO does not offer a definition of sustainable development, the term needs explanation and for the purposes of this work the approach used is that as defined in Our Common Future – the Brundtland Report:

> Sustainable development is development that meets the needs of the present without compromising the ability of future generations to meet their own needs. It contains within it two key concepts:
>
> - the concept of needs, in particular the essential needs of the world's poor, to which overriding priority should be given; and
> - the idea of limitations imposed by the state of technology and social organization on the environment's ability to meet present and future needs.[11]

Essentially the concept sees the inter-relation of decisions made today with impacts beyond the immediate time frame and also across geographic boundaries. This is a systems approach to global development, where a decision taken in one place and time has consequences, foreseen and unforeseen, in other areas. Hence trade policy decisions can have an impact on environmental protection policies now and in the future, and vice versa.

Protection of the global environment is seen as necessary for the preservation of humanity in the future, and for future generations' well-being. Reconciling these two interests can seem challenging when certain countries value economic development more than others who have perhaps advanced along the economic development continuum and have now put more of a value on the protection of the natural environment.[12]

Given this global situation it is, with reflection, no surprise that the debate on the interaction of the WTO with environmental policy through its

9 See R. Carson, *Silent Spring*, 40th Anniversary Edition, Mariner Books, New York, 2002, as the first recognised book relating to the new environmentalism of the late 20th century.

10 The preamble to the Marrakesh Agreement Establishing the World Trade Organization contains a reference to using the world's resources in accordance with the principles of sustainable development. See http://www.wto.org/english/res_e/booksp_e/analytic_index_e/wto_agree_01_e.htm (accessed 24 January 2010).

11 World Commission on Environment and Development (WCED), *Our Common Future*, Oxford University Press, Oxford, 1987, p. 43.

12 See the findings in the two polls mentioned in op. cit. 6 and 7.

dispute settlement activities creates a split between different and vocal schools of thought. The pro-environmental protection school (referred to as the environmentalists hereafter) consists of a number of academics, non-governmental organisations (NGOs) and civil society groups from across the globe.[13] The protagonists on the trade furtherance side are not opposed to environmental protection, but see it as a consequence of free market activity and therefore resist any attempts to suggest that there needs to be more regulation of the global trade system to protect the environment.[14]

Some commentators view both environmental protection and free trade as an equally worthy pursuit of global regulation, and it is here that this study fits most comfortably.[15] Whilst protection of the environment is hugely important, the need for a fair and transparent global trading system is equally valuable. These two objectives are not irreconcilable, they are complementary, and the WTO has its role to play in achieving both outcomes. As mentioned, the WTO parties have included reference to sustainable development as one of the guiding principles of the organisation, therefore recognising the role that the WTO can play in achieving both the goals of improved global trade transparency and environmental protection.

Nevertheless, the WTO has become notorious in environmentalist circles as a watchword for injustice and environmental ignorance.[16] Why is this so? One of the main reasons is surely the concerns that have been generated around the activities of the previous GATT and the WTO in relation to trade–environment cases. The *Tuna-Dolphin* case,[17] the *Shrimp-Turtle* case,[18] and perhaps the forthcoming seal product ban case all draw the attention of environmental activists to the workings of the WTO. In these cases the workings of the dispute resolution system of the WTO has been scrutinised by environmentalists in order to determine its suitability for dealing with environmental concerns. Whilst it has been noted here that the WTO has a commitment to sustainable development in its preamble, it does not have any specific mention of the environment in the main articles that relate to dispute resolution nor are there any references to the environment in the DSU. This lack of reference to the environment concerns environmentalists, who feel

13 D. Esty and F. MacMillan, op. cit. 5.

14 ibid.

15 See G.P. Sampson and J. Whalley, op. cit. 4.

16 See Friends of the Earth, 'What's Wrong with World Trade? An Introduction to the Trade and Sustainability Debate', Briefing, London September 2005; see also the World Development Movement website's campaign against the WTO, http://www.wdm.org.uk/wto (accessed 24 January 2010).

17 WTO, *United States – Restrictions on Imports of Tuna*, DS29/R, 1994.

18 WTO, *US – Import Prohibition of Certain Shrimp and Shrimp Products*, Report of the Appellate Body (AB-1998-4), WT/DS58/AB/R, 1998.

that the WTO in its dispute resolutions rides roughshod over environmental protection needs.[19]

So the question arises: is the WTO competent to deal with environmental matters in its dispute resolution system? This is a question of real importance given the new power that the DSU appears to have since the inception of the WTO, which may have ushered in a more legalistic form of dispute resolution. The level of the judicialisation of the dispute system is an important consideration when determining the competence of the WTO to address policy matters that interact with trade. In the context of this study judicialisation is used to refer to the process that has been identified in international dispute resolution in the last 20 years, whereby diplomatic dispute resolution systems relying on negotiation have been replaced with more legalistic systems that behave like courts.[20]

Where there are high levels of judicial behaviour in a legal system it could be argued that more reliance is put on the decisions of these systems by the parties interacting with the dispute settlement systems.[21] If the WTO DSU is found to be more judicialised in its dealings with disputes, it could also be the case that the members will adhere to the decisions more closely and allow the system to influence their policy choices. As each decision under the DSU builds further the jurisprudence of the WTO and its particular dealings with policy areas outside of trade, so the contracting parties may choose to look to the WTO to determine what they can and cannot do. This could be applicable to environmental policy and therefore impact the environmental policies that individual states pursue.

The importance of WTO decisions is also clear if the preceding decisions of the WTO also influence the outcomes of cases currently before the panels and Appellate Body (AB). If the weight of previous decisions is large, the panels and AB may be reluctant to depart from the cases readily. This could mean that each decision adds to the practice of the WTO when dealing with environmental issues. If the decisions are not concluded with sufficient consideration for the impact on international and national environmental laws, the WTO could be accused of endangering not just environmental protection, but also the rights of its contracting parties to determine their own responses to environmental challenges. The combination of a strong judicial system and reliance on panel/AB decisions increases the concerns of

19 Friends of the Earth, op. cit. 15.

20 See A. Mondre et al., Between Law and Politics: The Judicialization of International Dispute Settlement in the Fields of Security, Trade and the Environment, Transtate Working Papers No. 71, 2008; and for a general overview of judicialisation, see M.M. Shapiro & A. Stone Sweet, *On Law, Politics and Judicialization*, Oxford University Press, Oxford, 2002.

21 For a review of the impact of judicial decisions in an international context, see M. Shahabuddeen, Precedent in the World Court, Press Syndicate of the University of Cambridge, Research Centre for International Law, Cambridge, 1997.

environmentalists that the WTO is a danger to environmental protection.[22] But is the WTO really a danger to the environment? Are there safeguards that exist in the WTO and are the decisions that have already been made under the DSU so one-sided in their conclusions? The answers to these questions are complex and require an examination of the practice of the WTO through its DSU, but also require an examination of the general means with which the WTO interacts with the environment.

In examining the relationship between the WTO and the environment this study will set out to determine the extent to which the WTO DSU has created a judicialised system of dispute resolution. The purpose of this is to determine whether the weight of the judgments in environmental disputes is such that the decisions of the WTO could be construed as a challenge for environmental protection. To clearly determine this holding, it is also necessary to examine how the WTO's DSU and its components work to create a body of law. In this sense, do the outcomes of the decisions influence the behaviour of the states? Do they also influence the behaviour of subsequent panellists and AB members? The weight of the decisions is crucial as, if the decisions are generally ignored by contracting parties and if the subsequent panels and ABs ignore the outcomes of previous cases, then it may be that the WTO poses no threat to the environment. It is the answers to these questions that help shape the debate of the WTO and its interaction with environmental policies at both national and international levels.

Therefore, this study begins with an examination of the current status of the WTO dispute resolution system in relation to whether it is judicialised or not. Chapter 2 then compares the WTO to other international dispute resolution systems, to add an extra dimension of argument to determining the status of the panels and the AB in the international legal regime. The subsequent section of the study examines whether the outcomes of cases are in fact relied on by contracting parties and subsequent panels and ABs. Does this also impact on the trade and environment debate, and to what extent? If precedent of a form exists in the practice of the WTO, do the outcomes of cases have extra significance when dealing with controversial subjects such as environmental protection?

Following analysis of the legal nature of the system, the effect of decisions and the impact that they have on contracting parties' behaviour will be explored; this study examines the broader trade and environment debate to further the understanding of the perceived problem of reconciling environmental and trade objectives at both the national and international level.

22 See, for example, J. Bleifuss, 'Taking Care of Business: the World Trade Organization, In These Times', July 1997, Third World Traveler website, http://www.thirdworldtraveler.com/WTO_MAI/WTO_ITT.html (accessed 24 January 2010); and P. Costantini, What's Wrong with the WTO?, November 2001, http://www.speakeasy.org/~peterc/wtow/wto-case.htm (accessed 24 January 2010).

Furthering the understanding of the challenges that are faced both philosophically and practically through the interactions of trade and the environment supports the next sections of the study, which examine the specific nature of the WTO and the key sections of relevance for the environment. The examination of the arguments regarding trade and environment against the backdrop of the understanding of the legal nature of the WTO system supports a thorough examination of the WTO in its interactions with the environment. The arguments that are made by different schools of thought around the trade–environment conflict need to be understood in the context of the legal background of the WTO to truly appreciate the subtleties of the complex relationship.

Having established the basis of the trade and environment debate, the international legal order relating to the environment should also be examined to clarify if the operations of those multilateral environmental agreements' (MEAs') systems could really be threatened by the WTO DSU and its operations. A brief review of the key MEAs with trade components supports an analysis of the relative strength of the WTO in comparison to those MEAs. This can also be used to assess the threat posed by the actions of the WTO in relation to the environment. This is a crucial debate at an international level as it is often reported that the WTO poses a threat to such MEAs. If the WTO is in some way attempting to mitigate the danger of its operations having a negative impact on the MEAs, it is important to consider the real chances of such impacts occurring.[23]

Having reviewed the current situation in the debate around trade and environment, the actual interactions of the WTO will be examined to finally determine whether the WTO has now begun to interact more effectively with environmental concerns. There are three focuses of this study: how the WTO interacts with MEAs, how the WTO has attempted to address environmental concerns, and finally an analysis of the cases that the WTO has determined with trade-related environmental measures. This provides a comprehensive analysis of the nature of the WTO in its dealings with the environment, and assesses whether the WTO has grown to deal with environmental concerns within its operations.

This is the central tenet of the research question: has the WTO evolved through its dispute resolution system operations and the actions of its contracting parties to offer any competence in dealing with trade-related environmental concerns? As secondary and tertiary concerns, further questions will be asked, such as: Can the application of institutional development theory to the WTO demonstrate that over the last 15 years the WTO has adapted to better deal with environmental concerns? Do we still need to find alternatives to the WTO to deal with trade-related environmental

23 R. Eckersley, 'The Big Chill: The WTO and Multilateral Environmental Agreements', *Global Environmental Politics*, Vol. 4, No. 2, May 2004, pp. 24–50.

disputes and challenges? These are the key issues that are addressed within this study.

The questions addressed here remain valid as the WTO and its dispute resolution system continue to be a focus for assessing the interaction of trade-related environmental measures and their legitimacy as seen through the lens of the panels and ABs. Recently the European Union (EU) has discussed a number of environmental policy objectives that have an impact on global trade relations and have therefore raised the interest of the WTO, not least the recent filing of the Canadian complaint at the WTO on the EU's ban on trade in seal products, due to concerns about the methods used to kill seals and the sustainability of the seal cull.[24] The EU, in response to concerns raised by animal welfare organisations, has agreed a law banning the trade in seal products in the EU member states.[25] The Canadians, who are one of the main producers of products containing seal derivatives, have therefore responded by initiating proceedings at the WTO.[26] Therefore, the WTO could be the forum for a trade–environment dispute in the near future. Once again the WTO DSU will be called into action to determine the validity of the trade-related environmental measures.

Likewise the EU recently considered the use of a 'border adjustment mechanism' to protect its industries from unfair external competition when enacting its own emissions trading system law.[27] The USA also has similar plans under its own draft climate legislation.[28] Such suggestions from the EU and the USA have already drawn criticism from emerging economies and developing countries, who would consider WTO action should the USA and the EU take such action.[29] The WTO dispute resolution system would be once again faced with determining the relative value of the systems to protect the environment against their trade-related nature.

The EU emissions trading system is designed to reduce the level of CO_2 emissions from various industrial sectors, to support the EU reduce its CO_2

24 See S. Petitjean, 'Ottawa Lodges Complaint on EU Seal Ban', *Europolitics*, No. 3853, 4 November 2009.

25 EC, Regulation (EC) No. 1007/2009 of the European Parliament and of the Council of 16 September 2009 on Trade in Seal Products, Official Journal of the European Union, L 286/36, 31 October 2009.

26 This was followed quickly by the Norwegians. See 'Seals: Norway Lodges WTO Complaint', 6 November 2009, Europolitics website, http://www.europolitics.info/externa-policies/seals-norway-lodges-wto-complaint-art253771-42.html (accessed 24 January 2010).

27 See 'Carbon Leakage Concerns Dominate EU ETS Debate', 11 September 2008, ENDS Europe website, http://www.endseurope.com/15480 (accessed 24 January 2010).

28 See 'Copenhagen Countdown: Border Carbon Adjustment', *Bridges Weekly Trade News Digest*, Vol. 13, No. 39, 11 November 2009, ICTSD website, http://ictsd.org/i/news/bridgesweekly/59235/ (accessed 24 January 2010).

29 See 'China, India Lash out at Talk of "Carbon Tariffs"', *China Programme*, Vol. 13, No. 25, 8 July 2009, ICTSD website, http://ictsd.org/i/news/bridgesweekly/50301/ (accessed 24 January 2010).

and greenhouse gas emissions in line with the requirements of the United Nations Framework Convention on Climate Change (UNFCCC). The system requires EU-based industries to buy permits for the greenhouse gases they emit. This is not a global system and some EU politicians fear that the system will put EU industries at a competitive disadvantage. The proponents of the border adjustment mechanism recognised that it would be necessary to determine if such a policy option is WTO compatible.[30] This argument continues to be held within the EU today, and it is possible that should the EU pursue this option it may fall to the WTO DSU mechanisms to determine if such a border adjustment tax is acceptable under international trade law. In this situation it is the relationship between climate change and international trade that is under scrutiny. Hence the interaction between trade and environment remains an ongoing and current concern, especially in relation to the operations of the dispute resolution system of the WTO.

Taking this current and vibrant debate on the role of the WTO in relation to international and national environmental legislation, it is clear to see that there remains a degree of controversy in the policy development relating to trade and environment objectives. This study aims to identify solutions to the problem that are practical and realistic in their potential application, bearing in mind the constraints of international law making and the need for political will and capital to see through reforms. The debates that have been taking place at the political, philosophical, legal and academic levels influence the research outlined here and guide the outcomes of the work. Nevertheless, the principle of this study remains firmly to identify international legal solutions that are workable and achievable in the global legal framework, including that of the WTO.

30 See 'Sarkozy Renews Pressure for CO_2 Border Tax', 14 September 2009, EurActiv website, http://www.euractiv.com/en/climate-change/sarkozy-renews-pressure-co2-border-tax/article-185387 (accessed 24 January 2010).

1 The development of a judicialised international trade dispute resolution system at the World Trade Organisation

1.1 Introduction

In the context of this book the starting point for determination of the competence of the World Trade Organisation (WTO) in dealing with environmental matters will be an overview of the nature of the dispute resolution system that the WTO operates. The central tenet of this book depends upon the notion that the legalised nature of the WTO drives contracting parties' policy choices. Therefore, it is first important to determine how legalistic the WTO dispute settlement regime is and the power it has to enforce its decisions. Thus this chapter explores the role of the Dispute Settlement Body (DSB). It also discusses the historical development of dispute resolution within the General Agreement on Tariffs and Trade (GATT) and the WTO, and examines the issues concerning the judicialisation of the WTO dispute resolution process.

The examination of the judicialisation of the WTO's dispute resolution mechanisms is reviewed in relation to the consideration of trade–environment issues in the WTO (this will be reviewed in detail in Chapter 4). The key aspect of this study is to determine how the development of a judicialised dispute resolution system in the WTO impacts on environmental policy at a global level, and to determine whether the WTO has the competence to deal with broad environmental policy issues. This chapter sets the scene for the body of this book, outlining the background against which the development of environmental rulings at the WTO can be examined.

Once the theoretical workings of the DSB processes have been reviewed, this chapter considers the practical implementation of the Dispute Settlement Understanding (DSU) since 1995. This provides an opportunity to look at the likely consequences of the changing workings of the DSB on the judicialisation or otherwise of the WTO dispute resolution process.

This chapter further examines whether the development of the dispute resolution process through the DSU represents a judicialisation of that process. In this sense it has been well argued that judicialisation is implied when certain conditions are met within a process – ostensibly judicialisation can be deemed to be present if GATT/WTO dispute settlement has become a triadic dispute resolution mechanism that has authority over the member states, and if the decisions of that body come to influence the way that members interact with each other.[1] Other conditions should also be seen to be met: there needs to be a judicial power with the authority and power of a triadic dispute resolver within the WTO context;[2] parties to the WTO use the litigation process to settle disputes; dispute resolution is de-politicised; dispute resolution bodies treat their rules as legally enforceable; the dispute resolution body treats its own decisions as precedents; and there is an emergence of a system of compulsory adjudication.[3]

1.2 Definition of judicialisation

As stated above, the term judicialisation can be applied to a dispute resolution procedure that has as its main tenet the presence of binding third party enforcement.[4] Historically, prior to the GATT, this principle had not been present in international trade law. In the international trade regime, judicial power had been initially, and by design, excluded.[5] Judicial power in this context refers to the capacity of the dispute resolver to authoritatively determine the content of the treaty's rules-based structure. In the GATT the use of the dispute settlement procedures led to the development of a new regime, based around panel interpretations.[6]

The term judicialisation can be applied to the development of a dispute system from a basis of there being no judicial process to a rules-based system.[7] As states gained experience of the GATT dispute settlement procedures, and as panels performed their dispute resolution functions, the member states found that a stable case law enhanced legal certainty. The GATT members could therefore afford to view the panels' rule making as a useful, cost-effective guarantor of regime effectiveness. This process has been evidenced in other international arenas.[8] There are now 'islands' of international institutions structured by rules and a well developed dispute resolution system that

1 A. Stone Sweet, *Governing with Judges: Constitutional Politics in Europe*, Oxford University Press, 2000, p. 13.
2 W. Sandholz & A. Stone Sweet, 'Law, Politics and International Governance', in C. Reus-Smit (ed.), *The Politics of International Law*, Cambridge University Press, Cambridge, 2004, pp. 238–71.
3 ibid.
4 D. De Bievre, *Governance in International Trade: Judicialisation and Positive Integration in the WTO*, Max Planck Institute, Bonn, 2004.
5 A. Stone Sweet, op. cit. 1, p. 13.
6 R.E. Hudec, 'The Role of the GATT Secretariat in the Evolution of the WTO Dispute Settlement Procedure', in J. Bhagwati & M.Hirsch, *The Uruguay Round and Beyond: Essays in Honour of Arthur Dunkel*, Springer-Verlag, 1998, pp. 101–20.
7 ibid.
8 See A. Mondre et al., 'Between Law and Politics: The Judicialization of International Dispute Settlement in the Fields of Security', Trade and Environment, TranState Working Papers, No. 71, University of Bremen, 2008.

include among others the EU, the WTO and the International Court of Justice.[9] Nevertheless there remain differing contentions over the extent to which the GATT/WTO dispute resolution system is truly judicialised. In this context judicialised refers to the conversion use of decision making into a more legalistic style.

In the context of the creation of the WTO DSU, the negotiators did not necessarily regard the new WTO system as a court or court-like institution.[10] This is in spite of the fact that the Leutwiler Report prior to the Uruguay Round recommended structural improvements in the GATT, mainly to achieve improved dispute settlement in terms of obligatory adjudication.[11] The arguments for not describing the system as judicial alleviated the fears that may have existed in supporters of a more diplomatic and less rules-based dispute resolution system. In fact, by not overtly stating that the process was judicialised, this approach facilitated the adoption of the Uruguay Round agreement.[12] It is only through the adoption of the Uruguay Round and the DSU that it is possible to argue in favour of judicialisation. Renato Ruggiero, a former Director General of the WTO, commented on the creation of the DSU: 'I suspect that neither governments nor industries have yet appreciated the full scope of the guarantees (creation of the DSU).'[13] This hints at the awareness of the impact the DSU could have. This is in line with the view that a judicialised system has been developed without formal introduction.

1.2.1 Quasi-judicial?

There are many commentators who still see the system as quasi-judicial.[14] Is it not the case that referring to the system as quasi-judicial simply acted as a veil to the fact that the system had the qualities of a judicial body – an

9 A. Stone Sweet, 'Islands of Transnational Governance', in M. Shapiro & A. Stone Sweet, *On Law, Politics and Judicialisation*, Oxford University Press, Oxford, 2002.

10 R.E. Hudec, op. cit. 6.

11 R. Dunkel (ed.), *Trade Policies for a Better Future*, Dordrecht, Nijhoff, 1987.

12 See D.H. Erskine, 'Resolving Trade Disputes, the Mechanisms of GATT/WTO Dispute Resolution', 2 *Santa Clara Journal of International Law* 40, 2004.

13 M. Dobbin, 'The World Trade Battle Heats Up', *Vancouver Sun*, 30 November 1999.

14 See J.L. Kenworthy, 'US Trade Policy and the WTO: The Unravelling of the Seattle Conference and the Future of the WTO', 5 *Georgetown Public Policy Review*, 2000, 104–105; D.C. Esty & D. Geradin, 'Market Access, Competitiveness and Harmonization: Environmental Protection in Regional Trade Agreements', 21 *Harvard Environmental. Law Review*, 1997, 329: this refers to quasi-judicial panels, but to a judicial AB. P. Sands, 'International Environmental Litigation and its Future', 32 *University of Richmond Law Review*, 1999, 1639: here the AB is referred to as quasi-judicial as it developed from the early GATT panel system. However, more recently Sands has stated that the WTO AB is an international court: see P. Sands, 'Good Trade, Bad Trade, Cheap Shrimp', in *Lawless World: America and the Making and Breaking of Global Rules*, Penguin, Allen Lane, 2005, p. 96. This suggests that he has shifted his view so that the WTO DSU is a judicial system.

international court? Ragosta puts an interesting slant on the debate, stating that quasi-judicial means as much as quasi-pregnant![15] Perhaps a useful point of view to explore is that of the people who actually work in the WTO dispute resolution system. Mike Moore, a former Director General at the WTO, described the WTO DSU as part of the growing development of International Courts and tribunals, such as the International Tribunal for the Law of the Sea, various war crime tribunals, and the International Criminal Court.[16] This places the WTO DSU on the same footing as judicial international systems.

Alternatively, Ehlermann concludes that there are pieces of the system that are judicial, but not the system as a whole.[17] This is based on the fact that Appellate Body (AB) decisions have to be adopted by a political organ to have legal effect.[18] A contemporary of Ehlermann, Bacchus stated:

> Whether our work is described as judicial or quasi-judicial and whatever we may be called, we have much to do around our table in Geneva. We have much to do because, among all the international tribunals in the history of the world, the Appellate Body of the WTO is unique in two ways: it has compulsory jurisdiction and its judgements are enforceable.[19]

There is a strong body of opinion that supports the notion that the WTO DSU is a judicial system.[20] The press have also expressed their view that the

15 J.A. Ragosta, 'Unmasking the WTO – Access to the DSB System: Can the WTO DSB Live Up to the Moniker "World Trade Court"?', 31 *Law & Policy in International Business*, 2000, 741–23.

16 WTO, 'M. Moore, Speech opening the Advisory Centre for WTO Law', 5 October 2001, http://www.wto.org/english/news_e/spmm_e/spmm71_e.htm (accessed 29 November 2009).

17 C.D. Ehlermann, 'Six Years on the Bench of the "World Trade Court"', 36(4)*J.W.T.*, 2002, 605–40.

18 C.D. Ehlermann, 'Experience from the Appellate Body', 38 *Texas Journal of International Law*, 2003, 479.

19 J. Bacchus, 'Table Talk: Around the Table of the Appellate Body of the World Trade Organisation', 35 *Vanderbilt Journal of Transnational Law*, 2002, 1021–39.

20 See T. Cottier, 'WTO Dispute Settlement and Multilateral Trade Negotiations: Is there Need for Inter-Round Negotiations?' Paper presented at the 2002 World Trade Forum: Dispute Settlement and Decision Making in the Multilateral Trading System – Current Operation and Options for Reform, 16–17 August 2002, as quoted in C.D. Ehlermann, 'Experience from the Appellate Body', 38 *Texas Journal of International Law*, 2003, 469. Also, P.-M. Dupuy, 'The Danger of Fragmentation or Unification of the International Legal System and the International Court of Justice', 31 *New York University Journal of International Law & Politics*, 1999, 792; and J. Davey, cited in P.C. Reed, 'Process, Compliance and Implementation Issues in WTO Dispute Settlement', American Society of International Law Proceedings, ISSN 0272-5037, 1997, April 9–12, 277–88, p. 278. He considers that the DSU '*is a very strong option toward a juridical approach*'. See also P. Lindsay, 'The Ambiguity of the GATT Article XXI: Subtle Success or Rampant Failure?', 52 *Duke Law Journal*, 2003, 1282; and J. Pauwelyn, 'Public International Law in the WTO System: How Far Can We Go?', 95(3) *A.J.I.L.*, 2001, 552.

DSU has created a 'Supreme Court of World Trade'.[21] A review of the development of the system of dispute resolution through the GATT and the WTO is necessary to determine the extent to which the DSU has created a formal judicialised dispute resolution process (see section 1.3). There follows an examination of the theoretical structures within which the WTO DSU could be placed.

1.2.2 International Law dispute resolution models

Public International Law has tended to divide international dispute settlement into two different camps: *diplomatic* (political) and *legal* (judicial) means to resolve disputes.[22] It is possible to arrange international institutions' dispute settlement processes along a continuum.[23] Sandholz and Stone Sweet have described it thus:

> At one end of the continuum are institutional settings that are relatively informal [sic] these are the diplomatic dispute resolution institutions. These institutions [sic] dispute resolution processes would be characterized with imprecise rules that are not binding on actors, and would have no centralised monitoring or enforcement mechanisms. (This is not to say that these settings lack rules, just that the norms in place are relatively informal and imprecise.) At the other end of the continuum are institutional contexts defined by rules that are highly formal, specific, and authoritative; these have the attributes that people associate with highly developed legal orders. Other institutions would fall between these two extremes.[24]

At one end of this continuum you have the diplomatic tools of negotiation, enquiry, mediation, coercion and conciliation. At the other you have a legal framework characterised by litigation and judicial settlement. It can be argued that the WTO has now become part of the legal end of the continuum, on the basis of the workings of the DSB and the AB.[25] It cannot be denied that the emphasis on negotiated resolution prior to this instigation of the formal dispute resolution process remains somewhat in the domain of the diplomatic system. Nevertheless, in a number of national legal procedures emphasis is being put on negotiation prior to the instigation of formal legal proceedings, for example divorce law in the United Kingdom now expresses

21 M. Hornblower, 'The Battle in Seattle', *Time Magazine*, 29 November 1999.

22 See P. Malanczuk, *Akehurst's Modern Introduction to International Law*, Routledge, London, 1997, 272–305.

23 See W. Sandholz & A. Stone Sweet, op. cit. 2.

24 ibid.

25 E.-U. Petersmann, 'The Dispute Settlement System of the World Trade Organization and the Evolution of the GATT Dispute Settlement System since 1948', *Common Market Law Review*, 1994, 31, 6.

a conciliatory process prior to formal proceedings.[26] Thus, it is not the case that having the option for negotiation excludes a dispute process from being at the legal end of the continuum.

The legal end of the continuum revolves around systems that have compulsory dispute resolution. Two important factors must exist for this to operate: constraining behaviour and the development of a normative system.[27] Constraining behaviour refers to the context in which a dispute is settled – there needs to be a framework and a compulsory system of dispute settlement. In the GATT/WTO context this means that no unilateral measures can be adopted in dispute resolution. Enforcement of dispute resolution in the WTO still relies on the self-help of retaliation, but the automatic right of enforcement in non-compliance has ensured an effective mechanism to change state behaviour.[28] In the context of the GATT/WTO, the development of the normative framework will be reviewed in section 1.3.

To briefly look at the process, it is clear that whilst the GATT gradually built case law, the system was viewed as a conciliatory process rather than one with a neutral adjudication. This is because the founders of GATT had deliberately excluded lawyers from the process.[29] Diplomats rather than jurists operated the system, which implied a conciliatory approach to dispute resolution as opposed to legalistic resolution.[30] Nevertheless, GATT dispute settlements developed GATT law. This is the start of the development of the normative framework. The development of the DSU under the WTO has increased the importance of law making through the provision of compulsory jurisdiction. The legal quality of the decisions has also been improved.[31] The new DSU system forces political actors to engage in the process, and the new procedures strengthen, develop and refine the rules of the system. Therefore, it is possible to say that both a normative framework and constraining behaviour exist in the WTO.

1.2.3 Tomuschat taxonomy of an international judicial body

A useful conclusion to this section is to examine the principles laid down in the influential Tomuschat's taxonomy of an international judicial body.

26 See the UK Family Law Act 1996, Chapter 27, http://www.opsi.gov.uk/acts/acts1996/Ukpga_19960027_en_1 (accessed 29 November 2009).

27 O.J. Lissitzyn, *The International Court of Justice, Its Role in the Maintenance of International Peace and Security*, Carnegie Endowment for International Peace, 1951.

28 R.E. Hudec, 'The New WTO Dispute Settlement Procedure: An Overview of the First Three Years', 8 *Minnesota Journal of Global Trade*, 3, 1999.

29 See W. Sandholz & A. Stone Sweet, op. cit. 2.

30 ibid.

31 T.A. Zimmermann, *Negotiating the Review of the WTO Dispute Settlement Understanding*, Cameron May, London, 2005.

There are four parts to the taxonomy to establish whether an international body is judicialised:

1 Persons vested with adjudicatory functions are working independently.
2 The process must have a legal basis and pre-existing and generally applicable procedural rules that are not under the control of the parties (i.e. have a normative framework).
3 The decision is rendered in the basis of law.
4 The decision is binding.[32]

The WTO meets all of these principles: the panels comprise independent experts; the rules for dispute settlement are laid down in the DSU and are part of treaty law, and are based on developed law; the panel and AB decisions are taken in relation to the rules of the WTO and international law; the decisions are binding and enforceable.

It is therefore the contention of this research that the WTO has a judicial system for dispute settlement. This has developed over time but can be held to meet the general agreed principles necessary to be considered judicial.

1.3 Background to the GATT dispute resolution procedures

Having reviewed the position of the WTO DSU in the context of international legal theoretical frameworks, this section briefly considers the inception and development of the WTO DSU from its roots in the GATT system. Since its inception in 1947 the GATT as a treaty agreement has undergone much change, not least in the formal creation of the WTO and a review of the main principles of the international trading community in 1995.

As the precursor to the WTO, the GATT came into being as a provisional agreement solely involved with international tariff barriers and trade. It was designed to occupy a gap that had been left in the post-war strategy of three pillars of international economic co-operation. It was intended that an International Trade Organisation (ITO) would be part of the new economic world order, alongside the World Bank and the International Monetary Fund (IMF).[33] However, due to diplomatic wrangling no institutional framework was set up, but the GATT treaty was formulated and agreed. The treaty bound signatories to the articles of the agreement aimed at reducing barriers

32 C. Tomuschat, 'International Courts and Tribunals with Regionally Restricted and/or Specialised Jurisdiction', in *Judicial Settlement of International Disputes: International Court of Justice, Other Courts and Tribunals, Arbitration and Conciliation: An International Symposium*, 1987, 397.

33 J. Jackson, *The Jurisprudence of GATT and the WTO*, Cambridge University Press, 2000, p. 18.

to trade and national protectionism. The agreement was later widened to include subsidies and countervailing duties, anti-dumping duties and technical barriers to trade.[34]

Thus, although the post-war community had failed to create the ITO, through the operation of the GATT they had set up a body to tackle the thorny issue of tariff control and international trade. This was also an effective organisation that significantly reduced trade barriers during its operation.[35] The GATT effectively took over the role of the ITO as an organisation (rather than as a treaty, as the name GATT suggests), with principal authority on the legal framework for international trade.[36] With the operation of the GATT, the dispute resolution process came to the fore as the arbiter of disagreements between member states.

1.4 The development of the GATT/WTO dispute settlement procedures

To fully grasp the operation of the WTO DSU, it is important to understand the development of the GATT DSB procedures. The reform of the GATT procedures also lends weight to the fact that member states *can* show the willingness required to change a dispute system in need of reform.

In the GATT Treaty the resolution of disputes is touched on in a number of different Articles. Principally, Article XXII and Article XXIII dealt with the regulations relating to the operation of the DSB[37] – Article XXII provided for informal consultation on any issue relating to the GATT, while Article XXIII outlined the more formal mechanism for dispute resolution. The system operated in tandem – a member invoking Article XXII could also use Article XXIII if necessary. It was even contended that the GATT dispute resolution procedures 'worked better than those of the World Court and many other international dispute resolution procedures'.[38]

This is an interesting proposition given the views of many parties to the workings of the GATT panels. These groups have tended to view the dispute resolution outcomes of the GATT with disdain for their impact on

34 ibid, p. 35.

35 The 1947 Geneva round of negotiations alone resulted in 45,000 tariff concessions affecting $10 billion of trade, about one-fifth of the world's total: see WTO website, http://www.wto.org/english/thewto_e/whatis_e/tif_e/fact4_e.htm (accessed 29 November 2009).

36 D. De Bievre, op. cit. 4, p. 119.

37 WTO, *The Legal Texts: The Results of the Uruguay Round of Multilateral Trade Negotiations*, Cambridge University Press, 2004.

38 D. De Bievre, op. cit. 4, p. 170.

environmental, animal welfare and social issues.[39] Often, such organisations called for the limitation of power of the GATT trade dispute settlement regime.[40] More importantly, it is surprising that the dispute resolution system of GATT was thought of this highly, because the GATT had so many problems in its inception. After all, it was the Treaty around which an ITO was intended to be built. The GATT procedures were far from perfect, but given the nature of international dispute resolution at that time the contention that it worked well is a statement that can be supported to a certain extent.

It was not necessarily clear at the beginning of the GATT exactly how dispute resolution would be undertaken. It had been the foremost objective of the DSB to resolve disputes between the member states; this would be achieved through conciliation, negotiation or otherwise.[41] It was therefore a formal international negotiating body steeped in the tradition of dispute resolution through diplomacy, rather than a body designed for promoting clear interpretations of the Treaty text in a way that a court would do. The main drawback of this was the fact that predictability was not woven into the workings of the DSB. A member state was not able to rely on the outcomes of previous cases when approaching the DSB if a dispute were to arise.

If the GATT had been placed in its institutional context it was hoped that the DSB would become a rigorous dispute settlement procedure, which contemplated the effective use of arbitration.[42] It was thus intended that the workings of the DSB would then provide a basis for the development of a body of international law to govern trade relationships. Yet with no ITO the GATT DSB did not develop exactly in this fashion. With only small amounts of the GATT dedicated to dispute resolution there was no guidance on how the DSB was supposed to operate. Thus it operated in an informal manner. This is how Hudec described the DSB of the GATT system: 'Legal rulings were drafted with an elusive diplomatic vagueness. They often expressed an intuitive sort of law based on shared experiences and unspoken assumptions.'[43] This reflected the style of international dispute resolution that had existed for centuries. Nevertheless, the system was generally held to operate reasonably

39 See Friends of the Earth Trade Case Study: Tuna-Dolphin Dispute; A.M. Roberts, 'Everything You're Afraid to Know about GATT But Need to Ask', Animal Welfare Institute, http://www.awionline.org/www.awionline.org/freetrade/gatt.htm (accessed 29 November 2009); HR 408 Bill – the US response.

40 See Friends of the Earth, 'The Citizens' Guide to Trade, Environment and Sustainability', 2007, http://www.foei.org/en/resources/publications/climate-justice-and-energy/2000-2007/trade_activistguide.pdf/view?searchterm=GATT%20dolphin (accessed 29 November 2009).

41 WTO DSU, *The Legal Texts*, op. cit. 37.

42 D. De Bievre, op. cit. 4, p. 170.

43 R. Hudec, *Enforcing International Trade Law: The Evolution of the Modern GATT System*, Salem, Butterworths, 1993, p. 12.

well, though a more formal approach to dispute resolution was recognised as beneficial.[44]

1.5 The central tenet of the GATT system

The centrepiece of the GATT dispute settlement mechanism was Article XXIII. Article XXIII was entitled 'Nullification or Impairment' and laid down guidance for contracting parties (signatories of GATT) as to the action they could take if they perceived that benefits of the GATT were being denied to them.[45] The Article was fairly flexible and applied to situations where direct action had been perceived, but also to situations where indirect action could be argued to be interfering with the benefit accruing to a contracting party of the GATT.[46] This later application of Article XXIII could be argued to be one of the main reasons for the overhaul of the GATT dispute resolution process.[47]

The need for a more formal dispute resolution system to deal with indirect measures could be seen as a driving force for creating the WTO DSU. Certainly, environmental protection issues had been considered by GATT's DSB to be indirect barriers to trade, so enraging the environmental NGOs in the early 1990s.[48] Article XXIII contained guidance on the specific circumstances relating to the impairment or impeding of contracting parties' rights:

a) the failure of another contracting party to carry out its obligations under the agreement; or
b) the application by another contracting party of any measure, whether or not it conflicts with the provisions of this Agreement; or
c) the existence of any other situation.[49]

The Article could be interpreted to allow a wide range of measures to be considered by the GATT DSB. Most notably section c) contains the catch-all – the existence of *any* other situation that could impede trade.

44 See M.L. Busch & E. Reinhardt, 'Transatlantic Trade Conflicts and GATT/WTO Dispute Settlement', Paper presented to Conference on Dispute Prevention and Dispute Settlement in the Trans-Atlantic Partnership, Florence, Italy, 2002.

45 GATT 1947 in *The Legal Texts: The Results of the Uruguay Round of Multilateral Trade Negotiations*, Cambridge University Press, WTO, 2004.

46 ibid.

47 See W.A. Kerr & J.D. Gaisford (eds), *Handbook on International Trade Policy*, Edward Elgar Publishing, Cheltenham, 2007.

48 US-Restrictions on Imports of Tuna, 1992, GATT BISD (39th Supp.) (1993) (*Tuna-Dolphin I*); and Friends of the Earth, op. cit. 39.

49 GATT Article XXIII, *The Legal Texts – the Results of the Uruguay Round of Multi-lateral Trade Negotiations*, Cambridge University Press, 2001, p. 457.

Therefore, virtually any conceivable national policy that may have been enacted could fall within the remit of Article XXIII. With no guidance in the text and no formal interpretation, the DSB panels would be free to interpret the Article as they saw fit.[50] So if a contracting party should believe that any benefit accruing to it, directly or indirectly, from the GATT was being impaired, they could refer the matter to the contracting parties of GATT.

1.6 Practical implementation of the GATT dispute settlement process

The initial method used by the GATT in practice was to assign a working party to review a dispute; this evolved into a system of referring the issue to a panel of experts. This was recognised as a necessary step forward by the then Director General, Eric Wyndham-White, in 1955.[51] This first use of the panel shaped the future use of panels by the WTO, and shows the early steps taken towards judicialising the GATT/WTO dispute resolution system. The panel would consist of three to five members, just as the WTO panels do. Panel members would not act in national interest, but in relation to the facts and the evidence.[52] A quasi-judicial arbitration body was set up and so the dispute panel came into being.

With the shift from contracting party negotiation to this more legalistic approach of expert panel review, it can also be contended that not only the first steps towards judicialisation had been taken, but also that the contracting parties had recognised the need for stable clear results in GATT dispute settlement. The legal standing of the panel was not entirely clear and the further development of the role of the panel was objected to by parties from the European Community (EC).[53] It was therefore considerable time until progress was made with changes to the dispute procedure being recognised.

1.7 Understanding regarding notification, consultation, dispute settlement and surveillance

In the 1960s and 1970s the dispute resolution process started to undergo the process of judicialisation – panels were established, litigation-style disputes were heard, and procedures were evolving ruling the conduct of panels. In 1979, at the Geneva round of discussions, greater progress was made to secure

50 See J.R. Cannon Jnr & K.L. Bland, 'GATT Panels Need Restraining Principles', *Law and Policy in International Business*, Vol. 24, 1993.

51 J. Jackson, *Restructuring the GATT System*, Royal Institute of International Affairs, London, 1990, p. 63.

52 J. Jackson, *The Jurisprudence of GATT and the WTO: Insights on Treaty Law and Economic Relations*, Cambridge University Press, 2002, p. 121.

53 J. Jackson, op. cit. 51, p. 64.

the panel system of dispute resolution. A document entitled 'Understanding Regarding Notification, Consultation, Dispute Settlement and Surveillance' was adopted, which provided a procedural guide for the dispute settlement practices of GATT.[54] Though the legal status of the document was not apparent, it has been contended by an authority on the matter that it was a document to facilitate the operation of the further objectives of GATT.[55]

This document was the first to enshrine the principles of a dispute resolution procedure. It marks the first point that a formal dispute settlement procedure had been agreed by the contracting parties. Prior to this document only the vague direction of the Treaty itself offered guidance. The ending of the diplomatic dispute resolution procedure was beginning.

This can be interpreted as the contracting parties instigating the process of judicialisation in a more formal manner, as the document offered a clear procedure for the handling of disputes. This judicialising of the process may not have assured the setting up of reliance on case outcomes at this point, but it did create more certainty in the process and therefore more use of the dispute settlement procedure.

GATT dispute settlement procedures were invoked 115 times throughout the 1980s; in the entire period before then (from the inception of GATT until the end of 1979) the procedures were only invoked 92 times.[56] Membership of the GATT also increased dramatically in the 1980s. However, a further breakdown of statistics shows that in the 1950s (when there were the fewest members) 53 of the 92 pre-1980 dispute settlement instigations occurred.[57] Therefore, increased membership alone cannot account for the increase in the use of the dispute resolution system. In fact, the use of the dispute settlement procedures was actually decreasing as membership of GATT increased during the 1960s and 1970s.

It is worth noting that the document 'Understanding Regarding Notification, Consultation, Dispute Settlement and Surveillance' formally gave power to the panels and associated procedures for dispute resolution.[58] It also contained direction relating to non-governmental persons participating in panels. Such use was to be allowed but not all the time; preference was to be given to persons from member state governments. This direction set a precedent that experts could be used on panels to help inform decisions. This is a further indication of the judicialisation of the panels, that such individuals should be neutral and expert.

54 'Understanding Regarding Notification, Consultation, Dispute Settlement and Surveillance', GATT BISD 26 supp. 210, 1980.
55 J. Bacchus, op. cit. 19, p. 64.
56 J.A. Ragosta, op. cit. 15, p. 287.
57 ibid.
58 Understanding Regarding Notification, Consultation, Dispute Settlement and Surveillance, op. cit. 54.

This is an important decision as it acknowledges that the GATT contracting parties realised that they would need experts to give advice to panels on the wide-ranging nature of the issues being brought to the DSB. This was recognition that the disputes weren't just about technical and legal trade issues. The importance of this document is therefore two-fold: it demonstrates the consolidation of the work to judicialise the dispute settlement process under GATT, and it acknowledges the need for experts to be appointed to panels to advise on issues over which the panels did not historically have expertise.

1.8 Drawbacks of the GATT dispute settlement process

The dispute settlement process was by no means complete at this stage, and many issues remained to be resolved in relation to the process and workings of dispute resolution in GATT. Issues such as the length of time it took to resolve a dispute – often it was a very long process from the initial consultation to an outcome. This reduced the effectiveness of the system as some issues needed speedy resolution that was not available through the GATT DSB.

A drawback recognised by commentators was the fact that the decision to set up a panel had to be taken by consensus of all contracting parties.[59] This problem was compounded by the consensus rule which stipulated that once a panel had come to a decision in a particular dispute it could only be adopted by the contracting parties through a consensus vote.[60] This created a paradox whereby contracting parties who had been on the receiving end of an unfavourable panel report could block the adoption of the report through the operation of the consensus rule. This paradox was the Achilles heel of the GATT dispute system. This was not rectified until the inception of the WTO.

A further problem for the GATT dispute settlement process lay in the lack of enforcement of panel reports. There was very little in the way of enforcement other than using the traditional methods of diplomacy and negotiation.[61] In a legal system the enforcement mechanism is one of the most important. In fact without enforcement a legal system will become difficult to operate, as was the case with the GATT dispute settlement procedure. This deficiency shows how far from being a 'trade world court' the GATT dispute system was. A party that had been successful in the dispute resolution procedure had no way of making good its loss. The GATT would not sanction compensation, though it would allow individual states to retaliate with tariffs

59 J. Jackson, op. cit. 52, p. 123.

60 ibid.

61 S. Anderson & J. Cavanagh, 'Foreign Policy in Focus: The World Trade Organisation', 2 *Institute for Policy Studies*, 14, January 1997.

of their own.[62] Again, decisions to use sanctions could only be approved through consensus of the member states.[63] This meant the transgressor could block such an action through its own vote. With no credible enforcement process the GATT system was in need of reform to develop its judicialised structure.

Thus, it can be seen that the GATT dispute resolution system started as a very traditional international legal process and was slowly made more judicial. This also demonstrates that the contracting parties are willing to make changes to improve the dispute resolution system when it becomes necessary for such change.

The GATT system certainly had drawbacks for many of its members. With no enforcement mechanism, some states were more vulnerable than others, especially if a transgressor state refused to comply with a panel report. If a relatively small country only had the option to use retaliatory sanctions against a larger more powerful state, it would be unlikely to succeed in its action. This applied particularly to developing countries in the GATT – it was argued that they were especially vulnerable to the whims of larger economic powers (an argument still used in the WTO to a certain extent).[64] This goes against the rule of law, which aims to offer protection to all – especially to the vulnerable from the strong.

The recognition of this failure emphasised the need for judicialisation of the dispute resolution system. In the 1980s the 'rule integrity' of the GATT was identified as an area that needed to be improved.[65] The developing countries and the USA were recognised as the main drivers of this changing attitude to the judicialisation of the GATT. Ironically the EC was singled out as a main contracting party opposed to the further judicialisation of the GATT.[66] This can be seen in contrast to the position of the EU in the WTO.[67] Another main principle that can be understood from a judicialised dispute resolution is that like cases have the potential to be treated in a similar way. This gives rise to an informal precedential view to rule of law and the development of confidence in the system by those who will use it. Thus the pressures from within the GATT were driving for a more judicialised dispute resolution process.

62 See GATT paper, 'Compensation in the Context of GATT Dispute Settlement Rules and Procedures', Negotiating Group on Dispute Settlement, MTN.GNG/NG13/W/32, 14 July 1989.

63 J.H. Jackson, *The World Trading System: Law and Policy of International Economic Relations*, 2nd edn., Massachusetts Institute of Technology, London, 1997.

64 M.L. Busch & E. Reinhardt, 'Developing Countries and General Agreement on Tariffs and Trade/World Trade Organisation Dispute Settlement', 4 *Journal of World Trade Law*, 37, 2003.

65 J. Bacchus, op. cit. 19, p. 66.

66 ibid.

67 D.H. Erskine, op. cit. 12.

An examination of the figures relating to the cases reviewed by GATT reinforces the view that developing countries were pursuing the judicialisation of the GATT dispute process. Of the whole number of disputes brought by complaining parties to the GATT, 88 per cent were instigated against industrial countries; of the complaints brought by industrial countries only 13 per cent were against developing countries.[68] The developing countries could therefore see the benefit of creating a more rigorous dispute settlement procedure as they would be the benefactors in consistent rule application in the GATT. They certainly had much to gain from such an approach.

The GATT dispute resolution system also drew criticism of the compliance mechanism with panel reports.[69] As mentioned earlier, a panel report could only be adopted through *positive* consensus. Therefore, the compliance level with reports would be expected to be high, given that a transgressor of GATT rules could block the adoption of a report.[70] During the 1980s the adoption of the document 'Improvements to the GATT Dispute Settlement Rules and Procedures, Decision of 12 April 1989 (L/6489)'[71] removed the need for consensus to establish a panel. A further development in the judicialisation of the GATT dispute system had taken place.

The document further encouraged the removal of consensus for panel report adoption, and the use of multilateral authorised retaliation against members who did not comply with such reports.[72] Nevertheless, very few panel reports were adopted under GATT rules. Those that were adopted did have a very high level of compliance, as the losing party had de facto agreed to the demands of the panel report to allow it to be adopted by the GATT contracting parties. Thus it could be of little significance if compliance was high under the GATT rules. The many faults of the GATT dispute system did not stop its operation, and as mentioned earlier it had certain plaudits.[73] Yet the drive for a 'rules-based' judicialised system has been demonstrated to have been occurring throughout the development of GATT's dispute resolution system.

68 J. Bacchus, op. cit. 19, p. 67.

69 J.H. Jackson, op. cit. 63.

70 ibid., p. 67.

71 The Contracting Parties to GATT, Basic Instruments and Selected Documents, Thirty-Sixth Supplement, Protocols, Decisions, Reports 1988–1989 and Forty-Fifth Session, Geneva, GATT (July) 61–67.

72 ibid.

73 R.E. Hudec, *Enforcing International Trade Law: The Evolution of the Modern GATT Legal System*, Butterworth Publishers, Salem, 1993.

1.9 The WTO and the Dispute Settlement Understanding

The evolution of the dispute settlement procedures during the operation of the GATT became embodied in the 'Understanding on Rules and Procedures Governing the Settlement of Disputes'.[74] This agreement was one of the six pillars of the WTO legal framework as laid down in the creation of the WTO. It became known as the Dispute Settlement Understanding (DSU).[75] The DSU was one of the most significant outcomes in the creation of the WTO.[76] The creation of the DSU marks fully the shift from power-oriented diplomacy to rule-oriented resolution, thus signifying the judicialisation of the world trade dispute settlement rules.[77] Importantly the emphasis created by the DSU was in the spirit of multilateralism, moving away from unilateral and bilateral actions that had been the mainstay of the GATT procedures. The creation of the WTO had allowed the member states the opportunity to create a substantive dispute resolution system, a chance they did not miss.

The DSU brought in a significant change to the dispute settlement procedures. The DSU contained a formal system for dispute settlement that all members of the WTO had to adhere to. The system consisted of the following components: the DSB; panels that were appointed for each dispute; and the AB. Taking each in turn, it is apparent that the WTO DSU had created a judicialised dispute resolution system.

1.9.1 The Dispute Settlement Body

All WTO members are entitled to take part in the DSB. The DSB's main function is to ensure that dispute resolution at the WTO is operated effectively. The DSB supervises the function of the DSU.[78] The DSB, in fulfilment of these duties, is authorised to set up panels to review disputes arising from member states. The disputes may relate to actions taken by member states or can relate to a specific interpretation of international trade law.[79] The fact that the DSB deals with interpretations of trade law explicitly demonstrates that

74 *Understanding on Rules and Procedures Governing the Settlement of Disputes in the Legal Texts: The Results of the Uruguay Round of Multilateral Trade Negotiations*, Cambridge University Press, WTO, 2004; and see A.H. Qureshi, *The World Trade Organisation: Implementing International Trade Norms*, Manchester University Press, Manchester, 1998 for an overview of the WTO DSU.

75 R. Wilkinson, *Multilateralism and the WTO*, Routledge, London, 2000, p. 118.

76 G.P. Sampson, *Trade, Environment and the WTO*, Overseas Development Council, Washington, DC, 2000.

77 J. Jackson, *The World Trading System: Law and Policy of International Economic Relations*, MIT Press, London, 1997, p. 189.

78 See J. Jackson, op. cit. 33, p. 106.

79 R. Hudec, *Enforcing International Trade Law: The Evolution of the Modern GATT System*, Salem, Butterworths, 1993, p. 118.

the WTO DSU is now a formal rule-making process. This is compelling evidence to suggest that the process of judicialisation has come to fruition in the DSU.

The DSB is also responsible for referring disputes to the AB – formed under the DSU – and finalising the process of 'court' procedures. The DSB also monitors the level of compliance by member states with the decisions from both panels and the AB.[80] The DSB is also active in enforcement – it represents the guardian of the DSU. Article 2 of the DSU gives the DSB the power to suspend illegally acting members' procurement of Most Favoured Nation (MFN) benefits, and may request compensation for such activities.[81] This strengthens the mechanism with which the WTO can regulate its member states' compliance with the outcomes of the dispute settlement procedure. The success of any legal process depends upon its ability to enforce the judgments of its decision-making process. Thus the DSB can be seen to have been judicialised successfully with the inception of the WTO.[82]

There still remain similarities to the GATT dispute system, especially that of the 1980s. Bilateral negotiations are still held between member states as the first step in dispute resolution. The DSB establishes these discussions as the GATT parties had facilitated discussions in the pre-WTO process. The emphasis is on conciliation at this stage so that parties have an opportunity to air their grievances prior to a formal panel, very similar to GATT procedures. The Director General may also be involved at this point as in GATT. However, this process is now strictly time bound, and if by the end of 60 days' negotiation no mutually acceptable outcome has occurred, the member states involved have the right to request a formal panel hearing. This provides necessary structure and limits to the negotiation stage.[83]

1.9.2 The panel

The dispute resolution panel is constituted by the WTO, and the members are normally individuals who have been former trade diplomats.[84] There are normally three members of the panel and they may not be representatives of the member states in dispute. This shows some similarity to the GATT procedures, though the right of access for a member to a panel is now enshrined in the DSU.[85] The disputing parties may also submit written reports to the panel before the case is formally heard. The panel has the power

80 WTO, DSU, in op. cit. 74.

81 DSU 1994, Article 2.1, in op. cit. 74.

82 A. Helmedach & B. Zangl, 'Dispute Settlement under GATT & the WTO: An Empirical Enquiry into a Regime Change', Paper for 5th Pan European Institutional Relations Conference, Den Haag, 2004, p. 4.

83 DSU 1994, Article 5, paras 4 and 5, in op. cit. 74.

84 J. Jackson, op. cit. 33, p. 107.

85 It is worth noting that this access was available post-1989 in GATT.

to set up expert review groups on scientific or technical matters to help inform the decision of the panel.[86] This allows for experts with an environmental perspective to be called for disputes involving environmental protection; it could also be possible to interpret this as a way to allow the Committee on Trade and Environment (CTE) to make deputations in disputes, where appropriate.

Once all the evidence has been presented the panel must make a decision, and all members on the panel must agree the outcome.[87] This must happen within six months of the panel receiving the submissions. Again, this is a time-bound procedure, strengthening where GATT had been weak, and helping to build confidence in the dispute system guaranteeing that an outcome would be issued relatively swiftly.

The members involved in the dispute may comment on the draft report before it is confirmed and submitted for all members to review. The outcomes are published on the WTO website for all non-governmental agents who may have an interest in the case to review.[88] The report is then adopted, effectively becoming the definitive interpretation of a rule of international trade law, within 60 days of the publication of the report.[89] The panel process has been fully time constrained, thus ensuring that parties can be sure of an outcome – something lacking in GATT and reflecting the more judicial nature of the WTO DSU process.

1.9.3 The Appellate Body

The AB is a standing body of seven experts appointed by the DSB. The AB members serve terms of no more than four years and may only be re-appointed once.[90] The AB has a maximum of 90 days to review the case in question; after such time has elapsed it must make a decision. The introduction of the AB represents the introduction of a check and balance to the panel and is comparable to national legal systems in operation globally.

The AB can only consider issues relating to law covered in the panel report and legal interpretation developed by the panel.[91] Once it has made its decision the AB may uphold, modify or reverse the conclusions of the panel; it may not add or subtract any right or obligations of members provided under the WTO agreements. The AB report must be adopted by the DSB

86 J. Jackson, op. cit. 33, p. 107.

87 DSU 1994, Article 8, paras 1–7, op. cit. 74.

88 See the WTO website, http://www.wto.org/english/tratop_e/dispu_e/dispu_e.htm#legal basis (accessed 29 November 2009).

89 DSU 1994, Article 16, op. cit. 74.

90 WTO News, 'WTO Completes Appointment of Appellate Body Members', 2000, WTO website, http://www.wto.org/english/news_e/pres00_e/pr179_e.htm (accessed 29 November 2009).

91 J. Jackson, op. cit. 33, p. 107.

within 30 days of its circulation to the member states. This addition of an appeal process in itself suggests the fundamental judicialisation of the WTO dispute resolution system.

1.9.4 Negative consensus

A major beneficial change that the DSU ushered in is the introduction of the use of negative consensus.[92] As explained earlier, the GATT had (until 1989) operated under the system of positive consensus – that all parties had to agree to adopt a report or initiate a panel. The DSB operates a mechanical procedure under the DSU – gone are the requirements of positive consensus, replaced with negative consensus. This means that DSB procedures are followed, unless all member states object.

The following sections of the dispute procedure are conducted under the principle of negative consensus: establishment of a panel; adoption of a panel report; adoption of an AB report; and authorisation for retaliation.[93] The WTO DSB has turned the GATT dispute procedures on its head; for each of the above processes (where applicable) positive consensus had been employed. Thus the member state found to be in breach of WTO regulations cannot block the adoption of the report or the imposition of retaliatory sanctions. This represents the evolution of the rule of law in international trade law at the WTO.

Not all actors on the international stage have been enamoured with these changes.[94] The fact that the process moves forward in a more automatic fashion means that the lack of third party involvement and the emphasis on trade is felt more keenly amongst some groups.[95] In fact the change means that more pressure is being put on the WTO to review its dispute process, especially in relation to panel membership and third party depositions. Concern has also been noted over the new enforcement procedures and their relative strength.[96]

1.9.5 Enforcement

Article 22 of the DSU allows member states who have been successful in the dispute resolution system to pursue a number of options should the losing party/parties fail to comply with the report.[97] For example, compensation can be sought for the negative impact of the measure deemed 'illegal' under the

92 See G. Sacerdoti, et al., *The WTO at Ten: The Contribution of the Dispute Settlement System*, Cambridge University Press, Cambridge, 2006.
93 J. Jackson, op. cit. 33, p. 104.
94 M.L. Busch & E. Reinhardt, op. cit. 64.
95 ibid.
96 ibid.
97 DSU Article 22, op. cit. 74.

panel/AB ruling. Article 22 also allows the aggrieved member state to withdraw its MFN policies in relation to the transgressor. As mentioned above, the enforcement procedures are adopted through negative consensus. For an international organisation these powers of enforcement represent some of the strongest measures available.

The DSU does state that the enforcement measures are only to be temporary alternatives to the resolution of the dispute, which remains the aim. Panel and AB rulings need to be implemented within a reasonable time, again placing time limits on the process of the DSB.[98] Only if the DSB deems that the report has not been implemented can the aggrieved party initiate enforcement measures. This gives the DSB considerable power. In the DSU it is compensation that is suggested as the first alternative to resolution; disputing parties would be expected to discuss mutually acceptable compensation. If after 20 days no agreement is forthcoming the party having invoked the dispute settlement procedures may make a request to the DSB to suspend the concessions/obligations the other party would expect under the WTO.[99]

It is here that the DSU shows the qualities that have led to it being described as a very effective dispute resolution system at an international level.[100] The DSU enforcement mechanism is very developed in the tools available to members who are successful in seeking compliance from a member who has not responded to an adopted report. Compensation and the withdrawal of the MFN obligation are two very powerful measures. Article 22.3(a) of the DSU states that:

> The complaining party should first seek to suspend concessions or other obligations with respect to the same sector as that in which the panel or appellate body has found violation or other nullification or impairment.[101]

Article 22.3(b) goes on to state:

> If that party considers that it is not practicable or effective to suspend concessions or other obligations with respect to the same sector(s), it may seek to suspend concessions or other obligations in other sectors under the agreement.[102]

98 DSU 1994, Article 22.1, op. cit. 74.
99 DSU 1994, Article 22.2, op. cit. 74.
100 M. Matsushita, T.J. Schoenbaum & P.C. Mavroidis, *The World Trade Organization: Law, Practice and Policy*, Oxford University Press, Oxford, 2004.
101 DSU 1994, Article 22.3(a), op. cit. 74.
102 DSU 1994, Article 22.3(b), op. cit. 74.

Further, Article 22.3(c) widens the sectors to concessions or other obligations under all the WTO agreements. This gives the enforcement mechanism an unusual level of power compared with other international agreements.[103] In essence the DSB/AB can allow the complainant to apply trade sanctions on an unrelated area of trade activity to the issue under review. This means that the complainant can theoretically apply sanctions to an area of more sensitivity to the opposing party.

There are guidelines in the DSU that explain how the DSB/AB must adjudicate the request to apply a measure resulting from impairment or nullification of the complainant's rights under the WTO agreement. The DSU will seek to guarantee that the measure pursued is not disproportionate to the loss of rights under the WTO agreements.[104] Of course, the member whose concessions or obligations are under threat of retaliation may object. In this case the matter is referred to the original panel for arbitration to determine whether the level of suspension of obligations is equivalent to the original nullification or impairment.[105] The decision of the arbiter is final; there can be no further appeal/arbitration. The DSB is informed of the decision and appropriate action taken. The suspension of the obligations will be temporary until the inconsistent measure is removed or the recommendations have been implemented. This process is monitored by the DSB.

In theory, the implementation of the recommendations could take a considerable amount of time, depending on the nature of the change/amendment that needs to be made. For example, the repealing of legislation and enactment of new suitable WTO consistent legislation in a national/regional government could be a lengthy affair. Nevertheless, until such action is taken, the measure imposed to redress the imbalance (be it directly or indirectly related to the nullification/impairment) or the compensation awarded is enforceable by the successful member. So the WTO has at least in theory created a strong dispute settlement process to enforce the rules of the WTO, which has considerable impact on national legislation that needs to be WTO compatible.

1.10 Judicialised dispute resolution at the WTO

The WTO dispute resolution system certainly gives the impression of a formal judicial system. The parties come before a panel of experts and present arguments that will be considered on their merits in relation to the law of the WTO. The experts consider them and make a decision, which can be appealed until a final adjudication is made. This judicialisation of trade rules is part of

103 For example, few Multilateral Environmental Agreements (MEAs) have such powerful enforcement mechanisms; see further discussion in Chapter 2.

104 DSU 1994, Article 22.4, op. cit. 74.

105 DSU 1994, Article 22.7, op. cit. 74.

the growing phenomenon of the judiciary acquiring a greater role in developing rules-based systems in international law.[106] The system is also becoming more open. Recently the DSB has allowed the public to be present at its hearings, and *amicus curiae* briefs can also be accepted by panels from interested third parties.[107] However, there is still a long way to go before the WTO DSU could be contended to be 'open' and a certain degree of secrecy may be the preferred option for some contracting parties. Hence the DSB and AB tend to fulfil their role with modesty and discretion.

It has also been argued that there is a legitimacy crisis in the WTO dispute settlement procedure caused by two opposing strains of criticism. The first group reject the rule-making process of the WTO adjudicative bodies on the basis that it is contrary to the role and function of dispute settlement in the organisation. This relates to fears of erosion of state sovereignty.[108] The second group does not reject the strong international law-making powers of the WTO DSU. However, they abhor the apparent one-sidedness of the decisions and want greater transparency and access to change the process from within.[109]

The first group can be said to be based around practitioners of the ideas of the Chicago School of Economics. They view the WTO narrowly, in that its main purpose is economic liberalisation and that it should not veer from this course. The WTO should be closed off from other social interests, such as the environment. They also reject the rule-making power or function of the dispute resolution system. Instead the rule making should be left to the diplomatic forum. Members of this broad group include R. Posner, K. Dam, E. Posner and A. Sykes.

The second group believes that the WTO process should be made more democratic. This is in the sense that all views should be protected at the WTO dispute resolution level. The WTO is viewed as a long-term institution that uses free trade techniques to achieve the WTO objectives, but in a balanced manner. The inclusion of scholars and NGOs in the fabric of the WTO dispute resolution system is proposed.

There are also calls for the linkage of rights – such as environmental, labour and human rights – to the WTO system, using economic sanctions to their infringement. Whilst this is a desirable outcome from the perspective

106 P. Sands, *Lawless World: America and the Making and Breaking of Global Rules*, Penguin, Allen Lane, 2005.

107 See WTO website on *amicus curiae*, http://www.wto.org/english/tratop_e/dispu_e/disp_settlement_cbt_e/c9s3p1_e.htm (accessed 29 November 2009); and WTO news on public access to hearings, 2009, WTO website, http://www.wto.org/english/news_e/news09_e/hear_ds367_16jun09_e.htm (accessed 29 November 2009).

108 P. Stephan, 'International Governance and American Democracy', 1 *Chicago Journal of International Law* 251, 2000.

109 J. Atkin, 'Democratizing the WTO, Loyola Law School Public Law and Legal Theory', research paper 2001-1; also published in 33 *George Washington International Law Review*, 2001, 451.

of improved environmental dispute resolution at the WTO, the current climate of questioned legitimisation of the WTO system seems to preclude this. This system would perhaps offer the best long-term solution to the problems faced by dispute resolution and social interests at the WTO. P. Sands and S. Gaines could be described as members of this group.

Another system is based on the theory of constitutionalisation of international organisations. Advocates include J. Jackson, E.-U. Petersmann and J.H. Weiler, among others who could be considered members of this group. The theory suggests that the WTO judiciary, AB and its jurisprudence act as a form of constitution. These commentators look to the US Supreme Court and the European Court of Justice (ECJ) for their inspiration. The way these two organisations develop constitutional rules is being compared to the actions of the AB and the judiciary of the WTO.

A caution to this relates to the fact that the WTO's ability to embrace and integrate these social elements into its dispute resolution system is not yet proven. Avoiding a pro-trade bias would be the yardstick of the DSB and the AB's own success.[110] Also, the US and EU represent a fairly homogeneous group of states: there is no such polity at the WTO – non-democratic countries are allowed to be members; not to mention the possibility of further attacks from pro-national sovereignty-oriented groups.

The AB, which could be contended to be the main driver of the judicialised WTO process, does not refer to its techniques as constitutional – instead it refers to them as judicial.[111] This in essence provides the basis for a judicialised system argument at the WTO. The AB is mindful of its role and tends to refer to the preamble to the Marrakesh Agreement and public international law when determining general direction.

International judicial settlement of disputes can be defined as 'the utilisation of the judicial function of international courts or other tribunals in order to resolve the disputes between parties subject to international law'.[112] The determination of whether an international organisation operates a judicial system depends upon the level of institutionalisation or permanency of the procedural law.[113] If there is no historical basis then the system may be more likely to be considered arbitration as opposed to judicial. Judicial means are therefore more institutionalised.[114] There needs to be a standing court/forum in which pre-selected judges are available and the procedure is fixed.[115]

110 H.L. Schloeman & S.L. Ohlhoff, 'Constitutionalisation and Dispute Settlement at the WTO: National Security as an Issue of Competence', 93 *A.J.I.L.*, 1999, 424–51.

111 J. Jackson, op. cit. 33, p. 181.

112 J.R. Fox, *Dictionary of International and Comparative Law* 235, Oxford University Press, USA, 1992. See also op. cit. 2.

113 J.S. Martinez, 'Towards an International Judicial System', 56 *Stanford Law Review*, 2003.

114 I. Brownlie, *Principles of Public International Law*, Oxford University Press, Oxford, 1998, 707.

115 ibid.

This is the case for the WTO. A judicial body also transforms into constants most of the variables inherent in international arbitration.[116]

1.11 An arbitration or judicial system at the WTO?

As the above argument examines why the WTO can be described as a judicialised system, it is important to draw a distinction with the process of arbitration. Arbitration is also a process for settlement of disputes. The International Law Commission emphasises that arbitration is a procedure for settlement of disputes between states by a binding award on the basis of law and as a result of an undertaking voluntarily accepted.[117]

What makes it different to judicial is that the parties are free to determine the arbitrators, the competence of the tribunal and the procedure to be followed. Under a judicial system you are not free to choose these things,[118] as per the dispute settlement system at the WTO. The more control the parties have over the system the less judicial it is. The greater the independence of the judiciary and the level of institutionalisation, the more judicial the system is.[119] It is also crucial to determine if the 'defendant' can be compelled to engage in the process – is it compulsory dispute resolution?

At arbitration there may be no agreed outcome for enforcement of a decision. A judicial body applies international law even though it may be a court of specialised jurisdiction. This is because the judicial process is pre-determined by the relevant treaty, whereas arbitration rules are free to be interpreted by the parties.[120] This is a distinguishing feature of judicial settlement of disputes. In arbitration the parties may agree the law and the interpretation of the law which the adjudicator must follow in making their decision.[121] Therefore arbitration is based on a derivative of international law, whereas judicialised systems settle disputes in accordance with international law. Any international tribunal settling disputes in accordance with international law can be called judicial.[122] This must apply to the settlement of disputes at the WTO. The judicial system will also create some jurisprudence, which is lacking in an arbitral system. Again this is apparent in the WTO dispute resolution system.

116 S. Rosenne, *Practice and Methods of International Law*, Oceana, New York, 1984, 12–13.
117 International Law Commission, *Year Book 1953*, [1953-11] ILCYB (doc A/2436) at p. 202.
118 P. Reuter, *International Institutions* (translated J.M. Chapman), Allen & Unwin, London, 1958.
119 See S. Charnovitz, 'Judicial Independence in the World Trade Organisation', in L.B. De Chazournes et al., *International Organisations and International Dispute Settlement: Trends and Prospects*, Brill Academic Publishers, 2002.
120 D.H. Ott, *Public International Law in the Modern World*, Pittman, London, 1987, p. 336.
121 ibid.
122 I. Brownlie, *Principles of Public International Law*, Oxford University Press, Oxford, 1998, p. 707.

However, it is important to note that the WTO DSU does set up a process for 'alternative dispute resolution'. By this it is not meant that the provisions are alternative to the DSU, as they are explicitly part of the DSU. It is simply that they are an alternative to panels and the AB. Article 25 of the DSU allows parties to resort to arbitration rather than taking the immediate steps to panel resolution. The parties of the agreed arbitration are free to depart from the standard procedure of the DSU and agree their own rules and procedures. The parties must agree to abide by the arbitration award, which when issued is notified to the DSB and the relevant Councils or Committees overseeing the agreements in question. The provisions of surveillance and implementation of the DSU apply to the arbitration award.[123]

To date only one dispute has gone through the process of arbitration, but this related to the use of the arbitration clause to determine the level of nullification/impairment to their rights.[124] Therefore the parties had already gone through the panel and the AB; the arbitration was used on a technical issue. Incidentally the panel report had already been adopted when the arbitration had begun, so the arbitration simply looked at the level of remedy available.[125]

It is also worth mentioning that emphasis is placed on allowing parties to a dispute to find a mutually satisfactory solution whilst going through the dispute resolution process.[126] The DSU provides the possibility for parties to a dispute to voluntarily employ other means of resolution, such as good offices, conciliation and mediation.[127] These procedures may also begin at any time of the dispute process, but do not preclude the use of the formal dispute settlement mechanism (DSM). In fact they may run in tandem to a dispute resolution panel/AB investigation.

The process normally requires the WTO Director General to offer these services, though it can be delegated by him to a senior WTO official; through this mechanism a neutral third party is involved in the dispute settlement procedure.[128] Obviously there are differences between each of these forms of dispute resolution: good offices provide a channel of communication between the parties; a conciliator investigates and makes a written

123 'Articles 21 and 22 of the DSU, Dispute Settlement without Recourse to Panels and the Appellate Body', WTO website, http://www.wto.org/english/tratop_e/dispu_e/disp_settlement_cbt_e/c8s1p1_e.htm (accessed 29 November 2009).

124 See United States – WTO, section 110 (5) of the US Copyright Act, WT/DS160/ARB25/1, 9 November 2001.

125 ibid.

126 'Article 11 of the DSU, Dispute Settlement without Recourse to Panels and the Appellate Body', WTO website, http://www.wto.org/english/tratop_e/dispu_e/disp_settlement_cbt_e/c8s1p1_e.htm (accessed 29 November 2009).

127 DSU, *Article 5, The Legal Texts: The Results of the Uruguay Round of Multilateral Trade Negotiations*, Cambridge University Press, Cambridge, 1999.

128 ibid., DSU, Article 5.6.

proposal for resolution; and a mediator is an active participant in the dispute settlement process.

Therefore, it is clear that there is some basis for arguing that the DSU represents a quasi-judicial system, but only if parties choose the alternative dispute resolution methods offered. As has been shown, this has only been the case once, and then after a panel decision. In fact it is almost automatic that parties choose the formal panel route for dispute resolution because the system offers more certainty. This confirms the opinion that the 'WTO has unabashedly adopted the judicial model of dispute settlement'.[129] However, it also shows that some of the dispute resolution methods offered can be outside the judicial framework. This is common with the growth of alternative dispute resolution in national legal frameworks, especially with regard to issues such as divorce and child custody.[130] Therefore by having these mechanisms it is arguable that they lessen the judicial nature of the DSU – in fact they enhance its reputation.

1.12 Effectiveness of the WTO DSU

Whilst much of the preceding text has been concerned with the workings of the dispute resolution system and its development and propensity to deliver a judicial style of dispute resolution, it is important to address the question of how the WTO system has worked in practice. A number of studies into the workings of the WTO dispute resolution system have taken place since its inception.[131] These have tended to generally show that the use of the dispute settlement system has increased and that compliance with the recommendations of panel/AB reports has been high (or at least higher than it was under the GATT system).[132]

The WTO statistics show that between January 1995 and June 2003 there were 295 requests submitted for consultation.[133] Of the 295 requests, most were received in one year, 1997: 50. This is probably due to the increased profile of the new system. Since then there has been a gradual reduction in

129 M. Matsushita, T.J. Schoenbaum & P.C. Mavroidis, op. cit. 100, p. 43.

130 UK Family Law Act 1996, op. cit. 26.

131 See, inter alia, M. Oesch, *Standards of Review in WTO Dispute Resolution*, Oxford University Press, Oxford, 2004; M.L. Busch & E. Reinhardt, 'Testing International Trade Law: Empirical Studies of GATT/WTO Dispute Settlement', in D.M. Kennedy & J.D. Southwick (eds), *The Political Economy of International Trade Law: Essays in Honour of Robert Hudec*, Cambridge University Press, Cambridge, 2002; B. Zangl, 'Judicialization Matters! A Comparison of Dispute Settlement under GATT and the WTO', 52 *International Studies Quarterly*, 4, 2008; A. Helmedach & B. Zangl, 'Dispute Settlement under GATT and the WTO: An Empirical Enquiry into a Regime Change', in J. Christian (ed.), *Constitutionalism, Multilevel Trade Governance and Social Regulation*, Hart, Oxford, 2006.

132 See C.M. Vazquez & J.H. Jackson, 'Some Reflections on Compliance with WTO Dispute Settlement Decisions', 33 *Law and Policy in International Business*, 2002.

133 WTO website, DSB evaluation, http://www.wto.org/ (accessed 29 November 2009).

requests and the annual number has fluctuated between 23 and 40.[134] The DSB established 110 panels in the same period. This demonstrates that the system, though judicialised, has been able to resolve issues without resorting to formal procedures. This implies that the dispute process still has the traditional international law mechanics of diplomatic resolution at its heart.

However, where the negotiations fail, the option of going to a further level, the panel, exists. In 37 per cent of the instances that are brought to the WTO, panel proceedings are invoked. Of these (110 panel disputes) 71 (65 per cent) have had adopted panel reports and there have been 47 AB reports.[135] This represents an appeal rate of 43 per cent, which is in part due to the high number of appeals just after the instigation of the DSU. The WTO state that in the early years of the dispute settlement system almost every decision was appealed, though this phenomenon has now decreased.[136]

On only 14 occasions have there been compliance disputes relating to the implementation of recommendations and on only seven occasions has the DSB granted authorisation to a complainant to suspend obligations.[137] In all seven cases, arbitration took place as the respondent disagreed with the complainant's proposal for the suspension. These figures reflect a vast increase in the members' use of the dispute resolution process in comparison to that of GATT – the total number of disputes at GATT was 207 for over four decades' worth of operation. More members have brought issues for consultation in the first decade of the WTO DSU. This could represent a statement of confidence in the WTO DSU from its users.

The numbers must, however, be reviewed. Numbers alone do not prove that the system is effective; there are cautions to bear in mind when treating the figures alone as a signal of success. In the consideration of other factors one must remember that the number of members has increased from 95 in the mid-1980s to 149 in 2006.[138] This is an increase of some 52 per cent in members in a relatively short period; the number of cases considered represents an increase of 43 per cent in ten years since 1995.

It could be contended that the increase in numbers of WTO members led to more dispute settlement in this context as a natural proportionate increase. However, a review of the parties involved in the cases tends to suggest that most cases involve members who were contracting parties to GATT, rather than the new joining member states.[139] Therefore the use of the DSU by the

134 ibid.
135 ibid.
136 ibid.
137 ibid.
138 WTO website statistics; and Busch & Reinhardt, 'Testing International Trade Law: Empirical Studies of GATT/WTO Dispute Settlement', in D. Kennedy & J.D. Southwick, *The Political Economy of International Trade Law: Essays in Honour of Robert Hudec*, Cambridge University Press, New York, pp.457–81.
139 The EU and US are involved in the majority of the cases as they were in GATT.

previous GATT parties represents a nullification of the increase in membership as a reason for more requests for consultations. It is possible to infer that more confidence has been placed in the arrangements of the DSU. It could also be contended that the WTO DSB is more effective because of the number of consultations that it has considered in a relatively short period of time. This represents a very dynamic and swift system for dispute resolution.

Another factor to consider as to whether the DSU is effective is the increase in global/international trade in the last ten years. World Bank figures show that global trade has increased from an annual average of $3,500 billion in the 1980s to an average of $6,500 billion in the 1990s. Certainly an increase in the volume and value of world trading would suggest a potential reason for the number of disputes considered at the WTO to rise. The monetary value alone would be enough to encourage states to seek arbitration if this lucrative activity were compromised. However, the fact remains that the WTO membership has increased dramatically over the same period, suggesting that nations have turned to the WTO and its DSU rather than trying to fight trade wars over international trade disputes. This in essence is an endorsement of the international standing of the DSU. Nations would rather join the WTO and use its DSU than seek unilateral or bilateral resolution.[140] The analysis of the figures and the constraining information demonstrates that the judicialised WTO DSB has a high standing and high rate of efficiency.

The WTO rather modestly state: 'On the whole, the operation of the dispute settlement system has been a success.'[141] They also conclude that members have faith in the system. Naturally this can hardly come as a surprise.

Other commentators have come to the same conclusion. The University of Washington's web page states: 'The WTO's increasing caseload of disputes may well be a sign of the dispute settlement systems [sic] success and growing international trust in the WTO.'[142] Even the United States Department for Agriculture (USDA) states that the WTO dispute system is a significant improvement over its GATT predecessor.[143] Especially pleasing for the USDA is the success in resolving disputes in a timely and effective manner. This statement is backed by the claim 'that there have been significantly more agriculture-related disputes brought *and* adjudicated in the last three

140 As evidenced by the ever growing number of members and the applications of those outside of the system.
141 WTO website, evaluation of the WTO DSU, http://www.wto.org/ (accessed 29 November 2009).
142 University of Washington website, WTO dispute resolution process, http://www.washington.edu/ (accessed 29 November 2009).
143 K. Brosch, Improvements in WTO Dispute Resolution, Agriculture in the WTO, WRS-98-44, Economic Research Service, USA, December 1998.

and a half years than during any comparable period in the past.'[144] This faith in the new dispute resolution system is only tempered by the fear that members whose practices have been successfully challenged do not live up to their obligations.

Before addressing the issues relating to enforcement, it is necessary to review the operation of the system in the adjudication and implementation of disputes. Since the mid-1990s more than 100 dispute resolution panels have been established; of these nearly 80 panel reports have been issued.[145] Of the 207 cases brought before the GATT dispute resolution body, 88 resulted in panel reports. This averages to about two reports a year. In the WTO the average number of reports is ten per year. This represents a greater emphasis on creating legal rulings and is a further indication of the judicialisation of the WTO DSU.

The WTO system has a certain automaticity in its system, similar to that of a national court. Once the panel has been established the route to adopting the report follows efficiently and effectively. There is a greater certainty that the report will be adopted. In relation to the implementation of adopted reports it is clear that most have been respected by the losing party. From the 81 cases, only 18 have led to complaints by the 'plaintiff' member that the defending member is in a state of non-compliance with an adverse ruling.[146] Importantly the traditionally more 'powerful' members (the EU, Japan and the USA) also comply with the decisions – a recognised fundamental necessity to allow the system to operate effectively. That smaller state members are able to win disputes within the WTO against the traditionally more powerful states, and that the rulings are complied with, shows the remarkable acceptance that the WTO dispute settlement procedures enjoy.[147]

As for the use of the enforcement mechanism within the WTO, this has happened on some occasions since the DSU was implemented.[148] This can be argued to be a success of the system – that parties have stayed within the WTO process so that serious disputes are arbitrated at the WTO rather than escalated through bilateral sanctions imposed outside the DSU process (as happened under the GATT system). However, it has also been noted that even if sanctions have been authorised by the DSB panel, the successful complainants have been unwilling to enforce sanctions, due to the difficulty this could bring to the defending party.[149] This tends to suggest that though enforcement is a possibility under the WTO, its practical use may be limited.

144 ibid.

145 K. Leitner & S. Lester, 'WTO Dispute Settlement 1995–2003: A Statistical Analysis', 7 *Journal of International Economic Law*, 1, 2004, pp. 169–81.

146 ibid.

147 J.H. Jackson, op. cit. 63.

148 J. Nzelibe, 'The Case Against Reforming the WTO Enforcement Mechanism', *University of Illinois Law Review*, 2008, 319.

149 J.H. Jackson, op. cit. 63.

Nevertheless, overall it can be seen that the enforcement procedure offers suitable leverage to make the whole system work.

1.13 A study of the effectiveness of the WTO DSU

A 2004 study by Helmedach and Zangl of the University of Bremen attempted to assess the facts as to whether the WTO had been more effective than the GATT in dealing with international trade disputes.[150] The study took a sample of cases of trade disputes, some that had occurred without the WTO system. The cases were picked by category and type, including agriculture/textiles, disputes where complaints were made about unjustified import restrictions, and those that appeared in public. The time frame was set between 1980–1985 for GATT and 1995–2000 for the WTO. The study also looked at cases of trade disputes that were not brought to the attention of the GATT/WTO – established through studying newspaper reports.

The preliminary findings of this study suggest the following trends:

1. The percentage of disputes brought to the attention of the dispute settlement procedures has increased remarkably under the WTO system.
2. In 65 per cent of cases brought to the WTO a panel report has been made and adopted, compared to just 50 per cent in the GATT system. This, they suggest, is evidence of more co-operative behaviour among WTO members.
3. In the implementation of panel reports the WTO also has a much more satisfactory performance: 68 per cent of rulings have been successfully implemented, whereas the GATT system has a zero rating for implementation of reports during the specified period in question. Only 18 per cent in the WTO have not resulted in corresponding behaviour by the defeated party. This reflects a highly successful system under the WTO DSU.
4. In the period for GATT all the cases have involved the use of bilateral sanctions at least. Of course none of this is permitted by the GATT. Under the WTO the parties involved in dispute do not use sanctions at all, at least prior to the instigation of the DSB panel to discuss the matter. Parties prefer to participate in the full DSB process, but in 50 per cent of the cases sanctions are initiated before the panel ruling to allow sanctions has been made. Where sanctions have been authorised, 50 per cent of the cases involve sanctions prior to the ruling.

This, it is contended, means that the enforcement process is the Achilles heel of the DSB provision, presumably because sanctions have been applied before

150 A. Helmedach & B. Zangl, op. cit. 82.

the DSB has allowed this, suggesting that parties still take their own action when a member does not implement a ruling.

On the other hand, it could be pointed to the success that sanctions, so often used prior to the WTO DSU, now only occur at the very end of the DSB process when non-implementation has occurred, and then only in 50 per cent of the cases (and sanctions were later approved by the DSB). It might therefore be imprudent to call the enforcement mechanism an Achilles heel.

Nevertheless, their conclusion, if somewhat cautiously delivered, is that the old GATT procedure was only partially successful in de-escalating trade conflicts, whereas the WTO system is much more efficient and effective.

1.14 Conclusion

This chapter has contended the creation of a judicialised dispute resolution system in the WTO. This has been seen through the numerous legalistic changes that the WTO DSU has ushered in, and indeed through the practice of the parties. The WTO has gained a certain standing in the international legal sphere, although it is not universally agreed that it has evolved into a full court. Nevertheless, the fact that there are two stages of legal process and a semi-professional roster of panellists, demonstrates that the DSU has created a system that appears to have the trappings of a judicialised system.

This chapter has also shown the development of the judicialisation of the WTO dispute settlement process from its origins in the GATT through to the operation of the DSU under the WTO. The jurisprudence of the system has been examined and the relative success of the system outlined. The operation of the WTO dispute settlement system has also been examined and found to be, in general, an effective and efficient system for international dispute resolution.

The findings support the general consensus that the judicialisation of the DSB has improved the mechanism of dispute resolution at the WTO. It has also supported the notion that judicialisation has occurred in the WTO dispute resolution system. The AB and the panels take their authority from further afield than simply the WTO treaty articles. This is explicitly stated in the DSU, and therefore the AB and panels are creating their own jurisprudence.

What this means for environmental decision making in the international arena will be considered in the following sections. It will also be important to examine the impact of the new legalistic decisions on parties' behaviour in policy fields, at both national and international levels. To assess the level of judicialisation of the WTO, a brief review of the position of the WTO in international dispute resolution systems follows.

2 The WTO dispute resolution mechanism in comparison to other international regimes

2.1 The context of the WTO DSU in international dispute resolution organisations

To establish the level of judicialisation of the WTO DSU, it should also be considered in relation to other international dispute resolution bodies. A comparison with the characteristics of these bodies will help determine the extent to which it can be truly claimed that the DSU represents a judicialised system of dispute resolution. As there are many organisations involved in dispute resolution at the international level the following cross-section of organisations will be considered: the European Court of Justice (ECJ), the International Court of Justice (ICJ), the North American Free Trade Agreement (NAFTA), the Common Market for Eastern and Southern Africa (COMESA), the Convention on International Trade in Endangered Species (CITES) and, finally, the Convention on Biological Diversity (CBD).

These organisations and agreements have been chosen as they represent a good cross-section of international organisations and a variety of dispute resolution styles. They also cover the areas of international trade, international environmental protection and general international law. Therefore these bodies represent a broad base of the many international organisations and treaties with dispute resolution, but also maintain relevance for this study. The WTO can be considered against globally recognised legal institutions, international trade treaties and international environmental treaties. This covers the main areas of this study.

2.2 The WTO DSU in the context of the International Court of Justice

The ICJ and the ECJ have been considered to be fully judicial international dispute resolution systems.[1] The ICJ is an organ of the United Nations (UN), and the Statute of the ICJ forms an integral part of the Charter of the UN.

1 Both have legal statutes declaring their rights and procedures.

The Court has functioned since 1945 in its present state. It does not have compulsory international jurisdiction for all countries, and its main function remains to decide in accordance with international law all disputes submitted to it.[2] According to Article 34 of the ICJ Statute, only states may be parties in cases before the Court. The Court has a dual role: to settle in accordance with international law the legal disputes submitted to it by states, and to give advisory opinions on legal questions referred to it by duly authorised international organs and agencies.[3] The Court's advisory jurisdiction is provided under Article 65 of the Statute. The ICJ can be considered an authority on international law, and indeed UN members and international organisations can ask the ICJ to provide advisory opinions.[4]

The basis of the Court's jurisdiction in contentious cases is given by the state party's consent.[5] The jurisdiction of the ICJ is compulsory for UN member states; this has been realised through successive rulings of the ICJ.[6] The ICJ jurisdiction *ratione materiae* is also regulated by its Statute and it covers legal disputes concerning:

a) the interpretation of a treaty;
b) any question of international law;
c) the existence of any fact which, if established, would constitute a breach of an international obligation;
d) the nature or extent of the reparation to be made for the breach of an international obligation.[7]

These powers given to the ICJ clearly mark it out as a body with strong judicialised features. Coupled to this the judiciary are also standing international

2 Article 38, Statute of the International Court of Justice, Charter of the United Nations, Statute and Rules of Court and Other Documents (Acts and Documents Concerning the Organisation of the Court), International Court of Justice, The Stationery Office Books, 1990.
3 D. Neacsu, 'The International Court of Justice Overview', Arthur W. Diamond Online Law Library, http://library.law.columbia.edu/ICJ/ICJ_Guide.htm#IL_IJ (accessed 29 November 2009).
4 International Court of Justice, 'How the Court Works', http://www.icj-cij.org/court/index.php?p1=1&p2=6#advisory (accessed 29 November 2009).
5 Article 36, Statute of the International Court of Justice, Charter of the United Nations, Statute and Rules of Court and Other Documents (Acts and Documents Concerning the Organisation of the Court), International Court of Justice, The Stationery Office Books, 1990.
6 International Court of Justice, 'Jurisdiction', http://www.icj-cij.org/jurisdiction/index.php?p1=5&p2=1&p3=1&sp3=a (accessed 29 November 2009).
7 ibid.

law specialists, totally independent of nation or other subjectivity in the conclusion of their work.[8]

Within the limits of its *ratione materiae*, as mentioned above, the ICJ has both contentious and advisory jurisdictions. For the last 60 years it has had the opportunity to render hundreds of opinions on a wide variety of topics and issues in international law. The judgments of the Court are binding in law, although states do not always comply with the ICJ judgments.[9] However, as statistics show, while the overall percentage of full compliance by states has decreased since the period 1946–1987 from 80 per cent to 60 per cent, for the period 1987–2004 partial compliance has increased.[10] This suggests that the ICJ represents a fully developed judicialised international legal body. It is certainly recognised as so by most nations and all members of the UN.

Compared to this the WTO does not have perhaps the same overwhelmingly obvious legal characteristics. The ICJ has a clear legal remit in its jurisdiction and its founding charter. It is called a Court and as such is a court of justice – like any court in any country, though obviously different in many ways. It is nevertheless similar to a national court of justice.[11] This explicitly distinguishes the ICJ from other international dispute resolution systems and methods. The DSU does not necessarily have such a clear guide, though it can be contended that the DSU has similar characteristics to that of the ICJ. The WTO DSU has developed a strong judicial authority, having replaced a 'power oriented approach' with a 'rule oriented approach'.[12] This may be a development, but nonetheless it conveys a sense of the creation of a judicial system.

Though the ICJ is widely held to be a judicial body it can also give advisory judgments, unlike the WTO DSB/AB that produce binding decisions on the parties to a dispute. Through its *ratione materiae* the ICJ is limited to similar tasks to the WTO DSU – both share formal rights to interpret law but within the context of the situation and the level of reparations that should be made in the case of breach by one party. Indeed, both the ICJ and

8 Article 2, Statute of the International Court of Justice, Charter of the United Nations, Statute and Rules of Court and Other Documents (Acts and Documents Concerning the Organisation of the Court), International Court of Justice, The Stationery Office Books, 1990.

9 For a detailed account of compliance with International Court of Justice decisions, see C. Schulte, *Compliance with Decisions of the International Court of Justice*, Oxford University Press, Oxford, 2004.

10 See C. Paulson, 'Compliance with Final Judgments of the International Court of Justice since 1987', 98 *American Journal of International Law*, 2004, 434, 458–459.

11 See *Fisheries Jurisdiction*, ICJ Rep 1974, pp. 23–24; M. Shahabuddeen, 'The International Court of Justice: The Integrity of an Idea', in R.S. Pathak and R.P. Dhokalia (eds), *International Law in Transition, Essays in Honour of Judge Nagendra Singha*, Martinus Nijhoff, Dordrecht, 1992, p. 341.

12 See J.G. Merrills, *International Dispute Settlement*, 3rd edn, Sweet & Maxwell, Cambridge, 1998, p. 218.

the WTO DSB/AB refer to their previous decisions to determine the course of action in a subsequent case. This exists without the formal need for precedent. The ICJ and the DSU also share a non-politicisation of judgment; both need judicial independence to operate effectively. Of course the main caveat is that the DSU is formally limited to trade law and the interpretation of one set of treaties within the ambit of the WTO; the ICJ can cover any international treaty.

Whilst this very brief overview cannot claim to cover all the similarities and differences between the ICJ and the DSU, it can be contended that the evidence laid out here suggests that there are considerable similarities between the DSU and the ICJ. Whilst the DSU lacks the overt title 'Court' it can be seen to possess similar powers, though on a smaller scale: the ICJ covers all matters of international law whereas the DSU covers trade and trade-related issues. This said, more and more issues are creeping under the auspices of the WTO, due to the inter-related nature of economic activity with other sectors of society. The case can be further strengthened by looking at similarities and differences between the ECJ and the DSU.

2.3 The WTO DSU in the context of the European Court of Justice

The ECJ was founded in 1958 and has a very large workload due to the broad areas of law that it covers.[13] It is based in Luxembourg and is composed of 27 judges, one judge from each EU member state. Since its inception it has heard many thousands of cases ranging over a wide variety of issues affecting the EU.[14] Essentially the ECJ deals with disputes and upholds the laws of the EU, i.e. the treaty provisions of the EU. In so doing it ensures that European law is uniformly interpreted and applied throughout the Union, so that there is a harmonious application of EU law in the member states.[15] It has a broad jurisdiction so that it can participate in disputes involving member states, EU institutions, businesses and individuals.[16] The ECJ also acts as a last source of appeal from member states' national courts. Again it can be seen that the legal nature of this Court is implicit in its very title: indeed all EU member states are bound by its interpretations of EU law and are required to be in conformity with its rulings. There is very little difference between EU law and international law; indeed Zurn and Wolf contend that there is

13 For a review of the workload of the ECJ, see R. Dehousse, *The European Court of Justice: The Politics of Judicial Integration*, Macmillan Press, London, 1998.

14 ibid.

15 See a broad account of the role of the ECJ in Cesare P.R. Romano, *The Price of International Justice. Loyola-LA Legal Studies Paper No. 2007–13; Law and Practice of International Courts and Tribunals*, Vol. 4, No. 2, pp. 281–328, 2005, Available at SSRN: http://ssrn.com/abstract=963441

16 ibid.

very little difference qualitatively between the law of the WTO and the law of the EU.[17] They go on to suggest that EU law might be better conceived as a mixture between domestic law and international law, existing on the middle of a continuum of legal quality from 'high' quality domestic law to 'low' quality international law.[18]

The ECJ is the body responsible for the legal order in the EU. EU law derives from international law and international organisational practice, and conversely in more recent times the dynamism of the EU has now affected the development of international Law, driving it forward.[19] Its external influence cannot be considered to be anything as dramatic as its influence on member states. Under the EU, Community law permeates the internal legal systems of the member states, giving direct effect to the directives of the EU. This creates rights and duties that are directly enforceable by – and on – businesses, citizens and national organisations. The ECJ defined its own sense of the nature of Community law as follows:

> This Treaty [of Rome] is more than an agreement which merely creates mutual obligations between the contracting states. This view is confirmed by the preamble to the Treaty that refers not to the governments but to peoples … the Community constitutes a new legal order in international law for whose benefit the states have limited their sovereign rights, albeit within limited fields, and the subjects of which comprise not only the Member States but their nationals.[20]

The rules of the EU are enforced through three different mechanisms. First, the European Commission acts as the EU supranational police, reviewing the compliance of members with the directives and regulations of the EU. The Commission has the power to initiate proceedings against a member state if the state is not complying with the laws of the EU, in the opinion of the Commission.[21] This would be taken to the ECJ.

This can be seen to be quite converse to the WTO DSU under which the DSB can only participate in disputes where WTO member states request such involvement. Secondly, the Commission can initiate actions against individuals and companies within the member states if it believes that these bodies are not in compliance with Community law.[22]

17 See M. Zurn & D. Wolf, 'European Law and International Regimes: The Features of Law Beyond the Nation State', 5 *European Law Journal*, 3, Sept 1999, pp. 272–92, p. 277.

18 ibid.

19 L. Azoulai, 'The *acquis* of the European Union and International Organisations', 11 *European Law Journal*, 2, March 2005, pp. 196–231.

20 Case 26/62 *Van Gend en Loos* [1963] ECR 1; [1963] CMLR 105.

21 See J. Tillotson & N. Foster, *Text, Cases and Materials on European Union Law*, 4th edn, Cavendish, London, 2003.

22 ibid.

Finally, Community law can be enforced through national legal systems of the member states.[23] This method of enforcement is not explicitly mentioned in the treaties making up the EU's basis. Rather it has been developed through cases such as *Van Gend en Loos*.[24] This demonstrates a degree of judicial activity in the ECJ; indeed there have been many accusations of overactivism of the judiciary in the ECJ.[25]

Looking at some of the issues that separate the WTO from the ECJ, a first point would be to state that there is no access for individuals or groups representing interests to the WTO procedures.[26] This is a major difference between what would be considered common in a national court and what is usual in an international court. The ECJ has crossed this usual divide and hears cases brought forward by individuals.[27] Naturally there are some limitations, such as the cost in the event of loss for an individual party – European Court hearings are expensive. Nevertheless the ECJ, as an international court, has similar access potential as national courts. This does not mean that the WTO DSU has not created a legal entity in the dispute mechanisms of the WTO, merely that they are not as advanced as the procedures of the ECJ. In other areas the WTO DSU can be held to be more similar to the ECJ.

When the ECJ deals with issues coming from national courts its decisions are binding and must be followed by the national court submitting the appeal or hearing request. This is similar to the workings of the DSU, in that the DSU sets international rules that should be adhered to in national courts. Thereby giving effect to DSB or AB rulings in the WTO dispute process at a national level, the effect of rulings in both the WTO and the ECJ have the same effect.[28] Equally the ECJ can determine penalties for the failure to

23 ibid.

24 For example, see *Costa v ENEL* [1964] ECR 584; and *International Handelsgesellschaft v Einfuhr und Vorsstelle Getreide* [1970] ECR 1125.

25 See for a general review of the power of the ECJ, M. Howe, 'The European Court: The Forgotten Powerhouse Building the European Super State', 24 *Economic Affairs*, 1, March 2004, pp. 17–21.

26 Though in the recent *US – Imports of Certain Shrimp Products* case, the AB did allow the submission of *amicus curiae* briefs. In the case the panel declined to accept an *amicus curiae* brief; however the AB stated that Article 13.1 of the DSU confers power on panels to seek information from any individual or body. The AB further stated this should be interpreted to include *amicus curiae* briefs. In essence this ruling allows concerned third parties to submit information to the WTO dispute mechanism, though the panel or AB has the power to accept or reject any such interventions. Again these can only be submitted in cases between member states and cannot be used by individuals to start proceedings against a member state.

27 M. Cabak, *Actions for Judicial Review Brought Before the ECJ: Position of Private Parties*, VDM Verlag, 2008.

28 WTO Agreement Art II:2 states that the WTO Agreement provides that all agreements are binding on all members. Through this each WTO member has a legal obligation to ensure the conformity of its laws with WTO obligations.

implement laws in the member states. This is also a power of the AB and DSB in the WTO.[29]

Therefore there are clear similarities between the workings of the ECJ and the WTO DSU, although there are some significant differences. The similarities, it can be argued, suggest that the WTO, through the workings of the DSB and the AB, is an international judicial body in kind to the ECJ. The matter of access makes it less so, but it is also worth remembering that the ICJ can only deal with disputes between countries. This is something of an international law norm; the ECJ is more advanced than either the ICJ or the WTO in that sense. This is probably due to its more homogeneous make-up and common interests of the member states.

In this brief review of the WTO DSU in relation to the ICJ and ECJ, it can be seen that the DSU has similar powers and procedures to these two recognised legal entities (recognised legally, most importantly, by their members). The DSB and AB lack a direct legal title, such as for instance 'World Trade Court' or 'International Court for Trade Justice'. This has been a quite deliberate decision by the architects of the system, as was the decision to make the DSU more legalistic. Indeed some commentators do refer to the WTO DSU as a World Court.[30] This is probably going a little too far as of yet, but it does highlight the fact that important commentators see the DSU as having created a judicial system to rival that of the ICJ and emulate the development of the powers of the ECJ.

2.4 The WTO DSU, the North American Free Trade Agreement and the Common Market for Eastern and Southern Africa

Having reviewed the WTO DSU in relation to all encompassing international legal frameworks, it is also important to review its situation in relation to other international trade agreements. The two chosen represent one in the developed world and one in the developing world. They are regional by design but have application in an international legal sense. One important point worth noting is that all trade agreements that exist outside of the GATT/WTO must be notified to the WTO as soon as they are in effect.[31] This is because all other trade agreements outside of the WTO derive

29 The ECJ can stipulate a fixed or periodic penalty on a party found to be in breach of EU law, until compliance is achieved.

30 See P. Sands, 'Good Trade, Bad Trade, Cheap Shrimp', in *Lawless World: America and the Making and Breaking of Global Rules*, Penguin, Allen Lane, 2005. As we mentioned in Chapter 1, he refers here to the WTO AB as an international court (p. 96). On page 99 Sands refers to the AB as the most powerful court in the world.

31 Article XXIV, GATT 1947, The GATT, reprinted in *The Legal Texts: The Results of the Uruguay Round of Multilateral Trade Negotiations*, WTO, Cambridge University Press, Cambridge, 2004.

authority from the WTO. In other words, all the regional trade agreements must be WTO-consistent in their terms – The Committee on Regional Trade Agreements (CRTA) examines the compatibility of the trade agreement with the WTO rules.[32] In theory where the CRTA deems the agreement to be WTO-incompatible, it can strike it down.[33]

There are caveats to this consistency with WTO rules; in fact Article XXIV can also be considered to fall under exceptions to the GATT. This is because preferential trade terms can be offered under a regional trade agreement that do not have to apply to all WTO members (hence the wide use of regional trade agreements).[34] However, there are tests that have to be met to fall within this remit.

The two most important are that 'substantially all trade' should be covered by the regional trade agreement and that these agreements be concluded in a 'reasonable period of time'.[35] The meanings of these two phrases are fairly ambiguous and have never been tested in the WTO DSB. Broadly, 'substantially all trade' can be taken to mean 90 per cent of all trade between the parties, though the WTO has not provided a workable definition of this key phrase.[36] This figure has been derived from studies into regional trade agreements and the propositions put forward by WTO member states.[37] There is a stronger indication of what is meant by a reasonable period of time provided by the 1994 Understanding on the Interpretation of Article XXIV of the GATT. This states that the reasonable length of time should only exceed ten years in exceptional cases. What exceptional cases are is not defined.[38] These two tests must be met for a regional trade agreement to be able to operate preferential treatment to its members. If they are not then the agreement will be considered WTO-incompatible.

Therefore it can be seen that for other international trade agreements the WTO is the superior authority and can rule against their creation or their

32 Understanding on the Interpretation of Article XXIV of the GATT 1994, para.3 in *The Results of the Uruguay Round of Multilateral Trade Negotiations*, Cambridge University Press, WTO, 2004.

33 ibid, GATT Article XXIV:7(b).

34 ibid.

35 Substantially all trade is referred to in GATT Article XXIV:5(a) and the reasonable timelimit is referred to in Understanding on the Interpretation of Article XXIV of the GATT 1994, para. 3, op. cit. 32.

36 M. Matsushita, T. Schoenbaum & P. Mavroidis, *The World Trade Organisation: Law, Practice and Policy*, Oxford University Press, Oxford, 2004. See also R. Scollay & R. Grynberg, *Substantially All Trade: Which Definitions are Fulfilled in Practice? An Empirical Investigation*, Commonwealth Secretariat, London, 2005.

37 See the recommendations of Australia that 95% of all Harmonised System codes at the six-digit level be covered in the definition.

38 The Contracting Parties to GATT, Basic Instruments and Selected Documents, thirty-sixth supplement. Protocols, Decisions, Reports 1988–1989 and forty-fifth session, Geneva, GATT (July): 61–7.

activities if the CRTA or a member state believes their WTO privileges are being impaired through the regional trade agreement. This should be borne in mind when considering the dispute resolution methods of the two regional trade agreements covered in the following sub-sections, as they derive their powers from the WTO system.

2.4.1 The 1994 North American Free Trade Agreement

The NAFTA came into force in 1994 and has a number of dispute settlement mechanisms, some of which can be considered to be highly innovative and some of which are more traditional.[39] At least five major dispute settlement functions can be distinguished in the Agreement.[40] The NAFTA secretariat is responsible for the administration procedures of the Agreement. Unlike the EC and COMESA, there is no permanent international court set up under NAFTA to settle the various disputes within its ambit. It is considered that the dispute settlement is less institutionalised and more dispersed, relying on ad hoc arbitration.[41] The remainder of this sub-section focuses on each part of the dispute resolution in NAFTA and offers a comparison with the DSU procedures.

The dispute settlement resolution provisions are provided in Chapter 20 of the NAFTA.[42] This offers a process that starts with consultations and moves to formal panels if necessary.[43] The process outlined in Chapter 20 comprises three stages. First, consultation between the parties takes place. Secondly, where this fails to pacify the parties the matter is referred to the Free Trade Commission for mediation. The Free Trade Commission can take advice from technical or legal experts to help inform their decision. Thirdly, if mediation fails the parties have the right to request the formation of an arbitral panel to report on the issue.

The outcome of the arbitral panel is not binding and as such is only a recommendation, although in theory the parties are expected to resolve the dispute in accordance with the findings of the panel within 30 days of the

39 J. Kirton, 'NAFTA Dispute Settlement Mechanisms: An Overview' (paper prepared for an Experts Workshop on 'NAFTA and its Implications for ASEAN's Free Trade Area'), Asian Institute, Munk Centre for International Studies, 2004.

40 See S. McBride, 'Reconfiguring Sovereignty: NAFTA Chapter 11 Dispute Settlement Procedures and the Issue of Public–Private Authority', 39 *Canadian Journal of Political Science*, 4, December 2006, pp. 755–75.

41 North American Free Trade Area Dispute Settlement Procedures, Project on International Courts and Tribunals (PICT), PICTRes 5, 26 February 2004.

42 See P. Macrory, NAFTA Chapter 19, 'A Successful Experiment in International Trade Dispute Resolution', The Border Papers, C.D. Howe Institute, No. 168, September 2002.

43 NAFTA Chapter 20, http://www.sice.oas.org/Trade/NAFTA/chap-201.asp (accessed 29 November 2009).

release of the report.[44] This is considerably different from the WTO DSU: the WTO has jurisdiction to enforce its decisions and member states must comply with the finding of the panel or the AB, as provided through the process of negative consensus. So the main dispute resolution process under Chapter 20 of the NAFTA is more of an arbitral system than judicial.

One very important aspect of Chapter 20 is the ability for panels to set up scientific review boards, which provide a report on any factual issue concerning the environment, health and safety, or other scientific matters.[45] The WTO panels also have this power to set up expert advisory panels to guide the outcomes of decisions.[46] Therefore the NAFTA has similar general dispute resolution mechanisms, but it does not have the overall judicial nature of the DSU.

As of 2010 the use of Chapter 20 has been limited. Only three cases have been taken all the way to a panel-level resolution: Mexico's complaints against the USA over brooms and trucking, and US complaints against Canada's poultry and dairy practices.[47] The decisions in these cases have been considered as high-quality decisions.[48] This can be seen as an endorsement of the dispute process in NAFTA Chapter 20. Thus, despite the arbitration nature of the system, the outcomes have been acceptable to commentators. This shows that the NAFTA process, whilst not judicialised, is capable of making sound assessments and outcomes in disputes.

Other sections of NAFTA also include dispute resolution processes. Chapter 19 deals specifically with anti-dumping and countervailing duties; Chapter 14 addresses disputes relating to financial services; Chapter 11 provides a mechanism for the settlement of investment disputes between member states and nationals of one of the parties.[49]

There are also two dispute mechanisms in the environmental side agreement – the North American Agreement for Environmental Cooperation (NAAEC). Articles 14–15 of the NAAEC allow civil society actors to have direct access to dispute resolution.[50] This is through the process known as 'citizens' submissions', where any interested party can initiate an action against a national government that is allegedly not upholding its own

44 M. Crommelin, 'Dispute Resolution in Federal Systems', 53 *International Social Science Journal*, 167, March 2001, pp. 139–44.

45 Article 20.15 NAFTA, http://www.worldtradelaw.net/nafta/chap-20.pdf (accessed 29 November 2009).

46 See WTO website, http://www.wto.org/english/thewto_e/whatis_e/tif_e/disp1_e.htm (accessed 29 November 2009).

47 J. Kirton, op. cit. 39; and see also 'Decisions and Reports', NAFTA website, http://www.nafta-sec-alena.org/en/DecisionsAndReports.aspx?x=312 (accessed 3 February 2010).

48 G. Vega, 'The Experience of NAFTA Dispute Settlement Mechanisms: Lessons for the FTAA', Atelier ALENA, 20 March 2003.

49 S. McBride, op. cit. 40.

50 See A. Abel, 'NAFTA's North American Agreement for Environmental Cooperation: A Civil Society Perspective', IRC Policy Report, March 2003.

environmental laws.[51] In stark contrast to the DSU, which will only allow *amicus curiae* briefs from interested third parties, this is a highly innovative system which empowers environmental non-state actors. However, some critics have claimed that it gives less power to environmental groups than Chapter 11 of NAFTA gives to foreign corporations in relation to investment disputes.[52] On the other hand it must be seen in the context of international trade agreements where very few have such direct access for environmental NGOs or citizens.

Therefore, though it may have some drawbacks as a system, it has brought about some environmentally enhancing change.[53] Article 14 has been a well-used mechanism by interested parties; this suggests that the innovative mechanisms in the NAFTA are useful for consideration by the WTO. A reform of the WTO could include such a mechanism to allow interested parties to submit citizens' submissions to the DSB for consideration. In this respect the NAFTA offers more access to individuals than the WTO DSU. This may be a step too far at the current time, especially when considering the size of the WTO secretariat staff.

However, Part 5 of the NAAEC introduces a more realistic alternative. Therefore NAFTA offers an innovative solution to allow citizens an opportunity to engage in international decision making. Whilst this is not judicialised in the way the WTO dispute settlement mechanism operates, it is a way of enhancing democracy in the operation of the system. This is something the WTO could consider.

Part 5 of the NAAEC allows one government to litigate against another government if it alleges that the country in question is not enforcing its own environmental laws.[54] If the defending party is found guilty it can have trade sanctions imposed on it or in the case of Canada fines imposed through domestic courts.[55] This provision has not yet been used. Perhaps the strong

51 Articles 14–15, North American Agreement on Environmental Cooperation (NAAEC), 1994, http://www.naaec.gc.ca/eng/agreement/summary_prov_e.htm (accessed 29 November 2009).

52 C. Tollefson, 'Stormy Weather: The Recent History of the Citizens Submission Process of the North American Agreement for Environmental Co-operation', in J. Kirton & V. MacLaren (eds), *Linking Trade, Environment and Social Cohesion: NAFTA Experiences, Global Challenges*, Aldershot, Ashgate, 2002, pp. 153–82.

53 See O.G. Alanis, 'Public Participation within NAFTA's Environmental Agreement: The Mexican Experience', pp. 183–6; and S. Wilson, 'Article 14–15 of the North American Agreement on Environmental Co-operation: Intent of the Founders', pp. 191–7 in J. Kirton & V. MacLaren (eds), *Linking Trade, Environment and Social Cohesion: NAFTA Experiences, Global Challenges*, Aldershot, Ashgate, 2002.

54 See K. Opalka, 'Enforcement Indicators and Citizen Submissions on Enforcement Matters under the North American Agreement on Environmental Cooperation', Secretariat, Commission for Environmental Cooperation of North America, http://www.inece.org/conference/7/vol1/23_Opalka.pdf (accessed 29 November 2009).

55 J. Kirton, op. cit. 39.

penalties deter countries from using the mechanism or breaching the environmental laws. Indeed, both this provision and the financial services provisions have remained unused.

Nevertheless the principle that is espoused here has some significance for the WTO. There has been a clear link between trade and environment in the NAFTA agreements; the possibility to have direct challenges to governments through this trade agreement over environmental issues is highly innovative. The WTO could consider adopting this model if it were to deal with more trade–environmental disputes. This is a clear precedent for the linking of trade and environmental issues in a fundamental way, through a trade agreement such as NAFTA. The workability of it for the WTO would depend on political will as much as legal design.

To summarise, there are similarities between the NAFTA and WTO dispute systems. However, the NAFTA system has a much greater reliance on arbitration than legalistic mechanisms. In this respect the WTO represents a more judicialised approach than the NAFTA dispute resolution system. This is interesting given the multilateral approach of the WTO and the more regional approach of NAFTA; under the ECJ it has been seen that regions can be more inclined to stronger dispute resolution systems given the level of similarity between the parties.

2.4.2 The Common Market for Eastern and Southern Africa Court of Justice

To oversee the implementation of the COMESA Treaty a Court of Justice (CCJ) was established. The Court was established in 1994 under Article 7 of the COMESA Treaty. It became operational in 1998. The Court was modelled on the ECJ; therefore the mandate of the Court includes dealing with disputes between the member states, references from the COMESA Council or Secretary General and states or legal persons from the states who allege their benefits under the agreement have been infringed.[56]

To date the Court has had difficulty functioning due to logistical, financial and administrative difficulties, common for such courts in Africa and the developing world.[57] The Court has two levels: the lower court and a court of appeal. This structure gives the Court a judicialised mandate, not dissimilar to the WTO DSU. There are seven judges in the lower court and five in the court of appeal. These are permanent appointments who are supposed to act

56 Court of Justice of the Common Market for Eastern and Southern Africa – Description, Project on International Courts and Tribunals (PICT) Resources, PICTRes 14, 18 April 2004.

57 The Court has been beset by problems relating to location. Set up in 1998 in Lusaka, Zambia, it has recently moved to Khartoum, Sudan. In the transition period judges were sitting in different venues.

beyond the constraints of political considerations. The judgments are also binding on the parties to the dispute and have precedence over national courts.[58]

So far there have been 40 cases heard by the Court covering most of the mandate of the Court. There are, however, other cases pending before the Court that have not been dealt with yet due to the logistical problems encountered through the setting up of the Court in Khartoum.[59] This is a process that has been in permanent delay and the Court has re-opened in Lusaka for the time being.[60] Nevertheless the Court has a strong judicial approach; it also has the ability to appoint experts to report back to the panel of judges on the issue under scrutiny.[61]

There are many features of the CCJ that reflect the practice of the ECJ. However, the Court has been less effective than the ECJ and indeed even compares poorly in comparison to some other African courts.[62] Not withstanding the institutional capacity difficulties, the CCJ offers an example of a highly judicialised international trade court. Of course the Court is relatively new and therefore the quality of its decisions is yet to be truly tested. However, the cases that have been decided so far appear to be in accordance with its mandate.[63] So far the judges have been able to apply an effective system of safeguards where the law has been challenged or applied and the judges have ensured that the law is not interpreted or applied differently in each member state.[64]

With regard to its position in relation to the WTO DSU, the CCJ is similar to the ECJ, but it does have a narrower remit as it theoretically is limited to trade-related issues rather than broader considerations such as social, cultural and environmental concerns. However, the legal decisions have standing over the member states' national laws. Nevertheless, on issues of trade law the CCJ will be required to uphold the rules as applied by

58 See International Labour Organisation website, http://actrav.itcilo.org/actrav-english/telearn/global/ilo/blokit/comesa.htm (accessed 29 November 2009).

59 See Tralac website, http://www.tralac.org/cgi-bin/giga.cgi?cmd=cause_dir_news_item&cause_id=1694&news_id=43127&cat_id=0 (accessed 3 February 2010).

60 See COMESA website, http://www.comesa.int/lang-en/component/content/article/253-comesa-court-of-justice-holds-session-in-lusaka (accessed 29 November 2009).

61 Article 18 of the Legal Notice No. 2 of 2003: Arbitration Rules, COMESA Secretariat, 2003.

62 Email from Irving Williamson, Chief of Party USAID WTO Accession Team – Ethiopia 2006. In this email it is commented that the COMESA Court compares poorly with the Abuja-based ECOWAS Court of Justice, which has a reputation for resolving trade and political disputes among its members in a timely and effective manner, 30 March 2006.

63 See K.J. Alter, *Delegating to International Courts: Self-Binding vs. Other-Binding Delegation, Law and Contemporary Problems*, forthcoming, available at SSRN: http://ssrn.com/abstract=1001949 (accessed 29 November 2009).

64 F. Maonera, 'Dispute Settlement Under COMESA', Tralac Working Paper No. 7, October 2005.

the WTO. Again the authority for overall trade law remains with the WTO. The process is highly judicialised, on a similar line to the ECJ and perhaps more so than the WTO DSU. More time will be needed to see exactly how the Court now develops before a full indication of its judicial nature can be given. The CCJ therefore sits at the judicial end of the taxonomy of international dispute resolution. More so than the WTO, but the test of time would need to be passed to determine if the CCJ can effectively resolve and uphold disputes.

2.5 The WTO DSU in the context of the Convention on International Trade in Endangered Species and the Convention on Biological Diversity

Having considered two international courts and two trade-specific dispute resolution bodies, the final part of this chapter looks at the dispute resolution mechanisms of two important international environmental treaties that currently exist.

CITES came into force in 1975. One of the oldest international environmental treaties, it aims to protect species of plants and animals and control the trade in these goods. Over 30,000 species are covered by CITES – not all are endangered and indeed not all endangered species are covered.[65]

CBD was an outcome of the UN 'Earth Summit' of 1992, perhaps one of the most ambitious environmental treaties of the modern era. Essentially the CBD is concerned with the protection of the world's biological resources and their equitable use, and fair sharing of the benefits of genetic resources.[66] It has over 175 signatories and strong links with the WTO through the CBD's interest in intellectual property rights and its potential conflict with the WTO Trade Related Intellectual Property Rights (TRIPS) agreement.[67]

These two environmental treaties will be reviewed in terms of their dispute resolution mechanisms, and a comparison with the WTO dispute settlement mechanism will be made.

65 J. Ginsberg, 'Issues in International Conservation CITES at 30 or 40', 16 *Conservation Biology*, 5, October 2002, pp. 1184–91.

66 CBD Article 1, 1992, https://www.cbd.int/doc/legal/cbd-en.pdf (accessed 29 November 2009).

67 For a review of the potential areas of conflict that could arise between the WTO and the CBD, see K. Ni, 'The Incorporation of the CBD Mandate on Access and Benefit Sharing into TRIPS regime: An Appraisal of the Appeal of Developing Countries with Rich Genetic Resources', *Asian Journal of WTO and International Health Law and Policy*, 2006, 433.

2.5.1 The Convention on International Trade in Endangered Species

As previously mentioned CITES is one of the oldest international environmental treaties, and currently it has 175 members.[68] The prime objective of the Convention is to ensure that trade in plants and animals does not threaten their survival. The principal article concerned with dispute resolution is Article XVIII, which has just two short paragraphs. Article XVIII 1 states that disputes between parties shall be subject to negotiation between the parties. Paragraph 2 provides for arbitration if the negotiations are unsuccessful; this arbitration is completed at the Permanent Court of Arbitration (PCA).[69] The Convention provides that the parties will be bound by the decisions of the PCA and will adhere to the decision.

At the surface level it appears that CITES is symptomatic of international treaties in that it lacks a clear dispute resolution process and a means to enforce the decisions that bind parties – even through the PCA. However, the dispute resolution and compliance mechanisms of CITES are highly evolved and effective.[70] In practice the parties to CITES are responsible for the enforcement of the Convention, through their Customs authorities. It is their job to monitor and impose any bans agreed under the Convention. Parties submit reports and trade records on an annual basis to the Secretariat, which is run by the United Nations Environment Programme (UNEP).

Alongside compliance monitoring through the annual reporting mechanisms, trade sanctions are also used to enforce the decisions made by the CITES Conference of the Parties (COP), in relation to the species appearing on the various schedules of protection.[71] The trade sanctions take the form of licences for the export and import of wildlife and plant products that appear on the schedules of protection; indeed some species and plants are banned from international trade. This is a strong power for a multilateral environmental agreement (MEA). It is under these conditions that parties have been worried that a conflict with the WTO could arise, if a member of CITES was challenged over a trade ban in conjunction with that Convention at the WTO for prejudicing trade of a non-CITES WTO member.[72] Nevertheless, the

68 CITES, http://www.cites.org/eng/disc/parties/index.shtml (accessed 29 November 2009).

69 CITES, Article XVIII, http://www.cites.org/eng/disc/text.shtml#XVIII (accessed 29 November 2009).

70 See R. Reeve, 'Wildlife Trade, Sanctions and Compliance: Lessons from the CITES Regime', 82 *International Affairs*, 5, 2006, pp. 881–97.

71 ibid.

72 To date there have been no such conflicts. However, Zimbabwe did raise the issue of the banning of trade in African elephant ivory at the WTO. No formal proceedings were instigated. See P. Morici, *Reconciling Trade and the Environment in the World Trade Organisation*, Economic Strategy Institute, Washington, 2002.

Convention offers good protection for the species that are covered under the various appendices.[73]

Unlike some MEAs there is no formal compliance mechanism in the CITES provisions. Instead the development of compliance has been through secondary modes, such as COP decisions and practices of members under the Convention.[74] The practices have developed the system of compliance monitoring under CITES; as mentioned above the use of annual reports and trade statistics allow the Secretariat to monitor compliance with the Convention's regime. Practices also include recommendations made by the Secretariat to parties on implementation of the Convention – this requires the parties to respond with remedial action and report to the COP. In general this provides a lot of information and therefore the Secretariat has the power to review the compliance of the parties with the Convention.

The enforcement of decisions made under CITES is also a relatively powerful mechanism for a MEA. It allows the use of trade sanctions and trade suspensions on parties that do not conform to the Convention's requirements.[75] The COP held in October 2006 reviewed the use of financial penalties and considered the suspension of rights without coming to agreement. These two enforcement mechanisms would be a welcome addition to improving the strength of the Treaty in terms of its drive to ensure compliance with Treaty measures. The trade-related measures can be broken into two parts: suspensions of trade can be at country level and at Appendix II listed species level.[76] Under suspension against a country trade can be suspended in all species listed in CITES. However, the trade suspension is considered a voluntary measure by the other parties rather than a judgment against which the parties must abide.[77]

Since 1985 there have been seven cases of trade sanctions against members of CITES and three against non-members of CITES, who subsequently acceded to CITES.[78] In all these cases the parties responded and the sanctions were lifted from them. This suggests a high level of compliance and therefore an efficient enforcement mechanism. However, a major difference between the WTO DSU and the enforcement of compliance under CITES is that of member-to-member enforcement actions in the case of alleged breaches. These are not found under CITES; only the Secretariat brings measures to encourage compliance against countries in breach of CITES rules that are enacted by the members. This suggests a limited scope for judicial-style

73 R. Reeve, op. cit. 70.

74 ibid.

75 CITES, Article VIII, http://www.cites.org/eng/disc/text.shtml (accessed 29 November 2009).

76 ibid.

77 R. Reeve, *Policing International Trade in Endangered Species: the CITES Treaty and Compliance*, Earthscan/Royal Institute of International Affairs, London, 2002, p. 95 and p. 124.

78 ibid.

actions – only under the option of referral to the PCA can members challenge each other under CITES. To date this has not happened.

Nevertheless, the compliance mechanisms under CITES can suggest that there is an enforcement mechanism of some note to be found in this MEA. Often it is the lack of enforcement that hampers MEAs; under CITES the Secretariat possesses the power of trade sanctions to enforce its decisions. Disputes of a party-to-party nature can be heard by the PCA, though the PCA does not have such powerful enforcement mechanisms as economic sanctions in the form of trade suspensions. To date there have been no uses of the Article XVIII dispute resolution process.[79] This can be considered a success to a certain extent. The use of the threat of trade sanctions has been successful in making parties adhere to the recommendations of the Secretariat; where trade suspensions have been suggested the country in question has made the necessary changes to have the suspension lifted.[80] There is little evidence to throw light on how many countries actually suspend trade when the Secretariat bring trade sanctions on a non-compliant party, but the system seems to work.[81]

CITES differs from the DSU in that there is no judicial style of body set up under the agreement to deal with disputes between members. These are dealt with if they arise by the PCA. However, a significant mechanism is the power of the CITES Secretariat to initiate proceedings against parties who are in non-compliance with the Convention. Unusually for a MEA these powers are also effective economic sanctions. As discussed earlier, the potential for using financial penalties is also under consideration for cases of non-compliance.[82] These powers are similar to that of the DSB and the AB in the WTO, when it comes to enforcement.

However, the lack of a real panel dispute settlement system in CITES suggests that the methods used for resolving disputes are more focused on the negotiation and diplomacy end of the international dispute resolution continuum. Persuasion and the threat of sanctions seem to be the *de jure* choice. As mentioned, the formal Article XVIII procedures have never been used. Therefore it is possible to argue that although it is a relatively effective MEA, it does not have a judicialised dispute resolution system such as the WTO. It does, however, have a very effective system for dispute resolution.

79 M. Yeater & J. Vasquez, 'Demystifying the Relationship between CITES and the WTO', 10 *RECIEL*, 3, 2001, pp. 271–276.

80 Except in the recent case of Nigeria, where failure to respond to the CITES request resulted in a suspension of all trade in all CITES species from Nigeria. See http://www.terradaily.com/reports/Nigeria_is_suspended_from_CITES_wildlife_trade_pact_999.html (accessed 29 November 2009).

81 R. Reeve, op. cit. 70.

82 See CITES, Interpretation and Implementation of the Convention: Possible Measures for Non-Compliance, SC46 Doc.11.3, 2002.

2.5.2 *The Convention on Biological Diversity*

Article 27 of the CBD covers the settlement of disputes under its regime. Essentially Article 27 requires disputing parties to settle their differences through negotiation in the first instance.[83] Where this fails the parties have access to mediation and/or good offices to be provided by a mutually agreed third party.[84] Alternatively the parties can, at the point of signing, agree to have disputes that cannot be solved through negotiation or mediation referred to the ICJ, or to follow procedures in Annex II of the CBD.[85] Annex II lays down rules for arbitration of disputes.

Annex II requires parties to notify the CBD Secretariat that they are referring a matter to arbitration.[86] Following this, an arbitral tribunal is set up with a President to oversee the arbitration. The arbitral tribunal consists of three members, one appointed by each party to the dispute, and these appointees choose an independent chairperson to act as President of the tribunal.[87] This gives the tribunal some independence from the parties to the dispute, adding legitimacy to its work. The tribunal determines its own rules of procedure for determining the outcome of the dispute before it, though generally the issues are kept confidential.[88] The decision of the tribunal can be taken by a majority vote and the decision is binding on the parties to the dispute. There can be no appeal, unless the parties agreed an appellate procedure at the outset of the arbitration. It is required that the decision be submitted within five months of the start of the procedures.

Annex II also contains a conciliation procedure, not dissimilar to the arbitration procedure. However, the conciliation commission contains five members, two appointed by each country involved in the dispute and an elected chair. The conciliation commission takes its decisions by majority vote and expects the parties who referred the issue to consider the proposal in good faith. Again the conciliation commission chooses its own procedural rules.

The system operated under the CBD is an example of the type of arbitrational dispute resolution system operated by MEAs. There is no mechanism for enforcement of the outcomes of the arbitration panel, which leaves the CBD relying on the members to implement the decisions upon their own volition. This is where there is a large difference between the dispute resolution mechanism of the WTO and that of the CBD. Having no enforcement mechanism means that the CBD is much less like a legalistic dispute

83 United Nations, Article 27.1, CBD, United Nations Treaty Series, Vol. 1760 I-30619, 1992.
84 ibid., Article 27.2.
85 ibid., Article 27.3 and Article 27.4.
86 ibid., Annex II.
87 ibid., Annex II, Article 2.
88 ibid., Annex II, Articles 5 and 8.

resolution system than the DSU. In comparison to the dispute resolution system of the CBD the facets of the DSU compare well in a judicial sense. Comparing this MEA with the DSU it is possible to argue that in the international context the DSU represents a highly judicial model of dispute resolution.

2.6 Conclusion

In conclusion to this chapter, the argument can be made that the DSU has set up a system that is as legalistic as the ICJ, though without the formal title of a court. There are a number of commentators who give the WTO DSU system the title of court, which reflects its growing stature as a legal institution; indeed its very set-up with two levels of decision making reflect those of a court. In comparison to other international dispute resolution systems there can be seen to be a deficit at the democratic level. By this it is meant that the ECJ and the CCJ allow direct action by individuals rather than just by states.

However, this does not diminish the legalistic nature of the DSU; *amicus curiae* briefs are now submitted to panels allowing third-party access to the dispute resolution system. Standing for individuals is not a necessary component of a judicialised system. In comparison with the NAFTA and the MEA agreements the WTO DSU clearly represents a more legalistic system. Whilst the NAFTA, CITES and the CBD have innovative dispute measures and compliance mechanisms, they place a large amount of stress on arbitration and conciliation rather than formal dispute resolution.

Overall, in the context of the international treaty regimes within which the WTO exists, it is possible to suggest that the WTO system is judicialised in comparison to the treaties' dispute resolutions that have been reviewed. This can be applied more broadly and it can be contended that the system represents a highly judicialised dispute resolution mechanism in the context of international law.

3 The role of previous decisions in the WTO DSU and their impact on member state behaviour

3.1 Introduction

> Law develops by precedent, and it is that which gives it consistency and predictability. But legal precedents like any other must be seen in the light of history and of changing times.[1]

Having reviewed the process of judicialisation in the DSB in Chapter 1, and argued that the dispute process now resembles that of a recognisable legal entity, this chapter is concerned with the effect of the decisions of the DSB and the AB in the context of the international legal framework, and whether a form of precedent plays any role therein. To undertake this study, it is pertinent to review the status of precedent in international law in general and then to review the status of precedent in the most legal of international institutions, the ICJ. This will allow a reasoned opinion to be formed on the effect of decisions under GATT and the WTO DSU.

This comparison shall set the context of the chapter and provide the necessary benchmarks against which to assess the judgments under the GATT and the WTO. It is also useful to analyse the difference in the way the GATT disputes and the WTO disputes have been assessed as tools for interpreting international trade law. This also encompasses the reliance put on these decisions.

The question of precedent in international law is one that will provide many different answers, depending on the definition of precedent used and, of course, which actors are consulted for an opinion. International law does not have a history of accepting precedent as a basic legal principle, for example *stare decisis* precedents are not to be found in international legal

1 Judge Jennings, 'Military and Paramilitary Activities in and against Nicaragua', ICJ Rep, 1984, p. 547, dissenting opinion.

organisations.[2] However, this chapter will argue that other forms of precedent exist in international law and ultimately at the WTO. For this purpose it is necessary to define the concept of precedent as it is interpreted by various authorities, and to understand the varying forms of precedent that exist. Different definitions of precedent have been put forward:

> a decided case that furnishes a basis for determining later cases involving similar facts or issues.[3]
>
> a judgment or decision of a court normally recorded in a law Report, used as authority for reaching the same decision in subsequent cases. … A lower court is not bound by all respects of a previous decision but only by those parts of the judgment that constitute the principles of the decision and not merely passing comments of the judge.[4]
>
> In law, a precedent or authority is a legal case establishing a principle or rule that a court may need to adopt when deciding subsequent cases with similar issues or facts. The term may also refer to the collective body of case law that a court should consider when interpreting the law. When a precedent establishes an important legal principle, or represents new or changed law on a particular issue, that precedent is often known as a landmark decision.[5]

These definitions explain the basis of the notion of precedent, but the concept has many levels that will be examined. For example, precedent can be split into mandatory and persuasive precedent, and also between custom and case law.[6] It is also a feature of particular types of legal systems: precedent, and its most powerful notion, *stare decisis*, are found in common law systems such as those favoured by the English-speaking world. Classic constitutional and civil code forms of legal systems, described herein as the continental legal school of thought, do not follow any specific notion of precedent.[7] Instead, law is derived from statutes only and not open to re-interpretation by judges.

It is in this context that the WTO must be considered, as precedent has more influence on some members' legal systems than it does on others. It is

2 It is argued that Article 59 of the Statute of the ICJ rules out the application of *stare decisis* in the operations of the ICJ. This is covered in section 3.4. See also E.J. Powell & S. McLaughlin-Mitchell, 'The International Court of Justice and the World's Three Legal Systems', 69 *The Journal of Politics*, 2007, pp. 397–415.

3 *Black's Law Dictionary*, 7th edn, West Group, New York 1999, p. 1195.

4 *Oxford Dictionary of Law*, 4th edn, Oxford University Press, Oxford, 1997, p. 348.

5 Precedent and *stare decisis*, Wikipedia definition, www.wikipedia.com (accessed 20 December 2009).

6 See W.H. Putman, *Legal Research, Analysis, and Writing*, Delmar Learning, New York, 2004, p. 367.

7 See D.N. MacCormick & R.S. Summers (eds), *Interpreting Precedents: A Comparative Study*, Dartmouth Publishing, Dartmouth ,1997.

also likely that the legal system an analyst is most familiar with will influence their acceptance of precedent at an international level. Ultimately, where all factors regarding the meaning of precedent are concerned, the key to its interpretation and use lie in the value attributed to judicial decisions, and therefore the decisional authority determines the essence of precedent. This notion will be further examined below.

This chapter will examine whether a notional precedent can be discerned under the DSU at the WTO. However, the chapter will begin with an analysis of precedent in international law, and specifically precedent in the context of the ICJ. In this regard it is important also to review the reliance on *obiter dictum* and *ratio decidendi* in international law, where such practice exists and can be demonstrated.

The chapter will therefore set the context of precedent in the international legal environment, before offering suggestions on whether in fact a form of precedent can be distinguished in the WTO DSU rulings. The form of this precedent, if it indeed exists, will also be identified.

3.2 International law and reliance on dispute resolution decisions

> Judicial decisions particularly when published become part and parcel of the legal sense of the community.[8]

This statement supports the notion that reliance is placed on decisions wherever they are published. This should also apply in the context of international legal decisions made by institutes such as the ICJ and the WTO. Indeed this notion can be further supported by arguments that the international lawyer also relies on case outcomes: O'Connell noted that 'The practising international lawyer of today ... selects as his sharpest and most valued tool the judicial decisions that will support his case'.[9] Both these notions suggest that in theory and practice the decisional authority of judges in cases is a fundamental principle of legal systems, including the international legal system.

The quote from O'Connell is directly linked to the workings of international lawyers at the ICJ. Indeed, as a part of a settled and predictable legal system it is considered that consistency of decision is of paramount importance:

> It is a fundamental principle of the administration of justice that like cases should be decided alike. Inconsistency in judicial decisions affronts even the most elementary sense of justice. In this sense the principle of

8 E. Lauterpacht (ed.), *International Law, Being the Collected Papers of Hersch Lauterpacht*, Cambridge University Press, Cambridge, 1975, pp. 473–4.

9 D.P. O'Connell, *International Law*, Stevens & Sons, London, 1970, p. 32.

> *stare decisis*, of abiding by previous decisions, figures prominently in most legal systems, including all of those of the Member States of the (European) Communities.[10]

This suggests that reliance on legal decisions has a strong part to play in the international legal system, though the question of whether precedent is also in play is disputable:

> Precedents are not binding authorities in international law, but the English theory of their binding force merely elevates into a dogma a natural tendency of all judicial procedure. When any system of law has reached a stage at which it is thought worth while to report the decisions and the reasoning of judges, other judges inevitably give weight, though not necessarily decisive weight, to the work of their predecessors.[11]

Therefore the consideration of precedent in the international arena may well be different from that of a precedent with a binding nature at a national level, such as that in the UK or USA. It is out of a concern for consistency to consider like cases alike, rather than a bound duty. The process of international tribunals looking to previous decisions does not need a specific treaty provision to endorse it; this is simply a normal practice of decision-making bodies.[12]

It can also be stated that reliance on decisions in international law exists because the form of law often requires judges and advocates to determine whether or not they have dealt with a similar problem before.[13] If they have it is often the case that they will return to the reasoning of that case to determine if it can be applied to the present dilemma. This can be seen clearly in the words of King James I: 'Reason is too large. Find me a precedent and I will accept it.'[14]

The dictionary definition of precedent is followed by the common law systems, as described in the Introduction. Therefore it is arguable that precedent is applicable to all legal systems. Given that precedent remains a feature of common law systems it is questionable whether it can exist outside of these legal systems. The continental approach has been to restrict the use

10 L.N. Brown & F.G. Jacobs, *The Court of Justice of the European Communities*, 3rd edn, Sweet & Maxwell, London, 1989, p. 311.

11 J.L. Brierly, 'Regles Generales du Droit de la Paix', *Hag R*, 58, 1936-IV, pp. 5–237.

12 See J. Gerhardt, 'The System of Precedent in the English Legal System in Comparison to the European Court of Justice', GRIN paper, 2000. See http://www.grin.com/en/e/=/book/96633/the-system-of-precedent-in-the-english-legal-system-in-comparison-to-the#inside (accessed 20 July 2012). This paper points out that some form of precedent exists in the German legal system.

13 See E. Gaillard & Y. Banifatemi (eds), *Precedent in International Arbitration*, IAI Series on International Arbitration No. 5, Juris Publishing, New York, 2008.

14 G.J. Postema, 'Some Roots of our Notion of Precedent', in L. Goldstein (ed.), *Precedent in Law*, Oxford University Press, Oxford, 1987, p. 9.

of precedent in legal decision making, but it has not succeeded in removing the principle entirely.[15] Precedent therefore still has some use in the legal systems favoured by non-common law countries.[16]

It would seem then that precedent could have a place in the legal sphere, and in the international legal sphere, particularly at the ICJ. Indeed, judicial decisions have become highly important in the development of international law, so much so it is surprising that so little has been done regarding setting rules for the use of precedents in international law.[17] The fact remains that a decision of a court, even at the international level, has the strength to warrant consideration when a relevant case is under consideration. A decision makes the tribunal that is sitting consider what has gone before in similar circumstances. This holds true for international legal decision making as well as national legal decision making.

There is, therefore, a sense that a form of precedent exists even where *stare decisis* does not exist. As noted earlier, the practice of considering decisions in international tribunals when undertaking later decisions does not require specific sanction in the treaty setting up the decision-making body. Simply the fact that the legal community recognises the importance of judicial *decisions*, rather than legal opinion, lends to the operation of informal precedent in the international legal community.[18] Nevertheless, the ICJ explicitly mentions precedents in its Statute.[19] When the body of legal decisions are based on previous judicial decisions, it would be necessary to develop a set of regulations to determine how previous judgments could be used. A system including some form of precedents is inevitable where the law is influenced by previous judicial decisions.

It is contended that a system of precedents will arise where the following certain conditions are met: the main rules are unwritten, a court operates as a unifying force in a dispersed legal system, and there is a necessity to resort to principles.[20] This can be applied to international law as well as domestic national legal structures. In the following section the precedent of the ICJ will be reviewed. It is possible to argue that some or all of the conditions can be found in that institution and also in the WTO dispute settlement mechanism. In general the rules of international law are relatively flexible and in systems where codified law exists it has been possible to discern the

15 See C.K. Allen, *Law in the Making*, Clarendon Press, Oxford, 1964, p. 187; and see also A.L. Goodhart, 'Precedent in English and Continental Law', *LQR*, 50, 1934, pp. 45–60.

16 J. Gerhardt, op. cit. 12.

17 R.Y. Jennings, 'General Course on Principles of International Law', *Hag R*, 121 (1967-II), p. 342.

18 E. Gaillard & Y. Banifatemi, op. cit. 13.

19 UN, Article 38, 1 (d), Statute of the International Court of Justice, http://www.icj-cij.org/documents/index.php?p1=4&p2=2&p3=0 (accessed 20 December 2009).

20 T. Koopmans, 'Stare Decisis in European Law,' in D. O'Keefe & H.G. Schermers (eds), *Essays in European Law and Integration*, Kluwer Law, Deventer, 1982, pp. 14–17.

growth of a form of precedent.[21] Also the AB can act as a pinnacle of international trade law, exercising a unifying influence over the body of law under its protection. The recognition of the Vienna Convention on the Law of Treaties in the GATT fulfils the idea that principles are resorted to in international law.[22] Therefore, it is possible to argue that precedent, at least of a type, may exist in international law and international legal systems.

Precedent can operate in a number of ways: principally it can be said to act as part of the legal fabric that is available to a judge when considering the outcome of a case.[23] Alternatively it may oblige a judge to decide an identical case in the same way as a previous judgment.[24] The first type of precedent can be distinguished from legal systems whereby a judge must follow previous decisions slavishly, such as a binding (*stare decisis*) system, and is more similar to those systems where non-application of *stare decisis* is allowed.

However, even under systems of binding precedent, higher courts can depart from a precedent when it appears right to do so. This means that these courts are not strictly bound by previous decisions.[25] Common law courts are more likely to rely on cases than their continental counterparts; a single case can be relied on to establish a legal principle.[26] The continental law system uses cases and evidence to base a judgment upon, but refers to the codified law as the main consideration. Nevertheless, the outcomes of cases are considered and therefore the importance of judicial decisions remains, even in the continental system of law. This can be applied to international law and the institutions that operate in this sphere. An examination of the ICJ follows, and the role of judicial decisions in the ICJ jurisprudence is reviewed and analysed.

3.3 Judicial decision making in the jurisprudence of the ICJ

The ICJ is the UN's judicial organ; it shares in the responsibility to maintain peace.[27] In order to do so it must ensure the consistency of its decisions to

21 J. Gerhardt, op. cit. 12.

22 See E.-U. Petersmann, *The GATT/WTO Dispute Settlement System: International Law, International Organisations and Dispute Settlement*, Kluwer Law International, London, 1997, p. 126.

23 See K. Turcotte, 'Why Legal Flexibility is not a Threat to either the Common Law System of England and Australia or the Civil Law System of France in the Twenty First Century', 1 *Hanse Law Review*, 2, 2005, p. 190.

24 For a good overview of binding precedent, see L.H. Gaines & R.L. Miller, *Criminal Justice in Action*, 5th edn, Thomson Wadsworth, Belmont, 2009, p. 102.

25 R. Cross & J.W. Harris, *Precedent in English Law*, 4th edn, Oxford University Press, Oxford, 1991.

26 L.H. Gaines & R.L. Miller, op. cit. 24.

27 UN, Article 1, Statute of the International Court of Justice, http://www.icj-cij.org/documents/index.php?p1=4&p2=2&p3=0 (accessed 20 December 2009).

avoid creating controversy. The schools of thought prominent at the foundation of the ICJ were those of the common law and continental schools, with perhaps a greater influence from the civil law systems. However, it is possible that an individual schooled in the common law scheme may feel comfortable with the methods employed by the ICJ.[28] This is because the ICJ judges often have recourse to its previous decisions when determining the law. The main difference is that the principle of *stare decisis* does not apply.[29]

This fact alone means that one must take care when referring to precedent in the ICJ, as it is not precedent in the sense associated with the common law legal systems. However, the fact that precedents at the ICJ are not binding precedents in a *stare decisis* sense does not mean that the judgments are not precedents. The ICJ is a standing legal body and as such it has a role to play in developing international law and legal practice. Within this the development of a body of case law can give rise to a reliance on previous decisions. Indeed it has been commented:

> Permanent tribunals usually show themselves disposed to shape their decisions into a consistent body of case law ... The Court has not expressly been given the function of developing international law; yet if it holds the respect of Governments and of the legal profession, that must be an inevitable by-product of its functioning over a long period of time.[30]

With case law comes precedent. This should not be a surprise as the principles of coherence, consistency and predictability are the main objectives of the ICJ in decision making; and they are also the fundamental basis for precedents to be formed. The concern to ensure continuity in decision making is a fundamental principle of both the ICJ and precedent.[31]

The term precedent is part of the jurisprudence of the ICJ and has been referred to in its cases and the decisions relating to their outcomes.[32] It is also true that the ICJ uses its previous cases for guidance on decisions, as long as the cases can be considered reliable in interpretation of the law.[33] The ICJ is not of course directly similar to a municipal court as there are clearly

28 E.J. Powell & S. McLaughlin-Mitchell, op. cit. 2, p. 402.

29 M. Shahabuddeen, *Precedent in the World Court*, Cambridge University Press, Cambridge, 1997, p. 2.

30 M.O. Hudson, *The Permanent Court of International Justice, 1920–1942, A Treatise*, The MacMillan Company, New York, 1943.

31 M. Shahabuddeen, op. cit. 29.

32 See *Interpretation of the Greco-Turkish Agreement of 1 December 1926* (Final Protocol, Article IV), 1928, PCIJ Series B, No. 16, p. 15; and *Factory at Chorzow* (Merits), 1928, PCIJ Series A, No. 17, p. 7. See also *Certain Norwegian Loans*, ICJ Rep, 1957, p. 60, Judge Lauterpacht.

33 G. Fitzmaurice, *The Law and Procedure of the International Court of Justice*, H. Frowde, Cambridge, 1986, p. xxxii, footnote 22.

many differences regarding its organisational, jurisdictional and procedural processes. However, the differences must not be overstated as the fundamental nature remains the same – it is a court and its main function is dispute resolution.[34] Other methods of recourse are available to states besides the ICJ, yet when they seek resolution under the auspices of the ICJ they are following an inherently legal settlement system. This is like any court with rules, procedures and specific functions.

The judges at the ICJ have the power to depart from previous decisions, yet the judges have been careful not to do so over the period since the inception of the Court.[35] Indeed it is a power not lightly exercised. In this case it can be argued that the Court follows a more common law system approach to the interpretation of law and the formulation of decisions, which naturally gives much value to its previous decisions. Thus it can be accepted that the decisions are not *stare decisis* by nature, but this does not exclude the judges of the Court using previous decisions to determine the outcome of a case in hand. Rather, this suggests that an informal level of precedent exists – not such a *stare decisis* form of precedent but more one that is a persuasive precedent system. As has been argued previously, international lawyers use previous cases as a form of persuasion to support their arguments.

The jurisprudence of the ICJ which is founded in the juridical nature of the organisation, meaning that its functions are exercised in an independent and legalistic way, contributes to the proposition that a persuasive precedent exists in the rulings of the ICJ.[36] The ICJ has referred to its own settled jurisprudence and in essence this supports the notion that its decisions can be used in future situations and may be relied upon.[37] However, the freedom of the ICJ to follow a previous decision is influenced by the authority of the tribunal which proclaimed a particular decision.

Naturally in the international legal arena the ICJ considers its own authority (and its predecessors) as the ultimate authority when ruling on cases. If there is a clear precedent set by the ICJ the bench will not normally consider it necessary to have extra research on the topic under discussion.[38] In a case under current consideration it is the practice of the ICJ to refer to previous

34 For further discussion on this, see *The Fisheries Jurisdiction*, ICJ Rep, 1974, pp. 23–4, para. 53; G. Guillaume, 'L'Administration de la Justice Internationale', *Revue Francaise d'Administration Publique*, 57, 1991, p. 135; M. Shahabuddeen, 'The International Court of Justice: The Integrity of an Idea', in R.S. Pathak & R.P. Dhokalia (eds), *International Law in Transition, Essays in Honour of Judge Nagendra Singh*, Martinus Nijhoff, Dordrecht, 1992, p. 341.

35 C. Damgaard, *Individual Criminal Responsibility for Core International Crimes: Selected Pertinent Issues*, Springer, Heidelberg, 2008, p. 51.

36 M. Shahabuddeen, op. cit. 29.

37 *United States Diplomatic and Consular Staff in Tehran*, ICJ Rep, 1980, p. 18, para. 33; and *Interpretation of the Agreement of 25 March 1951 between the WHO and Egypt*, ICJ Rep, 1980, p. 87, para. 33.

38 S. Bastid, 'La Jurisprudence de la Cour Internationale de Justice', *Hag R*, 78 (1951-I), p. 631.

cases, as indeed it is the practice of the AB and DSB in the WTO (as demonstrated later in this chapter). As time passes the decision itself may not be recited, but the principle of law laid down in the judgment will be. Precedents are properly read and considered when making a judgment, but they are used for extracting the law, rather than to be reiterated time and again.[39]

Thus the ICJ does use its cases as the authority for determining the principle under consideration at a given time; not as a binding precedent as in common law systems but as part of the jurisprudence of the ICJ.[40] The ICJ will follow these decisions unless they can be distinguished, or if the fabric of the international community has been changed to render a decision obsolete. In essence the Court is building a rule of law that is in part based on its decisions that will become precedents to a similar extent in the way that successive decisions make up the common law in the United Kingdom.

In this vein it is important also to consider the difference between the reliance and use that can be made of ICJ judges *ratio decidendi* and *obiter dictum* in decision making. It is pertinent to consider and assess whether the judges of the ICJ have the power to create law through their decisions. This has particular relevance for the workings of the AB at the WTO.

Article 38, paragraph 1(d) of the Statute of the Court provides that the Court shall apply judicial decisions and the teachings of the most highly qualified publicists of the various nations, as subsidiary means for the determination of rules of law.[41] This means that the Court in its proceedings must take into account judicial decisions that might have some relevance for the case. As the UN's supreme legal body it is necessary that the ICJ follows the doctrines of its Statute and Charter; its legitimacy depends upon this. Indeed this is precisely what it does when applying previous decisions to cases under consideration, as provided through the explicit requirements of Article 38, 1(d). The Statute therefore implies some knowledge that previous decisions will play a part in the ICJ's jurisprudence, but it does not dictate a principle of *stare decisis*.

3.4 *Stare decisis* and the International Court of Justice

The principle of *stare decisis* does not apply in the ICJ; it is mainly found in common law legal systems. Its exact definition can be elusive, but it has been defined as follows:

> General orthodox interpretations of *stare decisis* … is *stare rationibus decisis* (keep to the *rationes decidendi* of previous cases).[42]

39 Lord MacMillan, 'The Writing of Judgements', *Canadian Bar Review*, 1948, p. 498.

40 H. Waldcock, 'General Course on Public International Law', *Hag R*, 106 (1962-I), p. 93.

41 Statute of the International Court of Justice, op. cit., 19.

42 R. Cross & J.W. Harris, *Precedent in English Law*, 4th edn, Oxford University Press, Oxford, 1991.

This does not apply to the ICJ and the case has been well made that this is so.[43] In fact the point is well made that decisions can be departed from at a later date. Maintaining consistency is a strong influence on decision making but it cannot be said to amount to binding precedent – *stare decisis* would be binding. The judges of the ICJ have made clear reference to the role of judicial decisions for the determination of law, but equally have stated that although Article 38, 1(d), requires them to do so there is no suggestion of binding precedent.[44] Notably Judge Read of the ICJ has stated that a precedent can be declined if a case can be distinguished, and if there were any reasons that would justify the rejection of the legal principles adopted by a previous case.[45] If this is taken to be the case then it is not possible to argue for binding precedents in the ICJ.

Therefore the role of *stare decisis* in the ICJ is clear – it does not exist. However, judicial decisions do affect the way in which the ICJ operates. The effect of a decision might not be on parties to a subsequent case, but rather the previous decision may have helped shape the law on an issue. Article 59 of the Statute states that 'the decision of the Court has no binding force except between the parties and in respect of that particular case'.[46] Not withstanding this, the judges of the ICJ have expressed a view that whilst *stare decisis* is not found in the ICJ, the Court's decisions cannot be taken in a narrow context; that is the decisions affect the international legal arena.[47] The decisions, arguably, have more power than a binding force.[48]

The point of Article 59 is to simply act as a safeguard against binding precedent; it does not in itself preclude precedent from existing in decisions that are made in subsequent cases. Thus, the effect of a decision can be to bind the parties subject to the decision and can also be seen to create a general precedential effect on international law. In fact the original Permanent Court of International Justice made the point about Article 59 that its main aim was to prevent legal principles accepted by the Court in a particular case

43 M. Bos, 'The Interpretation of International Judicial Decisions', *Revista Espanola de Derecho Internacional*, 33, 1981, p. 46.

44 See Sir G. Fitzmaurice, *The Law and Procedure of the International Court of Justice*, 2 vols, Grotius, Cambridge, 1986, pp. 583–4.

45 UN, *Interpretation of Peace Treaties with Bulgaria, Hungary and Romania*, ICJ Rep, 1950, pp. 233–44.

46 UN, Article 59, Statute of the International Court of Justice, http://www.icj-cij.org/documents/index.php?p1=4&p2=2&p3=0 (accessed 20 December 2009).

47 H. Lauterpacht, *The Development of International Law by the International Court*, Stevens & Sons Ltd, London, 1958.

48 *Barcelona Traction, Light and Power Company Limited*, ICJ Rep, 1970, p. 163, para. 9; see also *Aegean Sea Continental Shelf*, ICJ Rep, 1978, pp. 46–47.

being legally binding on other states or in other disputes.[49] Judge Jennings later pointed out that:

> This is no more than to say that the principles of decision of a judgement are not binding in the sense that they might be in some common law systems through a more or less rigid system of binding precedents. But the slightest acquaintance with the jurisprudence of this Court shows that Article 59 *does by no manner of means exclude the force of persuasive precedent*. So the idea that Article 59 is protective of third states' interests in this sense at least is illusory.[50] (emphasis added)

Through this statement it appears that Judge Jennings was discounting binding precedent, but that he accepted that a form of persuasive precedent exists in international law where a supreme law giver creates a decision. Therefore it appears that whilst *stare decisis* cannot be argued for convincingly in international law, there is nothing to stop rules being laid down through persuasive precedent.

Indeed it has further been commented that when the ICJ considers the decisions of the Court they are not considered as binding precedents because of both Article 59 and Article 38. As mentioned above, Article 38, paragraph 1(d) states that judicial decisions will be a subsidiary means for determining the law. However, this is prefaced with a caveat that it is subject to the provisions of Article 59. This ensures that decisions of the Court are only binding for the parties, subject to the decision.[51] The basis of the Court is not to create an unpredictable system, but neither is it intended to create a system that follows a common law understanding of binding precedent. It is simply important that each case can be considered on its own merits, with reference to similar cases and their outcomes.

Therefore, *stare decisis* is definitely not applicable at the international level, but a form of persuasive precedent is. A precedent can create law even if the doctrine of binding precedent does not apply as it does in the common law model. This is important for the workings of the DSU in the WTO in the sense that in the highest global legal institution there is a form of persuasive precedent, and also because although *stare decisis* does not apply, it does not stop the ICJ judges from making law. This has important implications for international dispute settlement decision making and its effect in the WTO.

To pick up on the point of judges creating law without reference to the principle of binding precedent, it is important to look at the English legal

49 UN, *Certain German Interests in Polish Upper Silesia*, Merits, PCIJ Series No. 7, 1926, p. 19.

50 *Continental Shelf (Libyan Arab Jamahiriya/Malta)*, ICJ Rep, 1984, p. 157, para. 27.

51 See G. Fitzmaurice, *The Law and Procedure of the International Court of Justice*, 2 vols, Grotius, Cambridge, 1996.

system. It can be held that the English legal system, whilst recognising the principle of binding precedent (though somewhat modified by the 1966 House of Lords Practice Statement), has allowed departures from this principle.[52] It appears that the level of the Court determines the level of strictness with which a decision will be followed. A House of Lords decision will be weightier than one from the Privy Council, as in the USA a Supreme Court decision will be viewed with absolute authority.[53]

Even so it is a recognised right of a judge to depart from a decision where it is right to do so.[54] This allows the judge the ability to create law by modifying the legal principle that is passed on through the case. Therefore judge-made law can come into being even in the absence of *stare decisis*. The fact that a previous decision of the House of Lords is law does not prevent judges from departing from it. Thus, it is possible to infer that a decision creates law without implying that *stare decisis* applies. This is applicable to the ICJ and also to the decisions of the WTO AB. Both systems do not apply binding precedent, but the decisions represent an interpretation of the relevant law that is considered as a supreme judgment on a particular issue.

Even if the decisions of the ICJ are not binding they still have a persuasive precedential effect:

> The enunciation by the Court of the legal rules or principles on which its decisions of the issue rests has weight as a precedent even though the principle of *stare decisis* is not regarded as obligatory on the Court.[55]

Thus, whilst it is not contended that binding precedent applies to international courts, the ICJ must take into account principles of international law. Where a decision is based on a principle of international law the Court cannot decide against it as long as the principle retains its value.[56] This in effect means that the decisions have a precedential effect. The judgment of the Court and even its advisory opinions bind all states by virtue of their quality as authoritative statements of the law.

This principle can also apply to the WTO AB, which is the definitive authority on international trade. The issue then appears to be whether or not the decision is part of international law rather than whether it causes binding precedent. In the case of the ICJ the judgments are considered as part of international law as referred to in the Statute. WTO AB decisions also form

52 E.J. Powell & S. McLaughlin-Mitchell, op. cit. 2.

53 A.P. Fachiri, *The Permanent Court of Justice, its Constitution, Procedure and Work*, 2nd edn, Oxford Univeristy Press, London, 1932, p. 104.

54 D. Keenan, *Smith & Keenan's English Law Text and Cases*, 15th edn, Pearson Education Ltd, Harlow, 2007, p. 211.

55 E. Lindsay, *The International Court*, Crowell, New York, 1931, p. 268.

56 UN, *Interpretation of Peace Treaties with Bulgaria, Hungary and Romania*, ICJ Rep, 1950, p. 104, Judge Zoricic, dissenting opinion.

part of the international trade law jurisprudence; therefore it is put forward that the decisions of the AB also form part of international law and so can be relied upon as a precedent might be.

3.5 Distinguishing a case at the International Court of Justice

The application of the decisions of previous cases can be set aside if it is possible to distinguish the current case from the previous one that was considered.[57] This can be done through distinguishing the case in hand: in the context of this study it shall be taken to refer to determining that factually or legally the cases are considered to be different. For example, where a case closely resembles a previous case that set up a legal principle, it may be possible to argue that the principle does not apply because of the circumstances of the new case.[58] In these instances it is possible not to refer to the precedent of the previous decision. It is possible to distinguish a case by showing that although the decision might be applicable it was different in the application of the specific legal point under consideration.

Differences in cases do not preclude the use of precedents if the legal principles can be applied. The use of precedents requires reasoning on the part of the judges to apply a method of analogy, and this is how precedents develop the law.[59] The judges themselves must determine when to apply precedent and when a case can be considered to be distinguished. The circumstance of the decision determines the application of precedent or the principle of distinguishing. Any dispute resolution system must be able to identify key similarities between cases and make a reasoning of whether to apply a common classification.[60]

The integrity of a legal system depends upon the ability to determine like situations in the same way, but also to be able to distinguish cases that are sufficiently different. In a case there may be many elements of similarity and difference; whether or not they are identical depends upon the interpretation of the judge.[61] In this case the difference would have to be shown to be an absence of a significant element which caused the reasoning in a previous case. Then it would be possible to distinguish the case and not apply the principle of precedent.

Even so where legal questions put before a court may be obviously different, the principles underlying the earlier decisions can still contribute to the

57 See D. Keenan, op. cit. 54 and M. Shahabuddeen, op. cit. 29.

58 D. Keenan, ibid.

59 J. Frank, *Courts on Trial, Myth and Reality in American Justice*, Princeton University Press, New Jersey, 1963, p. 275.

60 E. Levi, *An Introduction to Legal Reasoning*, University of Chicago Press, Chicago, 1949, p. 1.

61 UN, Judge Tanaka, separate opinion, *Barcelona Traction, Light and Power Company Limited*, ICJ Rep, 1964, p. 71.

determination of the current case.[62] Therefore the consideration and determination of the law is very much in the hands of the judge. In this respect the Court evaluates the context of a case, and the evaluation is based on the cases, looking at the differences and similarities between them. The decision is not necessarily affected by the differences in context.[63]

Of course this very fact demonstrates that the application of case-law precedents means that the formulation of judicial principles in international law is not rigid. Each case is determined on its combination of facts and principles. This is true of domestic courts in common law systems and also in the international arena. However, there is a tendency for the international courts to address the particular facts of a case, rather than address the general situation – an approach arguably present in common law system domestic courts.[64]

This infers that a decision in an international court is likely to be more flexibly interpreted than a decision made in a domestic common law court. Therefore the possibility of distinguishing cases in international law seems higher. Even so, at the national level it has been commented on numerous occasions that the wording of judgments are not the same as statutes.[65] It follows that the degree of flexibility associated with case law is greater than it is under statute law. It is not intended that the arguments espoused here should be taken to suggest that precedents are the same as statute rules; the principles of distinguishing and departing from a decision suggest otherwise. Nevertheless it is apparent that persuasive precedent exists in the ICJ and that the principle of distinguishing is used to treat cases as they come, based on their situations.

One final point on distinguishing cases at the ICJ is related to the value of the arguments put forward by the Councils of each party. At the international level, where the interpretation of each case is highly important, the arguments put forward by Council are of great relevance to the outcome of decisions, influencing the judges in favour of distinguishing or of maintaining a precedential principle.[66] Here it is argued that to understand the

62 UN, *Interpretation of the Convention of 1919 concerning Employment of Women during the Night*, PCIJ Series A/B, No. 50, 1932, pp. 374–5.

63 ICJ Pleadings, *Application of the Convention of 1902 Governing the Guardianship of Infants*, p. 267.

64 C. De Visscher, *Theory and Reality in Public International Law*, tr. P.E. Corbett, revised edition, Princeton University Press, New Jersey, 1968, pp. 391–2.

65 See Lord Reid in *Cassell and Co v Broome* [1972] AC 1027 (HL) 1085; and Lord Reid in *Goodrich v Paisner* [1957] AC 65 (HL) 88; see also *Mills v The Queen*, *The Times*, 1 March 1995 (PC) 38, in which the Privy Council stated that *R. v Turnbull* [1977] QB was not a statute.

66 C. De Visscher, op. cit. 64, p. 403.

judgments of the ICJ it is absolutely necessary to understand the arguments of the parties.[67]

This is also why the role of precedent and distinguishing are so important in the ICJ. Because of these principles the law is never ultimately stated in one particular case; it is likely to be modified or altered as time and new judgments progress. It can be argued that through the processes of distinguishing and applying previous decisions to similar – though not identical – cases, the Court develops law through precedent.[68] As Lauterpacht has succinctly stated: 'The power of judicial precedent is in the long run not greater than the inherent value of the legal substance embodied in it.'[69] Thus, even where common law *stare decisis* exists, a judge who is convinced that a precedent is wrong can distinguish the case and depart from that judgment.

This reasoning demonstrates that even where precedent exists in the ICJ it is possible to distinguish decisions in the name of keeping a consistent value of justice being applied. This does not mean that precedent is not applied, simply that there are means to avoid applying a decision in a case where it would not serve the interests of justice. It is further argued that this is easier to apply in international law than it is in domestic common law scenarios. This does not undermine the principle of precedent; it simply allows the function of the Court to make the best decisions. This can also be held to apply to the working of the WTO DSU.

3.6 Departing from a previous decision at the International Court of Justice

Another important constraint on the use of precedent in international dispute resolution is the ability of judges to depart from previous decisions, where appropriate. However, it is possible to see the power of a court being able to depart from previous decisions as an important part of the functioning of precedent, in the sense that where a decision no longer has relevance it can be set aside rather than stifling the development of the law or, more importantly, where it serves justice. For example it has been stated that:

> It is common knowledge that courts of law and other tribunals, however praiseworthy their intentions may be, are not infallible. In recognition of this fact appellate tribunals are usually provided.[70]

67 ibid.

68 E. Levi, op. cit. 60.

69 H. Lauterpacht, 'The so-called Anglo-American and Continental Schools of Thought in International Law', *British Yearbook of International Law*, 12, 1931, p. 52.

70 Judge Hackworth, *Effect of Awards*, ICJ Rep, 1954, p.86, dissenting opinion.

This is the case in the WTO, though not in the ICJ. Nevertheless, the highest authority usually has the power to depart to serve the purpose of justice. This is true of both the ICJ and the AB.

The power to depart is also important, as the position of the law needs to be flexible over time and between situations. It is the judges or the decision makers who determine whether a principle laid down in the past remains relevant today. Both the ICJ and the WTO AB recognise their right to depart or to maintain a previous position. However, both are careful not to reverse precedents established in previous decisions, and they also explain departures from such precedents.[71] It follows that the reasoning of a decision is more important than the decision itself, as this is the basis for a decision, and therefore reliance. It is recognised that the decision itself should not be maintained at the expense of justice or common sense.

Hence in international law decisions should be overruled and international tribunals should not be too pre-occupied with maintaining them.[72] There is no merit in the continuation of faulty reasoning through precedent. Therefore the right needs to exist to depart from previous judgments – this is true of common law systems as well as international legal systems.

In the ICJ when there is a departure from a previous decision the sitting bench usually acknowledge that there is a departure, even though this is not a necessary action to take.[73] This has been stated as follows:

> The present judgement undeniably represents a break with the 1959 precedent, of course there is nothing to hinder this, but it is well to be fully aware of this.[74]

It is unlikely that the ICJ would depart without giving reasons for its departure. This is perhaps different to the ECJ, which is free to depart without giving reasons for its departure.[75] This power to depart therefore limits the use of precedent in the international legal arena, but judicial precedent is not disregarded entirely. This is demonstrable from the ICJ judges' desire to explain the reasons for their departures: 'Precedents can be followed or

71 See UN, *Application for Review of Judgement No. 158 of the United Nations Administrative Tribunal*, ICJ Rep, 1973, p. 172, para. 414; and the WTO Appellate Body ruling in the US Final Anti-dumping Measures on Stainless Steel from Mexico, DS344, 2008.

72 UN, Judge Tanaka, *Military and Paramilitary Activities in and Against Nicaragua (Nicaragua v United States of America)*, Jurisdiction and Admissibility, ICJ Rep, 1984, p. 69.

73 M. Shahabuddeen, op. cit. 29.

74 Judge Ago, 'Military and Paramilitary Activities in and Against Nicaragua' (*Nicaragua v United States of America*), Jurisdiction and Admissibility, ICJ Rep, 1984, p. 526, para. 26.

75 See L.N. Brown and F.G. Jacobs, *The Court of Justice of the European Communities*, 3rd edn, Sweet & Maxwell, London, 1989, pp. 313–14.

discarded, but not disregarded.'[76] The effect of this power on the practice of the WTO AB will be considered in section 3.9.

The power to depart is exercised with caution in most legal systems, because previous judgments are considered to be of importance in a responsible legal system. It follows that the power to depart is used with care and not too frequently in the ICJ. It is also true that there must be good reasons for a departure from a principle that has been decided in a previous case.[77] Indeed in all judicial activities it is important that there is respect for precedents and maintenance of jurisprudence to serve the purpose of stability and confidence in a legal system such as the ICJ. These principles can also apply to the decisions of the WTO AB.

Conversely the ICJ does not use its power to depart very often, *if at all*.[78] Rather, due to the nature of explaining the reason for departure it has been contended that the ICJ simply applies the principle of distinguishing.[79] Therefore the ICJ judges reflect that the decision of a previous case is not applicable, rather than suggesting that previously the law was decided in an incorrect way. This demonstrates a very clear principle: the ICJ believes that it is preferable to determine that a case is distinguishable rather than depart from a decision. This can be argued to be a clear indication of the value that the ICJ puts on previous decisions.

It consequently follows that there have not been many occasions on which the Court has been asked to depart from its previous decisions by counsel. Even when this does occur the Court usually finds that the previous interpretation of the law or decision was correct.[80] Therefore the question arises as to when a bench of the ICJ may choose to depart from a previous decision:

> The Court would be unlikely to disown a previous decision unless it was satisfied that the legal rule or principle in question had undergone a subsequent modification.[81]

If this is the case it appears that departing from a previous decision would be somewhat exceptional; this supports the notion of precedent in the decisions

76 S. Rosenne, *The Law and Practice of the International Court*, 2 vols, 2nd edn, Martinus Nijhoff Dordrecht, 1985.

77 Judge Lauterpacht, *Interhandel* Case, ICJ Rep, 1959, p. 120, dissenting opinion.

78 See P. Weil, *The Law of Maritime Delimitation – Reflections*, Grotius, Cambridge, 1989.

79 ibid., p. 172; and see the remarks of Judge Gros, dissenting, *Continental Shelf (Tunisia/Libya Arab Jamahiriya)*, ICJ Rep, 1982, p. 151, para. 16.

80 See ICJ Pleadings, *Legal Consequences for States of the Continued Presence of South Africa in Namibia (South West Africa) notwithstanding Security Council Resolution 276*, 1970, I, p. 677, para. 3.

81 N. Singh, *The Role and Record of the International Court of Justice*, Eastern Law House, Calcutta, 1989, p. 138.

of the ICJ, as it shows that the ICJ judges recognise the importance of earlier decisions.

The Court is also capable of departing on the grounds of believing that a previous judgment did not serve justice; or that the judgment is now contrary to the needs of the international community. Thus, technically the ICJ is free to reconsider the substance of the law as embodied in its previous practice.[82] In some common law countries a court of last resort would only reverse a decision if it was satisfied that there had been a clear error or the decision would create a public mischief.[83] Normally the requirement is that the court has to be satisfied that the error is conclusively proved.[84] Thus it follows that the injustice of following the precedent must be greater than the injustice that could be done by disturbing the flow of a particular legal principle as espoused in a precedential decision. In general the principle of predictability and stability in law often prove more convincing than those persuading departure.[85]

Departing from a decision could also be considered where a previous holding's weight could be considered less, due to a lack of argument in the decision process. In common law the decision of a court is final and the degree of the arguments presented is considered very important.[86] If an argument is not made it is not considered, and this lack of consideration could therefore affect the outcome of the case. This is not the case in the ICJ, where the judges must be sure that the legal principle has been fully considered, whether or not the arguments are presented by counsel.[87]

This means that the ICJ will hear arguments to assist its decision-making process. Where these arguments are deficient the Court is duty bound to consider the law beyond the arguments.[88] However, this is not to say that Counsel does not play a part:

> Whilst it is true that it is for the Court to determine what the fact is and what the law is ... a claim to judicial omniscience which can derive no assistance from the submissions of learned counsel would be to my mind unfamiliar, indeed, a quaint but unconvincing affectation.[89]

82 Sir H. Lauterpacht, *The Development of International Law by the International Court*, Stevens & Sons, London, 1958, p. 19.

83 See C.S. Gibson & C.R. Drahozal, 'Iran-United States Claims Tribunal Precedent in Investor-State Arbitration', 23 *Journal of International Arbitration*, 521 (Suffolk University Law School Research Paper No. 07-15, 2006); and N. Duxbury, *The Nature and Authority of Precedent*, Cambridge University Press, Cambridge, 2008.

84 ibid., Duxbury.

85 See *Aerial Incident of 3 July 1988*, ICJ Rep, 1989, p. 158, separate opinion.

86 R. Cross & J.W. Harris, *Precedent in English Law*, Oxford University Press, Oxford, 4th edn, 1991, pp. 158–9.

87 L.F. Powell Jnr., 'Judge Hardy Cross Dillard',65 *Virginia Law Review*, 5, June 1983, p. 805.

88 ibid.

89 Judge Barwick, ad hoc, *Nuclear Tests (Australia v France)*, ICJ Rep, 1974, p. 442, dissenting opinion.

Weight is still applied to a decision of the Court where argument may not have been complete, but the arguments of counsel are still important to the outcome of the decision.

The absence of argument on a particular issue in a case does not mean that the Court will not rule on that point in its decision. Equally the practice of common law courts to make reference to the standing of a court or a judge when determining the weight to accord to a decision is not used in the ICJ. The standing of judges does not affect the weight of a decision of the ICJ.[90] This could also be applied to the WTO dispute resolution system – the standing of panel members does not affect the way in which subsequent panels will view the decision.

Another factor that could be taken into account when the Court considers whether or not to depart from a previous ruling is whether the preceding decision was made unanimously. Where this is not the case the decision may not have the same precedential effect, especially where the decision has been taken by the President's casting vote.[91] There is some doubt to the validity of the argument. Indeed, practice in other international courts does not take account of whether there are dissenting opinions.[92] The judgment is simply made irrespective of the size of majority.[93]

Therefore it appears to depend on the international tribunal in question. The European legal system tends not to concern itself with the decision's unanimity, but arguably the ICJ does so. This can be contended based on the comments of the Court and its judges themselves.[94] It has been shown that there is a greater willingness to reconsider majority cases than unanimous decisions, and this is reflected in the desire of judges to make a decision unanimously.[95] This supports the notion that departing from a decision would be more likely to occur where the decision is a majority one. Therefore the weight of the ruling could be deemed to be less where there is a lack of unanimity, which in turn would impact the reliance placed on the decision.

Equally it is worth noting that there is an interest in maintaining the consistency of rulings of the ICJ to ensure that there is no difference between the rulings of particular judges. Parties may be inclined to attempt to re-submit similar cases if they perceive that there could be a change in the ruling, following a change in the composition of the Court. In fact judges are

90 Given that the judges are of equal standing and that there is no appeal level, the outcomes are considered in their total judicial value.

91 G. Schwarzenberger, *International Law as Applied by International Courts and Tribunals*, Stevens & Sons London, 1986, IV, p. 178.

92 Indeed the WTO operates on a majority basis.

93 Judge Jessup, South West Africa cases (*Ethiopia v South Africa*; *Liberia v South Africa*), ICJ Rep, 1966, p. 325, footnote.

94 South West Africa, Preliminary Objections, ICJ Rep, 1962, p.334.

95 See *Continental Shelf (Libyan Arab Jamahiriya/Malta)*, ICJ Rep, 1985, p. 59, the declaration of Judge El-Khani.

changed every nine years in the ICJ; this change could indicate that a new panel would be inclined to depart from previous rulings. This would be a troublesome legal system if the change of composition of benches led to changes in the outcome of decisions. Speaking of the UK House of Lords' decisions, Lord Wilberforce remarked:

> Nothing could be more undesirable, in fact, than to permit litigants, after a decision has been given by this House with all appearance of finality, to return to this House in the hope that a differently constituted committee might be persuaded to take the view which its predecessors rejected ... it requires much more than doubts as to the correctness of such opinion to justify departing from it.[96]

Therefore, there are some strict rules in relation to departing from a decision. The example was applied to a national court, but it is no less relevant to the workings of the ICJ and indeed this can also be applied to the WTO DSB/AB.

The final question, which will be addressed with regard to limits on the power to depart from previous decisions in the ICJ, relates to the manner in which a bench does so. Does the bench depart or does it overrule? If the previous decision is not overruled it is possible that there could be two versions of the law existing simultaneously; this is considered to be against the principles of consistent law making.[97] It appears that overruling previous decisions is the actual practical application of the effect of departing; this removes the previous decision as a continuing part of the legal environment upon which subsequent decisions will be taken.

However, the Court and its judges are very reticent in using the language of overruling – even to the extent that when a decision is departed from, the judges responsible express explicitly that they have not overruled the previous decision.[98] However, other judges have expressed disquiet with the practice of not formally stating that a previous decision has been overruled.[99] Judge Tanaka has stated that the ICJ should not hesitate to overrule precedents when they are incorrect.[100] However, as has previously been argued, the

96 *Fitzleet Estates Ltd v Cherry (Inspector of Taxes)* [1977] 3 All ER 996 (HL) 999.

97 See Judge Anzilotti's comments, *Electricity Company of Sofia and Bulgaria*, PCIJ Series A/B, No. 77, p. 90. He stated that it was clear that there could not be two rules relating to the same facts with contradictory consequences existing at the same time in the same legal system. This suggests that the Court overrules rather than simply not following a previous decision.

98 Sir H. Lauterpacht, op. cit. 82, p. 62.

99 Judge Tanaka commented that the Court should have overruled a previous decision in *Barcelona Traction, Light and Power Company Limited*, ICJ Rep, 1964, p. 77.

100 ibid., p. 65.

effects of a decision are only precedents because they form part of the international legal environment.

Therefore decisions create law, and departing from them must be considered a major action to take – overruling a decision suggests a re-writing of an international legal principle. If it is accepted that the Court can make law it must surely be true that it can unmake it? *Stare decisis* is not present in the system; therefore judges should be free to overrule previous decisions. This is in fact a sign of a healthy and functioning judiciary. Overruling a decision means no more than that it shall no longer be taken to represent the law.[101]

It has been observed that despite the UK House of Lords Practice Statement of 1966, stating that the House has the power to depart from previous decisions, the House itself has used the term 'overrule' sufficiently to suggest that in the House there is no distinction between the terms when applied to departing from a previous decision.[102] The ICJ may by contrast avoid the language of overruling as a courtesy to previous benches. However, that does not mean that overruling does not occur; it is simply a different type of language employed in the international context. This is reflected by the practice of the ICJ (and the Permanent Court of International Justice before it) to never expressly disapprove of any of its precedents, and to reference and explain any departure.[103]

3.7 Summary of precedent in international law and the International Court of Justice

The arguments laid down in the previous sections are aimed at determining the possibility of the existence of precedent and precedential effects in international law. Whilst no formal recognition exists, other than the opaque language of Article 37.5 of the Statute of the ICJ, it is clear that through practice in the ICJ some form of precedent is applied. Indeed, when departing from a previous decision of the Court the current judges go to great lengths to explain why a new direction has been taken. This reinforces the notion that the law must be consistent and that there is vested interest in adhering to previous decisions.

Whilst precedent of the form of *stare decisis* is clearly not applicable to international law, and perhaps less and less so to common law systems, a form of persuasive precedent does exist. This part of the chapter has outlined the extent of precedent/reliance on past decisions in the ICJ and the means with which decisions are protected to ensure their integrity. The practical

101 See Sir Kenneth Roberts-Wray, *Commonwealth and Colonial Law*, Stevens & Sons, London, 1966, pp. 574–575.

102 R. Cross & J.W. Harris, *Precedent in English Law*, 4th edn, Oxford University Press, Oxford, 1991, p. 131.

103 M. Sorensen, *Les Sources du Droit International*, Munksgaard, Copenhagen, 1946, p. 166.

functioning of the ICJ system, and the opinions of the law makers themselves, strongly suggests that a form of precedent exists in international law. This is argued to be of a persuasive nature or a rebuttal nature of precedent. The emphasis could be placed on the term precedent, rather than on its persuasive nature, as the ICJ appears to highly regard its previous decisions.

The next section of this chapter will examine the possibility of precedent existing and being applied in the WTO, and whether it also takes the form of the persuasive precedent advocated in the ICJ. To start this examination the development of precedent throughout the history of the WTO and GATT will be explored, starting with a consideration of whether precedent existed under GATT, and the continuation of the tradition.

3.8 Precedent under the GATT 1947

While the GATT clearly did not operate a judicialised form of dispute settlement, as argued in Chapter 1, it can be seen that there were some practices that amounted to a form of precedent being used. It is not intended to suggest that the form of precedent used in the GATT dispute resolution system bears any similarity to a process of *stare decisis*. That is not applicable in international law, as argued previously. Nor is it intended to argue that the GATT used precedent in a similar way to the ICJ. However, a more informal sort of precedent existed, but with less weight given to decisions due to the less judicialised nature of the system. Commentators have suggested that precedent was being considered through the use of the GATT dispute resolution system.[104] This was because even under GATT, panels referred to previous reports when reasoning a dispute – acknowledging a form of precedent and the value of previous decisions.

There is no suggestion that binding precedent was being used, but the reference to previous decisions shows the value attributed to each panel report in the operation of the dispute settlement process. Of course not all panel reports were adopted and the status of non-adopted reports was unclear, though they may have been referred to. Jackson stated:

> It would seem that such reports (non-adopted) would not be particularly influential in the GATT and would not even bind the parties to the particular dispute as to that dispute itself.[105]

This position could be overcome if at a later time all contracting parties adopted the principles in the panel report itself. However, it is difficult to suggest that non-adopted panel reports could have a legitimate precedential effect.

104 J. Jackson, *Restructuring the GATT System*, Royal Institute of International Affairs, London, 1990, p. 67.
105 ibid., p. 68.

On the other hand, adopted panel reports had clear implications for the practice of the member states. Even though member states may rely on a ruling of a panel, and panels referred approvingly to earlier panels' outcomes, the existence of precedent cannot wholly convincingly be argued under GATT. In most systems of common law, a case and its judgment become binding law upon future cases with similar facts, unless there are a number of factors that can be used to distinguish the case. In international law no such principle of binding precedent exists.

Yet precedent is an important factor in building confidence in dispute settlement and establishing a rule of law. Certainly the contention here is that precedent works with a process of judicialisation to create certainty and a rule of law. It was argued by Jackson that whilst precedent did not exist in the GATT formally, the practice of the GATT dispute settlement system led to a situation where *informal* precedent existed.[106] An adopted panel report would be an endorsement of the interpretation of the GATT by the panel.[107] An adopted panel report becomes part of the practice history of the Treaty, so it can be relied on for interpreting the GATT as part of the legal environment upon which decisions are taken. Panel reports were accepted as definitive outcomes of disputes in this regard by the members who had endorsed them where they were adopted.

This is an agreeable notion and suggests that an informal precedent effect existed in the GATT, which was relatively powerful and influenced the behaviour of member states in interpretation of the GATT. We have seen in Chapter 1 that whilst the dispute settlement procedures of the GATT were flawed, trends were identifiable in the development of procedures over the first 40 years of GATT's existence. Judicialisation and reliance on panel decisions had both been occurring and were driving reform of the GATT dispute settlement procedures. It is contended that this process came to fruition in 1994 with the implementation of the Uruguay round of ministerial negotiations.

In 1995 the WTO was implemented. The DSU formalised certain rules and demonstrated that the member states had the will to alter the ailing GATT system for increased effective and efficient dispute resolution.

In GATT, as we have seen, there was no concept of *stare decisis*. The panel reports were not strict legal precedents, though they were considered by subsequent panels. Nevertheless, some legal principles were developed by GATT panels that have subsequently been confirmed by the WTO, through the AB.[108] An examination of some of the case law supports this notion. In the GATT *Brazilian Internal Taxes* case, the panel took the view that Article III(2) of the GATT should be interpreted to give the view

106 ibid., pp. 68–9.

107 ibid.

108 A. Chua, 'The Precedent Effect of WTO Panel and Appellate Body Reports', 11 *Leiden JIL*, 1998, p. 47.

that potentialities for exporters should be taken into account for assessing non-discrimination.[109]

In the later GATT *United States – Taxes on Petroleum and Certain Imported Substances* case, the decision in the *Brazilian Internal Taxes* case was relied on to determine the outcome.[110] The principle that potentialities and not trade volumes are protected by the national treatment provision was enshrined. In the *US – Section 337 of the 1930 Tariff Act*[111] case and the *US – Measures Affecting Alcohol and Malt Beverages* case,[112] the panels made their decisions in accordance with previous reports. These cases both related to Article III (2) of the GATT. The GATT decisions established a principle of law: the fact that a trade-related measure had no effect on trade volumes was irrelevant for the interpretation of Article III (2). This decision effectively removed a defence upon which a nation might look to rely and set up a principle in international trade law.

Therefore GATT panels were interpreting and defining the GATT law and creating rules relating to the operation of GATT through interpretation. The reliance by member states on these decisions also shows that the system was operating a form of precedent in dispute resolution decision making. The principle laid down in these GATT cases was confirmed in the *Japan – Alcoholic Beverages* case by the AB in the WTO.[113] This proves that law decided under the GATT also had applicability under the WTO, as long as the panel reports were adopted and applicable to a similar situation.

This reasoning is tempered with the acknowledgement that GATT panels were not bound to follow previous decisions or that GATT jurisprudence necessarily showed any consistency. An example of this inconsistency can be highlighted by examining the following cases. The interpretation of 'like product' as contained in Article I of the GATT, relating to the Most Favoured Nation Principle, has received different interpretations in different cases.[114] In the *Spain – Tariff Treatment of Un-roasted Coffee* case the panel rejected the notion that different types of coffee should have different tariff classification bands.[115] The panel did not agree that tariff classification was enough to determine whether products were 'like'.

On the other hand, in *Canada/Japan – Tariffs on Imports of Spruce-Pine-Fir Dimension Lumber*, the panel went back to tariff classification as the criteria for

109 *Brazilian Internal Taxes* case (GATT/CP.3/42 - II/181), 1949.

110 *United States – Taxes on Petroleum and Certain Imported Substances* (L/6175 - 34S/136), 1987.

111 *US – Section 337 of the 1930 Tariff Act* (L/6439 - 36S/345), 1989.

112 *US – Measures Affecting Alcohol and Malt Beverages* case (DS23/R - 39S/206), 1992.

113 *Japan – Alcoholic Beverages* (WT/DS8/R, WT/DS10/R, WT/DS11/R), 1996.

114 A. Chua, op. cit. 108, p. 48.

115 *Spain – Tariff Treatment of Un-roasted Coffee* (L/5135 - 28S/102), 1981.

determining the like nature of the products.[116] In *EEC – Restrictions on the Imports of Apples from Chile*[117] and *EEC – Restrictions on the Imports of Dessert Apples*,[118] the outcomes were diametrically opposed. The panel in the latter case did not feel that it was legally bound by all the details and legal reasoning of the prior case.[119] This does not mean that precedent was not being applied, but that the panel was distinguishing the case from the previous one.

Despite this inconsistency in GATT panel decisions, the persuasive importance of panel reports was recognised. Panels under GATT almost consciously limited their reasoning and decisions to the case in hand. References to previous cases were still made in passing. In a number of cases the panel made direct references to precedent under GATT, usually to distance itself from any formal commitment to creating such a principle.[120]

The standing of the GATT panel decisions was clarified in the *Japan – Alcoholic Beverages* case from 1996, mentioned earlier. The WTO panel stated:

> Adopted panel reports are an important part of the GATT acquis. They are often considered by subsequent panels. They create legitimate expectations among WTO members and therefore should be taken into account where they are relevant to any dispute. However, they are not binding, except with respect to resolving the particular dispute between the parties to that dispute.[121]

The panel also agreed that adopted panel reports are proof of subsequent practice as understood by Article 31 of the Vienna Convention on the Law of Treaties. Under this Article, to be considered subsequent practice, decisions must be consistent.[122] These statements acknowledge the value of GATT reports in the remit of the WTO dispute resolution process. Whilst acknowledging that they are not binding, they should be referred to where relevant. This recognises the legal heritage created by the GATT dispute resolution system. In Annex 1a of the WTO Agreement, the adopted GATT panel

116 *Canada/Japan – Tariffs on Imports of Spruce-Pine-Fir Dimension Lumber* (L/6470 - 36S/167), 1989.

117 *EEC – Restrictions on the Imports of Apples from Chile* (L/5047 – 27S/98), 1980.

118 *EEC – Restrictions on the Imports of Dessert Apples* (L/6491 – 36S/93), 1989.

119 A. Chua, op. cit. 108, pp. 49–50.

120 See *EEC – Regulation on Imports of Parts and Components*, 1990, where the panel stated that the case was decided without prejudice to any examination of these regulations in any other dispute settlement proceedings; and also *Japan – Restrictions on Certain Agricultural Products*, 1988, where the panel stated that its approach in this particular case should not be interpreted as precedent in other cases.

121 *Japan – Alcoholic Beverages* (WT/DS8/R, WT/DS10/R, WT/DS11/R), 1996, pp. 30–31.

122 UN, Vienna Convention on the Law of Treaties, Treaty Series Vol. 1155, 1969, p. 331.

reports are listed as 'such other decisions' that are part of the legal acquis of the GATT 1994.[123]

The WTO AB also rejected the argument that the GATT reports were binding, as it believed that the character and status of the decisions had not been altered in law by the instigation of GATT 1994. The AB footnote that accompanies their reference to the relative binding force of adopted GATT reports mentions Article 59 of the Statute of the International Court of Justice.[124] This explicit provision limits the binding force of a decision to the specific case, but observes that:

> this has not inhibited the development by that Court (and its predecessor) of a body of case law in which considerable reliance on the value of previous decisions is readily discernible.[125]

It is interesting that the panel limited its comparison to Article 59 and did not also look at Article 35.7, which would provide more recognition of precedential practice.

The underlying factor here is that the WTO AB equates itself with the ICJ – or at least the practitioners do. This suggests that the legal principles of the ICJ are also relevant under the WTO DSU.

3.9 The judicialised WTO dispute resolution system and the role of precedent

> If we regard precedents as decisions furnishing a basis for determining later cases involving similar facts or issues we can say without hesitation that large amounts of such precedents exist in the WTO dispute settlement system.[126]

The development of the WTO dispute resolution system represents the successful transition to a judicialised dispute resolution system, and its operations reflect this, as described in Chapter 1. The contention is that the WTO now has a judicial dispute resolution process, but can it be held with certainty that a notion of precedent exists? The above quotation seems to suggest that this is the case beyond doubt. However, it is necessary to review the facts of the matter.

123 WTO, Annex 1a of the WTO Agreement, 1994.

124 Footnote 30, *Japan – Alcoholic Beverages* (WT/DS8/R, WT/DS10/R, WT/DS11/R), 1996.

125 ibid.

126 Z. Lanye, 'The Effects of the WTO Dispute Settlement Panel and Appellate Body Reports: Is the Dispute Settlement Body Resolving Specific Disputes Only or Making Precedent at the Same Time?', 17 *Temple International & Comparative Law Journal*, 2003, p. 221.

Many commentators support the view that the WTO has experienced the judicialisation of its dispute settlement procedure.[127] To recap on Chapter 1, four further points can be identified to demonstrate the judicialisation of the WTO DSU. These can be summarised as follows:

1 The DSB is **politically independent** in that powerful states cannot exert influence to their advantage in the operation of panel decisions.[128]
2 **Compulsory jurisdiction of the adjudication procedure** is necessary or powerful states could co-opt less powerful states to adopt the procedures whilst refusing to accept the procedures themselves.[129] (As demonstrated earlier in the chapter, the procedures are applied equally to all.)
3 **Enforcement of decisions** through the use of effective sanctions to ensure that all parties take the decisions of the panel seriously.[130] (Again, the enforcement procedures of the DSU do have real 'teeth' to support panel decisions.)
4 **Access to the procedures**. Whilst this is only directly possible for states, third parties can submit *amicus briefs*. Member states also bring issues to the DSB on behalf of industries and companies that may be suffering from trade restrictions.[131]

Given that the process is considered as a highly judicialised system, one can thus address the question of whether there is precedent or a precedent effect of panel decisions.

In the legal texts of the dispute settlement resolution process there is no specific guidance as to the legal status of the outcomes and recommendations of the panel/AB. No provision of the DSU includes reference to precedent in the WTO legal system. To do so would have been a big departure from the traditions of public international law and also would have probably been unacceptable to WTO negotiators. Within the WTO's own material, published on the WTO website, the following statement can be found:

> Even if adopted, the reports of the panel and the Appellate Body are not binding precedents for other disputes between the same parties on other

127 A. Helmdach & B. Zangl, 'Dispute Settlement under GATT & the WTO: An Empirical Enquiry into a Regime Change', Paper of 5th Pan European Institutional Relations Conference, Den Haag, 2004, p. 4.
128 Keohane et al., 'Legalized Dispute Resolution: Interstate and Trans-national', 54 *International Organisation*, 3, 2003, 457–88.
129 ibid., p. 457.
130 ibid.
131 The *EC-Banana* case is an example of the US protecting its companies' interests.

> matters or different parties on the same matter, even though the same questions of WTO law might arise.[132]

This may seem to preclude the idea that a principle of precedent could be applied to dispute resolution procedure outcomes and reports. However, the passage does go on to state:

> If the reasoning developed in the previous report in support of the interpretation given to a WTO rule is persuasive from the perspective of the panel or the Appellate Body in the subsequent case, it is very likely that the panel or Appellate Body will repeat and follow it.[133]

While this is not openly extolling the principle of precedent, the qualification of 'very likely' does suggest that previous reports are good indicators of the likely outcome of similar disputes.

The AB and panels are not formally bound by precedent, but they are expected to follow their own reasoning unless there are grounds to justify distinguishing a case or departing from earlier interpretations or legal arguments.[134] Predictability of outcome is an important part of any legal system. Even in the formal operation of the rule of precedent in the UK's legal system precedent would only be guaranteed in a case that has *identical* facts. Distinguishing features of cases can be identified to allow judges and jurors leeway in determining the outcome of cases. This principle also has application in the WTO DSU. Apart from special circumstances the DSB/AB decisions should constitute persuasive precedents.[135]

The reliance that can be placed on previous WTO panel/AB reports suggests an informal commitment to a precedent principle in the system. Other commentators have also stated that the new DSU provides that like cases of breaches of WTO rules can be treated alike.[136] Further, the creation of the AB (described as a 'World Trade Court in all but name'[137]) has de facto taken over the interpretation of the WTO Agreements, provided the AB agrees by consensus its decision.[138] This means that it is unlikely that any

132 WTO website, http://www.wto.org/english/tratop_e/dispu_e/disp_settlement_cbt_e/c7s2p1_e.htm (accessed 20 December 2009).

133 WTO website, http://www.wto.org/english/tratop_e/dispu_e/disp_settlement_cbt_e/c7s2p1_e.htm (accessed 20 December 2009).

134 E. Reinhardt, 'Adjudication without Enforcement in GATT Disputes', 45 *Journal of Conflict Resolution*, 2, April 2001, pp. 174–95.

135 A. Chua, op. cit. 108, p. 61.

136 Keohane et al, op. cit. 128.

137 D. de Bievre, 'Judicialisation and Positive Integration in the WTO', Paper for the 5th Pan-European International Relations Conference, Den Haag, 9–11 September 2004.

138 ibid.

decision made by the AB would be easily overruled.[139] Naturally a majority decision may hold less weight, as considered in Chapter 1, regarding practice in the ICJ. This strengthens the argument to ascribe the unstated power of precedent to the panel/AB recommendations.

The WTO itself further strengthens this position of recognising the concept of precedent as an unstated principle. One of the key objectives of the DSU is to enhance the security and predictability of the multilateral trading system.[140] This in essence suggests that the WTO would encourage members to put faith in previous decisions of the panels and AB. In fact the AB itself has declared that adopted AB reports 'create legitimate expectations among WTO members, and, therefore, should be taken into account where they are relevant to any dispute'.[141]

The cause of predictability is best served by the development of WTO jurisprudence. The AB has an important role in developing this jurisprudence. Adopted reports have strong persuasive power and may be viewed as a form of non-binding precedent whose role is comparable to that played by jurisprudence in the contemporary continental system of many countries, such as France, and that played by decisions of courts at the same level in the United States. As a practical matter, parties will continue to cite prior reports to panels, and panels will continue to take them into account by adopting their reasoning – in effect, following precedent – unless panels conclude, for good and articulated reasons, that they should do otherwise.[142]

The conclusion one can reach from this evidence is that adopted panel reports should be considered as likely indicators of future dispute outcomes and influence the behaviour of member states; a system not dissimilar from that of the principle of precedent. It is argued that the system is not based on a doctrine of binding judicial precedent but on a rebuttal presumption of precedent, i.e. panels and the AB should respect precedent unless they can distinguish the case.

The position of unadopted panel reports is not quite so clear. Such reports have no formal legal standing in the WTO system. However, the reasoning in them has been deemed to be useful guidance for a panel or AB determining a subsequent case involving the same legal principle.[143]

139 J.H.H. Weiler, 'The Rule of Lawyers and the Ethos of Diplomats: Reflections on the Internal and External Legitimacy of WTO Dispute Settlement', Harvard Jean Monnet Working Paper 09/00, Cambridge, MA, Harvard Law School, 2000.

140 WTO, Article 3.2, DSU, 1994.

141 AB report, *Japan – Alcoholic Beverages* (II DSR) 1996, 1, 97 at 107–108.

142 D. Palmeter & P.C. Mavroidis, 'The WTO Legal System: Sources of Law', 92 *A.J.I.L.* 1998, 400–402.

143 ibid.

3.10 Arguments against the existence of precedent in the WTO

There are arguments against the existence of forms of precedent in the WTO dispute resolution system. Firstly, the DSU itself states that the AB and panel reports cannot create new rules for the WTO.[144] Equally the DSU states that the AB and panels cannot diminish the rights and obligations of the covered agreements.[145] As a formal matter the decisions of the AB and the panels bind only the parties to a particular dispute, not the whole membership. This is clear from the statements of the WTO. The binding nature of the AB/panel decisions has to be limited because only the WTO Agreement itself is binding on all parties.[146] The WTO also specifically accords the authority for definitive interpretations of WTO treaty language to the Ministerial or General Council. This right does not exist elsewhere.

The reason for these overt statements needs to be examined. WTO negotiators were keen to create a more formal legislative mechanism for solving disputes, but it is likely that they did not want judicial activism to run rampant and change the principles that the members had originally signed up to in the creation of the WTO. The DSU has incorporated elements of this notion by stressing that the dispute settlement procedure is central to providing stability and predictability to the multilateral trading system. Article 3.2 of the DSU also provides that the rulings made under the DSB cannot add or diminish the rights and obligations provided in the covered agreements.

This Article can be interpreted as a barricade against allowing any non-WTO principles into the DSB. It suggests that the system is closed to judicial activism on the basis that this would give the practitioners of the DSB power to change WTO law. Binding precedent could also be rejected on these grounds as it too could change the rights and obligations of member states through evolving WTO jurisprudence.

However, as we have seen, the AB and the panels have referred to principles of international law and previous cases in their decision-making process. Article 3.2 is merely placed to act as a warning against judicial activism.[147] The role of the panel members and the AB is to clarify ambiguous phrases or bridge gaps to allow a decision to be taken. They are limited in the amount they can develop the WTO legal system. Nevertheless, on balance of the arguments for and against the existence of precedent in the WTO dispute resolution system, it seems that the weight is slightly tipped in favour of the idea that some form of precedent exists.

144 Article 3.5, DSU, 1994.

145 Article 3.2, DSU, 1994.

146 Article IX (2), WTO Agreement.

147 R. Bhala, 'The Myth about Stare Decisis and International Law (part 1 of a trilogy)', 14 *American University International Law Review*, 1999, 845.

Even under the judicial confines of a continental system the predictability of decisions is valued highly. Certainly the AB refers to principles of international law when deciding cases, and the value of previously determined cases is apparent. It is not possible to claim that binding precedent exists, but a form of precedent does exist that can be classed as rebuttal precedent. As Lanye describes:

> The WTO Panels and the AB are not only resolving specific disputes between the Members, but are also making *de facto* precedent at the same time. Are the Panels and the AB acting beyond their authorization? Some textual support can be found in the DSU to show that the Panels and the AB have been performing their obligation under the DSU. Article 3.2 of the DSU provides that '[t]he Members recognize that it serves to preserve the rights and obligations of Members under the covered agreements, and to clarify the existing provisions of those agreements in accordance with customary rules of interpretation of public international law'.[148]

This supports the view that precedent is being created and that it is supported within the framework of the WTO, which refers explicitly to public international law.

3.11 Conclusion

The principle of precedent is not formally recognised in the WTO, but the practice suggests that much weight should be given to previous panel/AB rulings. The process is also recognised as providing a greater rule of law. The importance attached to predictability of rulings is considerable and this in turn makes it impossible to turn wholly aside from the values contained in precedent. This can be seen as a positive thing: an editorial in the *Washington Post* described the position of precedent at the WTO in the following way:

> Under the WTOs' [sic] rules, panels are not explicitly required to follow previous judgments; although precedent is enormously influential in practice, each case is supposed to be decided on its own merits. If the panels' deliberations were open to scrutiny, departures from past legal reasoning might attract so much criticism that they would become impossible. This, however, would be a good thing. The more closely the WTO follows precedent, the more authority its judgments would command. It would be harder for countries to paint adverse decisions as the work of a whimsical panel.[149]

148 Z. Lanye, op. cit. 126, p. 221.

149 Editorial, 'Open Trade', Washington Post.com, Thursday February 3, 2005, p. A26.

There is much support for recognising the existence of a form of precedent in the WTO DSB. Yet its lack of formal recognition suggests that at best the precedent that currently exists is more in line with the form of rebuttal precedent described earlier in the chapter. Therefore, in international law the principle of precedent can be said to have limited application, but it does nevertheless apply to some extent to WTO and ICJ decisions.

4 Trade and environment in the international legal order

4.1 Introduction

In the previous chapters it has been argued that the WTO DSB, with its panels and AB, together operate a judicialised dispute resolution system. Further, the operations of the DSB, and particularly the AB, have matured since the inception of GATT and the founding of the WTO, so that the decisions of the AB and panels have been relied on and influence the behaviour of the parties to the WTO. Therefore, decisions in the WTO DSB can have lasting consequences and influence not just the parties to a dispute, but also the members of the WTO as a whole. This is through the reliance that is put on the decisions of the DSB/AB by the members, as they expect consistency and reliability of outcome in the DSB system. This is endorsed by the WTO.[1]

This fact has far-reaching consequences for a number of sectors that interact with the WTO and its decision-making bodies. One of these areas is the environment. Whilst the environment itself is not explicitly mentioned in the GATT Treaty, in the preamble to the Marrakesh Agreement forming the WTO, the concept of sustainable development is clearly stated and committed to by all signatories.[2] In other agreements under the WTO the environment as a concept is clearly mentioned.[3]

Arguably this demonstrates that the WTO should have a certain competence for environmental and environmentally-related matters. The 1994 Marrakesh Agreement also set up the Committee on Trade and Environment (CTE). Originally this was intended to be temporary, but as a consequence of

1 WTO website, 'Dispute Settlement System training module', http://www.wto.org/english/tratop_e/dispu_e/disp_settlement_cbt_e/c7s2p1_e.htm (accessed 28 December 2009).

2 WTO, 'Marrakesh Agreement', in *The Legal Texts: The Result of the Uruguay Round of Multilateral Trade Negotiations*, Cambridge University Press, Cambridge, 1999, p. iii.

3 Article 27 of the Trade Related Aspects of Intellectual Property Rights Agreement (TRIPS) makes a specific exemption of patent rights on the grounds of environmental protection. See *The Legal Texts: The Result of the Uruguay Round of Multilateral Trade Negotiations*, Cambridge University Press, Cambridge, 1999, p. 333.

negotiations in the Doha Round the CTE has been given a permanent status.[4] The CTE has a broad mandate which includes, among other objectives, reviewing the relationship between the WTO and MEAs that employ trade mechanisms to enforce their measures.

In this chapter the development of the WTO's competence to deal with environmental issues will be examined, including an analysis of some of the relationships that exist between the WTO and other international environmental treaties. There will also be a review of the current negotiations around trade and environment and of possible developments in the future of this relationship.

4.2 Context of trade and environment in the international law arena

Over recent decades a number of factors have come together to focus the spotlight on the trade–environment debate. Much of the attention focuses on the compatibility of trade liberalisation and protection of environmental resources. Often the debate is portrayed as an either/or decision. This is partly due to a few high-profile conflicts such as the infamous GATT *Tuna-Dolphin* case,[5] but also due to the broader globalisation versus anti-globalisation political movements that have come to dominate the debate in the international economic–political sphere. In this arena commentators have represented the WTO as a body for the process of globalisation;[6] this in essence makes the WTO a target for a number of disparate groups with an anti-globalisation bent.

Since the Seattle ministerial meeting of 1999, with the exception of the Doha Round all the ministerial meetings have been marred with high levels of protest and violence. In the 2005 Hong Kong ministerial a number of South Korean farmers attempted to disrupt the proceedings by breaking into the discussion venue.[7] The 2009 ministerial in Geneva also saw demonstrations and civil unrest.[8] The reasons for this action related to a fear that trade liberalisation is increasingly taking precedence over other issues, such as agriculture, labour standards and environmental regulation. Over the last

4 See the Marrakesh Agreement and the Doha Round Negotiations on Trade and Environment, op. cit. 2; and http://www.wto.org/english/tratop_E/envir_e/envir_negotiations_e.htm (accessed 28 December 2009).

5 See *United States – Restrictions on Imports of Tuna*, WTO website, http://www.wto.org/english/tratop_E/envir_e/edis04_e.htm (accessed 28 December 2009).

6 J. Stiglitz, *Globalisation and its Discontents*, W.W. Norton & Company, New York, 2002.

7 'Trade Battle Starts in Hong Kong', BBC News website, 13 December 2005, http://news.bbc.co.uk/2/hi/business/4522794.stm (accessed 28 December 2009).

8 'Anti-WTO Demonstrations in Geneva turn Violent', Xinhua News website, http://news.xinhuanet.com/english/2009-11/29/content_12557389.htm (accessed 28 December 2009).

15 years developments in international environmental law and international trade law have interacted to bring these two spheres to form an important focus for global attention.[9]

The WTO has become the body to which the international community look to address the twin objectives of trade and environmental policy, both for dispute resolution and policy development.[10] Equally it is almost always considered that trade and environmental policy objectives are different fields.[11] Nevertheless, the essential linkages are apparent between trade and environment, not least due to the express commitments to sustainable development and environment in the WTO agreements.

A question that needs to be answered in this context is: 'Are trade and environmental positive objectives mutually exclusive?' Traditional views, particularly on the environmental protection oriented side, have tended to suggest that trade liberalisation is an outright disaster for the environment:

> The WTO has been a disaster for the environment. Threats – often by industry but with government support – of WTO illegality are being used to chill environmental innovation and to undermine MEAs. Already WTO threats and challenges have undermined or threatened to interfere with US Clean Air rules, the US Endangered Species Act, Japan's [sic.] Kyoto (global warming) Treaty implementation, a European toxics and recycling law, US long horned beetle infestation policy, EU eco-labels, US dolphin protection legislation and an EU trapping law. Things only stand to get worse ...[12]

On the other hand the trade liberalisation position seems to suggest that market economics will deliver environmental protection through drives to efficiency and removal of excess waste that is harmful to the environment.[13] It is at these two viewpoints that the debate regarding the position of environmental concerns and the WTO can begin. It cannot be disregarded that the WTO has many areas which relate to the environment, so the first

9 J. Cameron & K. Campbell, 'A Reluctant Global Policy Maker', in O Perez, *Ecological Sensitivity and Global Legal Pluralism: Rethinking the Trade and Environment Debate*, Hart, Oxford, October 2003, p. 23.

10 ibid.

11 See A. Hansclever, P. Mayer & V. Rittberger, *Theories of International Regimes*, Cambridge University Press, Cambridge, 1997; and also S. Krasner (ed.), *International Regimes*, Cornell University Press, Ithaca, NY, 1983.

12 L. Wallach & M. Sforza, *The WTO: Five Years of Reasons to Resist Corporate Globalisation*, Open Media Pamphlet Series, 2003.

13 P. Newell, 'The Political Economy of International Trade and the Environment', in D. Kelly & W. Grant (eds), *The Politics of International Trade in the 21st Century: Actors, Issues and Regional Dynamics*, Palgrave/Macmillan, Basingstoke, 2005, p. 108.

question to be answered is whether the WTO should be dealing with environmental-related issues at all.

4.3 Free market economics and the environment

The current school of economics in the ascendancy in global economic policy formulation is that of the free market/monetarist persuasion. Arguably the three pillars of global economics (the World Bank, the International Monetary Fund (IMF) and the WTO) pursue economic policies that reflect this school of economic thought. Free market economics are derived from the theories of Adam Smith and David Ricardo;[14] more recently the Chicago School of Economics have applied these theories in a modern context.[15] The principle of free trade lies within the borders of market economics and is therefore favoured by the economic proponents of the market economics model. A premise of free trade advocates is that environmental protection can be achieved through the workings of the market,[16] for the following reasons:

1 International trade generates the wealth and growth that can fund environmental protection programmes. The economic growth associated with trade liberalisation (free trade and tariff elimination) allows governments to tax and raise resources for environmental protection programmes, such as habitat protection or pollution abatement.[17]
2 Open markets create more competition and therefore encourage the efficient use of resources by individual firms. This means there is less waste, and production processes can be rationalised to improve efficiency. This itself promotes environmental protection.[18]
3 More generally the liberalisation of trade encourages the removal of wasteful activities – particularly envisaged are subsidies which support unsustainable industries or agriculture. Greenpeace reported in 1997 that US$15 billion of taxpayers' money had been used to support the fossil fuel and nuclear industries in Western Europe.[19] With trade

14 A. Smith, *The Wealth of Nations*, Prometheus Books, New York, 1991; see also D. Ricardo, 'On the Principles of Political Economy and Taxation', http://www.econlib.org/library/Ricardo/ricP.html (accessed 28 December 2009).
15 See the arguments of Milton Friedman, http://www.colorado.edu/studentgroups/libertarians/issues/friedman-soc-resp-business.html (accessed 28 December 2009); and K.W. Dam, *The Rules of the Global Game: A New Look at US International Economic Policymaking*, The University of Chicago Press, Chicago, 2001.
16 P. Newell, op. cit. 13.
17 J. Bhagwati, 'The Case for Free Trade', 265 *Scientific American*, 5, November 1993.
18 S. Schmidheiny (With the Business Council for Sustainable Development), 'The Business of Sustainable Development', in S. Schmidheiny (ed.), *Changing Course: A Global Business Perspective on Development and the Environment*, Boston, MIT Press, 1992, pp. 1–13.
19 Greenpeace International, *The Subsidy Scandal: The European Clash between Environmental Rhetoric and Public Spending*, Greenpeace International, 1997.

liberalisation it is argued that such practices would come to an end, as the industries would not be competitive nor the practices acceptable in a free multilateral trading system.

These arguments rely on a number of assumptions. For example, funding programmes to tackle environmental degradation represents an 'after the fact' approach to environmental protection. So the type of programmes the extra government revenue funds are also of critical importance. This is especially so when critics of these arguments claim that trade in itself is a cause of environmental degradation.[20] These arguments also assume that a government will use generated income on environmental programmes to address any externalities. This is often not the case, as a government's priorities cannot be second guessed.

In the Greenpeace study mentioned above, it was noted that in the same time-period that Western governments invested US$15 billion in fossil fuel and nuclear energy, only one tenth of the amount was invested in renewable energy resources.[21] Further assumptions include those that predict environmental consciousness follows development. That trade facilitates development therefore implies that more trade will lead to improved environmental protection, if a truly liberalised trade system is employed. This forms part of the notion that demand for environmental quality rises with income, known as the 'willingness to pay' theory, and reflected in the Environmental Kuznets Curve (EKC) model.[22] This again is deeply flawed as many developing countries have very strong environmental lobbies.[23]

The trade liberalisation argument also attacks eco-protectionism, on the grounds that it is harmful to developing countries through impacting exports and that it damages the environment through creating a sub-optimal resource allocation.[24] Further, the eco-protectionist measures may be deemed to be incompatible with the global trade rules. Behind this lies the belief that the gains of international trade liberalisation should not be easily surrendered

20 ibid.; and see section 4.4 for a comprehensive account of environmentalist views on the WTO.

21 Greenpeace, op. cit. 19.

22 See discussion of EKC later in this section.

23 India, for example. The Clemenceau incident required President Chirac of France to order an inquiry into the attempt to have the battleship broken in India (containing many toxic components and pollutants). This came about in part due to pressure from Indian environmental groups, including Greenpeace India. See 'Chirac Orders "Toxic" Ship Home', BBC News website, 16 February 2006, http://news.bbc.co.uk/2/hi/europe/4716472.stm (accessed 28 December 2009).

24 See R. Saez, 'The Case of a Renewable Natural Resource: Timber Extraction and Trade', in D. Tussie (ed.) *The Environment and International Trade Negotiations: Developing Country Stakes*, Macmillan Press, Basingstoke, 2000, pp. 13–33.

to new protectionism sanctioned by environmental concerns.[25] A better process, it is argued, would be to influence consumer demand which could actually suit both environmental protectionist policies and trade liberalisation policies.[26] Educating consumers not to choose mahogany, ivory or fur products can reduce demand for such products, therefore reducing supply of these commodities.

It is arguable whether encouraging consumers to alter their purchasing choices is the most effective way of changing economic behaviour; more positive action approaches, such as boycotts, may be more successful in encouraging the upgrading of social and environmental standards.[27] However, education and persuasion resonates more with the neo-liberal philosophy as consumer preferences would then determine environmental protection policies.

This premise may not be sufficient, as education and persuasion alone may not meet the necessary requirements of the environment, especially if the environmental option is more expensive than the environmentally harmful product. In relation to this, trade liberalisation proponents also argue against environmental concerns that unfettered market economics will result in the 'race to the bottom' with regard to environmental standards.[28] The 'race to the bottom' is an idea that has been put forward by environmental groups, which suggests that ever increasingly mobile companies will simply switch production from highly regulated markets to nations where environmental standards are more lax.[29]

In fact it is proposed by the liberal economists that the opposite happens. Companies try to locate in the most profitable markets; coincidently these markets tend to be the countries with the strongest national environmental legislation – often seen as a non-tariff barrier to trade by developing countries. To access these markets the exporters have to meet the higher environmental standards encouraging a global trend upwards in terms of environmental protection standards.[30] Again this assumes that

25 J. Whalley, 'Trade and Environment beyond Singapore', NBER Working Paper No. W5768, 1996.

26 R. Bommer & G.G. Schulze, 'Environmental Improvement with Trade Liberalisation', 15 *European Journal of Political Economy*, 4, November 1999, pp. 639–61.

27 N. Kabeer, *The Power to Choose*, Verso, London, 2000.

28 See G. Eskeland & A. Harrison, 'Moving to Greener Pastures? Multinationals and the Pollution-Haven Hypothesis', World Bank Policy Research Working Paper No. 1744, 1997; R. Letchumanan and F. Kodama, 'Reconciling the Conflict between the "Pollution-Haven" Hypothesis and an Emerging Trajectory of International Technology Transfer', 29 *Research Policy*, (2000): 59–79; D. Wheeler, 'Racing to the Bottom? Foreign Investment and Air Quality in Developing Countries', 10 *Journal of Environment and Development*, (September 2001), 225–45.

29 K. Polanyi, *The Great Transformation*, Beacon Press, Boston, 1944, p. 57.

30 D. Vogel, *Trading Up: Consumer and Environmental Regulation in the Global Economy*, 2nd edn, Harvard University Press, Cambridge, MA, 1997.

all companies are focusing their production on export to these markets, which of course may not be the case, especially in a global economy.

Indeed more trade is being focused between developing countries, with, for example, Brazil, South Africa and India investigating the possibility of setting up their own trade arrangement.[31] Equally true is the fact that repeated threats of relocation from industries who face increases in environmental legislation have been made. This has led to a regulatory standstill so that governments have lost their nerve in pushing through environmental protection methods.[32] It can also be argued that where national environmental laws have been strengthened, the government has followed these with competitive deregulations in other fields to attract investors.[33]

The views and arguments put forward by the neo-liberal economists are reflected in the global economic institutions. In 1992 the World Bank contended the following in its World Development Report:

> Liberalised trade fosters greater efficiency and higher productivity and may actually reduce pollution by encouraging the growth of less polluting industries and the adoption and diffusion of cleaner technologies.[34]

This view legitimises the neo-liberal view of environmental protection through economic means. These views are also backed up by technologists who support the notion that through human technological advancement environmental problems can be effectively tackled.[35] The model used in the past was known as the Environmental Kuznets Curve (EKC) (mentioned above). This model supported a hypothesis which stated that where there is social advancement from low-level incomes to higher standards of living there will necessarily be environmental degradation and harm. However, when the society has reached the higher level there will be money and assets free to invest in environmental goods such as pollution control and waste management.[36]

31 See K. Lai, 'India–Brazil–South Africa: The Southern Trade Powerhouse Makes its Debut', Council on Hemispheric Affairs, 15 March 2006, http://www.bilaterals.org/article.php3?id_article=4132 (accessed 28 December 2009).

32 The USA refusing to sign the Kyoto Protocol can be seen as an example of this.

33 C. LeQuesne, *Reforming World Trade: The Social and Environmental Priorities*, Oxfam Publishing, Oxford, 1996.

34 World Bank, *World Development Report*, Oxford University Press, New York, 1992.

35 See O. Maponga & C.F. Ngorima, 'Overcoming Environmental Problems in the Gold Panning Sector through Legislation and Education: the Zimbabwean Experience', 11 *Journal of Cleaner Production*, 2, March 2003, pp. 147–57; D. Austin & M.K. Macauley, 'Cutting Through Environmental Issues: Technology as a Double-Edged Sword', The Brookings Institution, 2001, http://www.brookings.edu/articles/2001/winter_environment_and.aspx (accessed 28 December 2009).

36 World Bank, op. cit. 34.

This suggests that investment in technology will occur to overcome any negative environmental impact. Indeed, the opening preamble of the WTO Agreement itself hints at this theory, suggesting that income generation for all provides the drive for sustainable development.[37] Of course not all commentators agree with the principles in the EKC theory, and evidence supporting the principle is limited.[38]

The WTO also commissioned a study on the relationship between trade and the environment.[39] This concluded that the impacts of the inter-relationship between trade and the environment were not unequivocal. The study also chose to isolate the action of trading goods to strengthen the position that trade does not harm the environment. This meant that all other processes involved in the production and consumption of goods were excluded. This would be taken to be a very narrow definition of trade, i.e. not including transportation, production, consumption and disposal of goods.

Interestingly the report concluded that the right environmental regulations and taxes could be used to ensure environmental impacts were covered by producers and consumers.[40] The study claimed that trade would benefit welfare if proper environmental regulations were in place, and that trade and environment could be harmonious, as long as the correct regulations were in place. What the correct regulations would be is not mentioned. The study further stated that the negative impact of trade on the environment was ambiguous and depended on three inter-connected factors:

1 Trade creates changes in the industrial make-up of a country, potentially increasing national output and increasing pollution;
2 Changes in the scale of economic activity;
3 Changes in production technology.

This complex set of inter-related issues would have to be considered before generalisations about trade and its effect on the environment could be contended. This is a fair point, and certainly Nordstrom and Vaughan agreed that where environmental harm occurred, gains from trade should be used to pay for abatement costs.[41] The study though, being limited, could not deal with the afore raised issue of government priorities and how domestic

37 See the opening paragraph of 'The WTO Agreement 1995', in *The Legal Texts: The Result of the Uruguay Round of Multilateral Trade Negotiations*, Cambridge University Press, Cambridge, 2004, p. 4.

38 See the review of studies in Lee, Ferraro & Barrett, 'Introduction: Changing Perspectives on Agricultural Intensification, Economic Development and the Environment', in D.R. Lee & C.B. Barrett (eds), *Tradeoffs or Synergies? Agricultural Intensification, Economic Development and the Environment*, CAB International, Oxford, 2001.

39 H. Nordstrom & S. Vaughan, *Trade and the Environment*, WTO, Geneva, 1999.

40 ibid.

41 ibid.

expenditure could be guaranteed to target environmental issues. The study could only suggest the course of action that national leaders would do well to heed.

With regard to the impact on competitiveness of environmental regulations, the study determined that costs of such regulations were minor for most industries. In fact, a good environmental profile was considered advantageous for a company competing internationally. Certainly it could lead to lower liability insurances and to less regulatory oversight. Importantly, for companies it could increase market access, as environmentally aware customers would be more inclined to buy the product. Therefore suggestions that companies would be inclined to migrate from developed countries to nations where environmental regulation was less stringent are refuted. Investment decisions would be more important than environmental decisions.

However, some anecdotal evidence contradicts this – as mentioned previously the Kyoto Protocol on climate change was not ratified by the USA in response to high-level lobbying from certain industries with market influence.[42] Specifically the carbon emissions reductions were considered constraining for industry due to potential increased production costs.[43] Essentially companies act in their own interests and thus can be inclined to fight any measures that may restrict their profits; yet if environmental regulations are introduced by governments the cost of relocation will be prohibitive.

Therefore the task of imposing the correct environmental regulations falls to the government, through multilateral, bilateral and national means. Most companies once located will install the most state-of-the-art technology, which will be easier and cheaper to install where the technology is developed. So upping and moving because of environmental regulations is considered an unlikely proposition.[44]

Returning to the EKC, the study found time to suggest that the implications of the EKC were limited to local application. This is a fair point given that many environmental pollution issues, like acid rain or global warming, are trans-boundary in their nature. These would not necessarily be detected by the community with increased wealth, so they would be disinclined to take action on these issues. The basic premise can be thus forwarded: economic wealth alone will not be sufficient to combat environmental problems.[45]

42 'How America Plotted to Stop Kyoto Deal', The Heat is Online website, 8 December 2005, http://www.heatisonline.org/contentserver/objecthandlers/index.cfm?ID=5627&Method=Full&PageCall=&Title=US%20Oil%20Lobby%20Sabotaging%20EU%20Kyoto%20Committments&Cache=False (accessed 28 December 2009).

43 See, for example, D. Adam, 'Oil Industry Targets EU Climate Policy', Guardian Unlimited, 8 December 2005, http://www.guardian.co.uk/climatechange/story/0,,1661741,00.html (accessed 28 December 2009).

44 H. Nordstrom & S. Vaughan, op. cit. 39.

45 ibid.

This brief overview contains the majority of the arguments put forward by the free market economists on the environmental benefits of trade liberalisation. These views are often rebuffed by environmentalists and some economists.[46] From this overview it has been demonstrated that the current dominant economic theory and its protagonists recognise that a relationship exists between trade and the environment. They may differ from environmentalists as to the nature of the relationship, or to the solutions to problems that arise from the trade/environment interaction. Nevertheless, the WTO, an organisation that is dominated by market economics, has undertaken a commitment to the environment through the various references to sustainable development and the environment throughout its agreements.[47]

The WTO study discussed earlier gave clear indication that environmental regulation was necessary, even within the neo-liberal framework proposed by the WTO. Yet the WTO continues to attract criticism from environmental groups despite this kind of official recognition of the impact of trade on the environment. An examination of the arguments of the environmental lobby and the orthodoxy upon which they are founded follows.

4.4 The environmental view of the trade–environment debate

The broad term 'environmentalist' is applied in this context to the groups of actors consisting of broad coalitions of policymakers, advocates and scientists, many of whom are united in their perceptions of environmental-related issues, i.e. causal ideas and prescriptive solutions to issues. Many are Non State Actors (NSAs) such as Friends of the Earth (FoE) or the Worldwide Fund for Nature (WWF). Not that they all necessarily agree on issues around trade and environment. For example, the WWF held that under certain conditions trade liberalisation could be made compatible with the goals of sustainable development.[48] Contrasted to this, FoE have described the current trade system as a 'tyranny'.[49]

Despite the differences in approach from actors within this sphere, for the purposes of this chapter the term environmentalist will be applied to this broad group of actors/organisations and individuals with a concern regarding all matters environmental. The philosophy that underlines the environmental

46 J. Stiglitz & A. Charlton, *Fair Trade for All: How Trade can Promote Development*, Oxford University Press, Oxford, 2004.

47 See the preamble of 'The GATS & TRIPS', in *The Legal Texts: The Result of the Uruguay Round of Multilateral Trade Negotiations*, Cambridge University Press, Cambridge, 2004, p. 286 & p. 321.

48 See WWF, 'The GATT, Environmental Protection and Sustainable Development', WWF discussion paper, November 1991.

49 Friends of the Earth, *The Tyranny of Free Trade: Wasted Natural Wealth and Lost Livelihoods*, FoE International, Hong Kong, December 2005.

debate in relation to economics is one of ecological limits.[50] That is to say that the environment has limits and cannot sustain economic development activities beyond a point that will irrevocably imbalance the ecosystem, to the extent that it will be damaged beyond repair. This is described as uneconomic growth and despite short-term benefits being potentially gained the long-term impact will be to reduce the quality of the global environment.[51]

These are the concepts that normal macroeconomics do not necessarily address, and that cause environmentalists to doubt that the current international trade law regime sufficiently addresses the real impact of the unquestioned imperative for economic growth. This is a realistic approach, as unfettered consumption of the planet's resources would leave little for future generations – and indeed there is species loss and resource mismanagement currently taking place. The concept of uneconomic growth requires serious attention, and there must be recognition that consumption of unreplenishable resources will lead to serious choices for future society. Nevertheless, the position does not seem to allow for technological advancement and scientific research that could support new inventions that will support society, a feature of humanities development. Trade is one aspect of economic development that could be considered as a 'threat' to the global ecosystem if it is sacrificed in order to fuel global trade.

Four main arguments have been put forward regarding the negative impact of trade on the environment.[52] Here are the environmental critiques:

1 Without environmental safeguards, trade may cause environmental harm by promoting economic growth that results in the unsustainable consumption of natural resources and waste production.
2 Trade rules and trade liberalisation often entail market access agreements that can be used to override environmental regulations unless appropriate environmental protections are built into the structure of the trade system.
3 Trade restrictions should be available as leverage to promote worldwide environmental protection, particularly to address global or trans-boundary environmental problems and to reinforce international agreements.
4 Even if the pollution they cause does not spill over into other nations, countries with lax environmental standards have a competitive advantage in the global market place and put pressure on countries with high environmental standards to reduce the rigour of their environmental requirements.[53]

50 See H.E. Daly, *Ecological Economics and Sustainable Development: Selected Essays of Herman Daly*, Edward Elgar Publishing, Cheltenham, 2007; and T. Prugh, R. Costanza & H.E. Daly, *The Local Politics of Global Sustainability*, Island Press, Washington, DC, 2000.
51 Ibid., p. 10.
52 D. Esty, *Greening the GATT: Trade, Environment, and the Future*, Earthscan, Washington, D.C., 1994, p. 42.
53 ibid.

These four arguments will be considered in the following review of the general issues environmentalists have with the WTO and trade liberalisation practices.

One issue this group would contend with trade liberalisation and neo-liberal economic theories is that of 'internalisation'. This is an economic term applied by economists to a process whereby full costs are borne by the producer of a good.[54] For the environmentalists a key flaw in the neo-liberal theory of free trade is the failure of the models to internalise the costs of production, i.e. pollution and waste. These costs are borne by the environment and therefore society in general; in economics these costs are known as externalities that companies do not bear the cost of, unless made to by governments. For the environmentalist these costs should be added to the cost of production, as should all activities related to trade – consumption, transportation, waste, etc. This would then give an accurate reflection of the cost of production.

An environmental concern linked to this is the concept of 'food miles', which evolved in the 1990s.[55] Basically it is a concern with the waste of resources used to move goods around the world, and this theory is not without justification. It is estimated that one tenth of oil production is used to move goods around the globe.[56] Given this fact and the cost of pollution associated with fossil fuel consumption, environmentalists see a truer reflection of the cost of pollution borne by the producer and the consumer. Therefore the net benefits of trade liberalisation are offset by the cost of non-internalised environmental degradation. Indeed an inverted model of the EKC has been alluded to. The European Community Taskforce on the Single Market stated:

> The favourable environmental effects of efficiency in the use of resources are likely to be outweighed by the growth in demand, with consequent increases in environmental pressures.[57]

This view opposes the theory that wealth will necessarily bring environmental protection. It is also noteworthy in that it came from an official European Community document, not from an environmental pressure group.

Linked to this is the dispute over the economic idea of comparative advantage. In economics it makes perfect sense to produce goods all over the world, depending upon the cheapest production costs. These goods should then be

54 See UNESCAP website, http://www.unescap.org/drpad/publication/integra/volume1/nepal/1np03d.htm (accessed 28 December 2009).

55 See M.H. Ho & R. Gala, *Food Miles and Sustainability*, Institute of Science in Society, United Kingdom, 2005.

56 P. Newell, op. cit. 13.

57 Quoted in C. LeQuesne, 'Profits and Pollution Havens', in *Reforming World Trade: The Social and Environmental Priorities*, Oxfam Publishing, Oxford, 1996, p. 73.

moved to the centres of demand. Like the above-mentioned theory of food miles, the overall notion of comparative advantage for production of goods poses problems to environmentalists. Economic logic dictates that transporting components across the world – utilising packaging, pesticides and preservatives, where necessary, to ensure a longer shelf life – is acceptable to meet demand.

The environmental movement generally disagree, arguing in favour of local production and local markets, reducing unnecessary environmental costs.[58] This theory has gained credence, especially in developed countries and in relation to food production and consumption.[59] Economists may argue that this preference for buying locally produced goods represents the phenomenon of consumers being willing to pay for environmental 'goods', a natural consequence of a high standard of living. This argument can then be taken forward to argue in favour of the concept of locating environmentally degrading activities amongst populations who can tolerate a higher level of environmental harm.

Some economists propose that this is a good idea and again an example of comparative advantage – a comparative advantage in pollution. This could create pollution havens where activities unacceptable elsewhere could be carried out. This is maintained as an example of comparative advantage and differences in value preferences.[60]

The WTO, World Bank and IMF face further criticism from environmentalists due to the emphasis each of the organisations put on export-led growth.[61] Certainly at the WTO exports are the main concerns for member states. The WTO is the embodiment of the idea that to gain advantages of the global trading system a nation needs to be heavily involved in the import and export of produce. Export produce by its nature can often be resource intensive. So the cost of production in environmental terms will be necessarily high.

58 'Save-on-Foods? Or Save-the-Environment?', Envirocommunications website, http://envirocommunications.wordpress.com/2009/12/07/save-on-foods-or-save-the-environment/ (accessed 28 December 2009).

59 See Friends of the Earth campaigns, http://www.foe.co.uk/campaigns/biodiversity/move.html; see also 'Prince Backs "Buy Local" campaign', BBC News website, 12 November 2001, http://news.billinge.com/1/hi/uk/1651138.stm: the article explains how the British food industry and agricultural lobby are backing a local produce campaign. The campaign also received Royal assent. This shows that it is not just the environmentalist lobby actively engaged in the anti-global food campaign. See also the Breaking the Chains campaign, Organic Consumers Association website, http://www.organicconsumers.org/btc.htm (all sites accessed 28 December 2009).

60 See D'Arge & Kneese, quoted in M. Williams, 'International Trade and the Environment: Issues, Perspectives and Challenges', 1 *Environmental Politics*, 4, November 1994, pp. 1–10.

61 Friends of the Earth, 'What's Wrong with World Trade? An Introduction to the Trade and Sustainability Debate', Friends of the Earth Briefing, London, 2005.

Linked to this concern is the fact that many developing countries are encouraged to engage in export growth that can have negative impacts, such as food shortages in domestic markets.[62] Whilst this is more of a social concern than an environmental concern per se, the argument is worth reiterating here. Export produce has been described as having the following attributes: it requires extra packaging, it requires forms of production which may be highly polluting (especially in agriculture), the processes can be damaging to health and often use land so intensively that it rapidly degrades.[63] Therefore it is natural that the global economic organisations attract such criticism from the environmentalist lobby.

Indeed exports are seen quite legitimately as a means of raising much needed foreign currency for developing countries to invest in development activities. The 'Trade, not Aid' campaign might consist of some groups who consider themselves part of the environmental lobby, yet it may also be the case that they are becoming marginalised.[64] This is because of the strong environmental opposition to the world trading system as it currently stands.

Localisation is now a much more entrenched principle for environmental groups. In the 1990s there was a growth in the principle of localisation and preferences for local exchange trading schemes' goods.[65] Self-sufficiency is now an important idea in the environmentalist camp as it reduces the need for global trade and the associated pollution problems that arise from the action of trading.[66] The environmentalist position draws attention to the shortcomings of export policies to truly reflect the cost of production of a good, and suggests a more practical solution would be to reduce trade and increase local consumption. This position is fundamentally opposed to the principles of economics in the prevailing philosophy of the global economic institutions.

A further criticism put forward by environmentalists about trade and global rules is that the WTO undermines both national and multilateral environmental laws.[67] Whether this is actually the case seems irrelevant to most environmental groups; GATT/WTO dispute rulings that relate to environmental measures are a cause célèbre in the environmentalist's sphere.

62 See L. DeRose et al., *Who's Hungry? And How do we Know? Food Shortage, Poverty, and Deprivation*, UNU Press, Tokyo, 1998.

63 J. Madeley, *Hungry for Trade: How the Poor Pay for Free Trade*, Zed Books, London, 2000.

64 See C.A. Preble & M.L. Tupy, 'Trade, Not Aid', Cato Institute website, http://www.cato.org/pub_display.php?pub_id=3873 (accessed 28 December 2009).

65 See D. Glover, 'Defending Communities: Local Exchange Trading Systems from an Environmental Perspective', IDS Bulletin, No. 30, 1999, pp. 75–81.

66 R. Douthwaite, *Short Circuit: Strengthening Local Economies for Security in an Unstable World*, Green Books, Devon, 1996, pp. 73–74.

67 Friends of the Earth, op. cit. 59.

There has been concern that trade rules would override environmental rules since the inception of the WTO (if not before):

> Current WTO rules provide an inadequate framework for sustainable development precisely because they do undermine governments [sic] ability to legislate in favour of environmental sustainability ... current trade rules discourage governments from pursuing a strategy of internalising costs precisely because they prohibit governments from protecting their domestic industry from cheaper competition from countries who have not internalised costs to the same extent.[68]

This claim is based on the outcomes of cases such as the GATT *Tuna-Dolphin* dispute. The case reviewed the legitimacy of environmental labelling of food products. In this case the GATT panel ruled against the labelling of the products on the basis that the process and production methods (PPMs) were irrelevant in like products.[69] However, environmental products rely on such labelling to allow the consumer to make informed decisions. At the time this was considered a serious threat to environmental product standards. However, following the WTO Hong Kong ministerial meeting it is clear that environmental labelling will be accepted in world trade standards.[70]

This new declaration does raise issues relating to PPMs; traditionally PPMs were kept outside of the trade remit. This development from an environmental perspective must be considered a positive outcome:

> There is no meaningful distinction to be drawn between environmental harm which is generated by a product, or the harm generated by its process and production methods.[71]

Certainly in the past any attempt to distinguish products and PPMs has been met with fierce criticism in some economic sectors:

> (The) distinction between products and processes may seem mere semantics; actually it is crucial if a liberal trading order is to be maintained. It is hard to see how GATT could sanction trade restrictions based on processes rather than products, without setting off a protectionist tide.[72]

68 C. LeQuesne, *Reforming World Trade: Ten Social and Environmental Priorities*, Oxfam Publishing, Oxford, 1996.

69 *United States – Restrictions on Imports of Tuna*, op. cit. 5.

70 This relates to the work on environmental goods and services in the ministerial declaration. It is not yet clear whether the goods will have to be listed to qualify for environmental status.

71 R. Douthwaite, op. cit. 66, p. 81.

72 The Economist, as quoted in J. Lee, 'Process and Product: Making the Link between Trade and the Environment', 6 *International Environmental Affairs*, 4, Fall 1994, 320–41.

This rather dramatic journalistic flourish seems less likely to hold weight in the post-Hong Kong ministerial meeting world. Nevertheless the agreement to allow certain environmental labels does not mean that products are likely to be distinguished on PPM grounds in general. This is more like a caveat for environmental products. This decision of the WTO members should go a long way to appeasing the fears of environmentalists, who have long contended that the WTO posed a major threat to their use in the global trading system. The decision to adopt this policy necessarily means that the distinction between PPMs and products will be more difficult to enforce, especially with the life cycle approach to production that a number of WTO members use.[73]

Previously the environmental lobby had been fearful that the WTO would deem eco-labelling contra WTO rules.[74] This fear is based on the problems that had arisen in GATT case law regarding the term 'like products'.

In the WTO under Articles I(i) and III(iv) a requirement is made for non-discriminatory treatment for like products originating from other member states. This is contentious to all parties, but especially so to the environmentalist argument, because an environmental product (be it a fridge, cooker, car, etc.) may not be similar to one that does not have an environmental pedigree. The question of what makes a product like or unlike another is a question of interpretation. Where it is sought to impose a tariff or taxes on a product on environmental grounds due to its poor environmental performance, so it is unlike domestic products which have environmental performance, it would be necessary to demonstrate the environmental harm that the product causes. It is here that the environmentalists have lost faith in the WTO process. The history of the treatment of 'like' products under Article III particularly has not given much in the way of hope to environmentalists to defend environmentally-motivated trade measures.[75] The case law on the interpretation of 'like' products has gone through a number of iterations to finally rest on the fact that PPMs are not relevant to determining likeness.

Under GATT law the *Japan – Customs* case emphasised the nature, quality and function of goods in determining likeness.[76] This excluded PPMs from determining whether products can be determined as like. Therefore the

73 See 'Life Cycle Costing', UK Office of Government Commerce website, http://www.ogc.gov.uk/implementing_plans_introduction_life_cycle_costing_.asp (accessed 28 December 2009).

74 'Eco-labelling, Forest Certification and the WTO' (originally on the FERN website), 2003, http://209.85.229.132/search?q=cache:ZwVfmf1FtpoJ:www.fern.org/pubs/briefs/WTOecolabel3.pdf+environmental+labelling+in+the+WTO&cd=11&hl=en&ct=clnk&client=firefox-a (accessed 28 December 2009).

75 See D. McRae, 'Trade and Environment: The Development of WTO Law', 1998, 9 *Otago Law Review*, 221, pp. 225–9.

76 *Japan – Customs Duties, Taxes and Labelling Practices on Imported Wines and Alcoholic Beverages*, panel report, Nov 10 1987, 34th Supplement, BISD 83, 1988, para. 5.6.

environmental effects of a product either through PPM or end use seemed to be excluded from this definition. This view was reinforced in the *Tuna-Dolphin I* case, where it was held that national regulations aimed at PPMs cannot be directed at a product.[77] Of course the panel report was not adopted, but the context could be referred to, if necessary, in later cases. Under the next case to consider the meaning of 'like' products a more purposeful approach was taken.

In the *United States – Taxes on Automobiles* case a tax on fuel-inefficient motor vehicles, which fell primarily on imported vehicles, was found not to breach Article III in determination of like products.[78] This was because the aim and effect of the measure was the issue being judged; the panel had determined that it was not a question of 'likeness' but rather whether the intention of the measure was protectionist. If the aim and the effect of the measure was not protectionist, then distinguishing between foreign and imported products is more legitimate. This interpretation seemed to be suggesting that it would be able to distinguish likeness on PPMs as long as the measure was not deemed to be protectionist. However, this piece of judicial activism was soon undone, and the panel report was not adopted.

In the *Japan – Taxes on Alcoholic Beverages* case, the test of aim and effect was rejected.[79] Instead the panel applied a test with regard to likeness of products based on the following issues:

1 the product's properties;
2 the product's nature and quality;
3 its end uses;
4 consumers' tastes and habits;
5 the product's tariff classification.[80]

The ruling was more in line with the *Japan – Customs* case, thereby signalling a return to the more straight 'likeness' rule. This closed the door on PPMs being considered under the rationale of like products. It appeared that the issue of environmental PPMs being used for discrimination in tariff duties was also ended – at least so it was widely believed. Certainly the AB broadly agreed with the original panel decision, though they were less inclined to include the fifth test for likeness.[81] The AB also stated that the concept of

77 *United States – Restrictions on Imports of Tuna*, panel report, August 1991 (1991) 30 I.L.M. 1594 (*Tuna-Dolphin I*).

78 *United States – Taxes on Automobiles*, panel report, October 11 1994 (1994) 33 I.L.M. 1397 (not adopted).

79 Panel report: WT/DS8/R, WT/DS10/R, WT/DS11/R, July 11 1996; AB report: WT/DS8/AB/R, WT/DS10/AB/R, WT/DS11/AB/R, October 4 1996, adopted (alcoholic beverages).

80 ibid.

81 AB report, ibid.

'likeness' should be reviewed on a case-by-case basis, with a narrow definition of 'like'.[82]

To recap, the 2005 statement on eco-labels raises expectations that the PPMs of environmental goods will still be advertised on products. This is a considerable positive for environmentalists, addressing some of the fears and criticism levelled against the WTO.

One further concern of the environmentalist lobby is the position of international environmental law in relation to the WTO rules and systems. For the purposes of this section it is sufficient to note that environmentalists contend that MEAs are at risk from the rules of the trading system. A number of MEAs employ trade-related environmental measures (known as TREMs), and it is these measures that could come into conflict with the WTO trade rules. Environmentalists claim that if these MEA provisions are contended in the WTO, the rules of global trade will override the principles of international environmental law.[83]

Indeed, the WTO members have recognised this and at the inception of the WTO the CTE was established. Its mandate included reviewing MEAs that employed TREMs to determine the risk. This work has resulted in a number of WTO studies.[84] The CTE identified 22 MEAs that require the signatory nations to implement TREMs that could violate the laws of the WTO. As of yet only one member has raised any issue in relation to TREMs and WTO rights.[85] It is not expected that there is likely to be a sudden rush of cases regarding MEAs and TREMs.

The work of the CTE has been something of a delicate operation, as often developed countries push for more environmental measures in the WTO and these are opposed by developing countries.[86] This has somewhat constrained the work of the CTE and has also led to rejection of the propositions that GATT Article XX be amended to include MEAs.[87] There are certainly

82 ibid.

83 R.G. Tarasofsky & S. Pfahl, *The Threats to Forests from Trade Liberalisation under the WTO*, Greenpeace, Netherlands, 2001.

84 MEA Database: 'Matrix on Trade Measures Pursuant to Selected MEAs', WTO, http://209.85.229.132/search?q=cache:SY6vpYMxy6kJ:www.tradeobservatory.org/library.cfm%3FrefID%3D25754+%E2%80%98MEA+Database:+Matrix+on+Trade+Measures+Pursuant+to+Selected+MEAs&cd=1&hl=en&ct=clnk&client=firefox-a (accessed 28 December 2009).

85 Zimbabwe requested compensation at the WTO for the inclusion of the African elephant on one of the CITES' endangered species lists. This, they stated, would compensate them for the loss of ivory revenue.

86 F. Macmillan, *WTO and the Environment*, Sweet & Maxwell, London, 2001, p. 14.

87 See WTO, Trade and Environment Bulletins, Nos 1–13 (1195–1996, Press/TE 001-13); see also R. Steinberg, 'Trade–Environment Negotiations in the EU, NAFTA and WTO: Regional Trajectories of Rule Development', 1997, 91 *American Journal of International Law*, p. 243; see also M. Williams, *In Search of Global Standards: The Political Economy of Trade and the Environment: Critical Perspectives*, Lynne Rienner Publishers Inc., Boulder, CO, 2001, pp. 39–63.

challenges posed by environmental inclusion in the WTO and the needs of developing countries. However, it is not just developing countries that object to the inclusion of particular environmental issues in the sphere of the WTO.

The Cartagena Protocol on biosafety has been devised in a way that represents a compromise between the EU, who were pushing for stronger measures, and the US, who favoured a subordination of the Protocol to WTO rules.[88] Therefore arguments relating to environmental measures can often be between developed nations. This kind of disagreement alarms environmentalists, especially when a nation such as the US argues in favour of WTO rules over environmental rules. Why should MEAs be subservient to the international trade rules? Certainly there is a perception that such protocols are secondary to the WTO and international trade rules; environmentalists would like to see no less priority for MEAs than there is for trade liberalisation.[89]

These issues broadly form the arguments of the environmentalists against the WTO and its workings with regard to the environment. They have some particularly strong points, such as the danger to MEA rules posed by WTO rules, but also there are some flaws in their arguments. As we have seen, the banning of eco-labels has not come to pass. The WTO has become the scene of the debate between the free market economists and the environmentalists. Before examining the record of the WTO on the environment to date, it is worth exploring the international environmental law context within which the WTO operates. This will help to explain some of the pressures on the WTO with regard to the environment and also why environmentalists perceive the WTO as an anti-environmental rules organisation.

4.5 The environmental law context

There follows a review of the international environmental law context which exists, including some of the organisations, treaties and NGOs that impact upon the WTO. In the context of this study it will be relatively brief, because there are a number of detailed reviews of the international environmental actors and their views on the WTO.[90] A number of conventions and

88 P. Newell & R. MacKenzie, 'The 2000 Cartagena Protocol on Biosafety: Legal and Political Dimensions', 10 *Global Environmental Change*, 2000, pp. 313–17.

89 See P. Morici, *Reconciling Trade and the Environment in the WTO*, Economic Strategy Institute, Washington D.C., 2002; see also C. Hines, 'Big Stick Politics', *The Guardian*, 8 October 1997, pp. 4–5.

90 See G.P. Sampson, 'Trade, Environment, and the WTO: The Post-Seattle Agenda', Policy Essay No. 27, Overseas Development Council, Washington, 1999; D. Esty, *Greening the GATT*, Earthscan, Washington D.C., 1994; and F. Macmillan, *WTO and the Environment*, Sweet & Maxwell, London, 2001.

treaties will now be examined to help provide a context of the international environmental law arena.

4.5.1 The Convention on Biological Diversity

Arguably the most significant environmental convention signed in the modern era is the one commonly known as the Biodiversity Treaty, which was opened for signing during the United Nations Conference on Environment and Development (UNCED).[91] Organised under the auspices of the UN, the conference resulted in an ambitious programme of environment and development objectives. The outcomes of the conference included the Rio Declaration on Environment and Development, the CBD and Agenda 21. This conference built on the earlier UN 1972 Stockholm Convention, which had initially recognised the environment as an entity for the first time.

Importantly, in the 1980s there had been further progress on environmental issues and the 1987 Brundtland Report, 'This Common Inheritance', which put forward the principle of sustainable development.[92] With growing public interest in the environment, and the recognition by states that numerous global environmental challenges lay ahead of them, the UNCED took place in Rio de Janeiro, Brazil, in June 1992. As mentioned above, one of the main achievements of that conference was the opening for signing of the CBD, which is concerned with the establishment of an international programme for the conservation and utilisation of the world's biological resources.[93] The CBD is also primarily concerned with the 'fair and equitable sharing' of the benefits accruing from the utilisation of genetic resources.[94]

The CBD has been ratified by 175 countries (more signatories than the WTO) and has important links with trade policy which will be examined later in this chapter. A notable absence, however, is that of the USA. Similarly, the USA has not signed the Kyoto Agreement, which will be examined later. This is a major problem for such environmental agreements – when the world's superpower refuses to ratify such conventions they lack that certain gravitas. The abstention of the USA aside, the CBD remains dedicated to preventing the continued extinction of species both plant and animal. Some of the aims have direct links with the work of the WTO.

91 See Columbia University Centre for International Earth Science Information Network, 'The Convention on Biological Diversity', http://www.ciesin.org/TG/PI/TREATY/bio.html (last accessed 20 February 2010).

92 The Brundtland Report, World Commission on Environment and Development, *Our Common Future*, Oxford University Press, Oxford, 1987.

93 See F. McConnell, *The Biodiversity Convention: A Negotiating History*, Kluwer Law, London, 1996.

94 UN, 'CBD Article 1', CBD website, http://www.cbd.int/convention/convention.shtml (accessed 28 December 2009).

The CBD is maintained by a COP held every one to two years. The third meeting of the COP proclaimed a decision on intellectual property rights.[95] The proclamation essentially requested more co-operation on issues relating to technology transfer and sharing with indigenous peoples. It also called for a re-examination of intellectual property rights, including generalised systems of ownership.[96] The relationship between the TRIPS agreement and the CBD is recognised by the members of the CBD; in fact the CBD has shown some deference to the WTO.

The fifth CBD COP held in Nairobi in 2000 invited the WTO to take into account the fact that the provisions of the TRIPS agreement and the CBD are inter-related and to further explore the relationship.[97] This can be seen as the CBD COP requesting the WTO to take a lead in the process. Indeed, the relationship between the CBD and the WTO continues to be a source of interest for many parties. Like most international conventions the CBD is not self-enacting and requires each signatory to adopt implementing legislation. It has no enforcement mechanism and no dispute resolution procedures. Its implementation has been slow, hampered by financial constraints and the reluctance of the USA to ratify the CBD. Conversely, TRIPS guarantees recognition and enforcement of intellectual property rights, backed by the power of the WTO dispute resolution system.

It has been documented that the TRIPS and CBD pose potential conflicts with one another.[98] These conflicts relate to the provisions of the CBD in respect of the sovereignty of genetic resources of plants and animals, and developing countries having the right to benefit from the development of these resources and the transfer of technology relevant to these resources. This has implications for the current intellectual property system with regard to bio-tech companies, pharmaceutical companies and agricultural industries. All follow rules of intellectual property agreed by TRIPS, where there is no real provision for protection of traditional knowledge and culture.

Interestingly, the provisions of the CBD were being devised at the same time as those in TRIPS. Yet the separate nature of the discussions led to very different outcomes. Almost ten years after the text for the two agreements were proposed there has been little systematic analysis of the potential conflicts between the two conventions. The WTO TRIPS committee have shown signs

95 UN, CBD, COP 3, Decision 111/17.

96 ibid.

97 Decision of the Contact Group on Access, UNEP/CBD/COP/5/WG.11?CRP.7, May 22 2000, Part B, para. 2.

98 See G. Dutfield, *Intellectual Property Rights, Trade and Biodiversity*, Earthscan, London, 2002; and B. Dhar, 'The Convention on Biological Diversity and the TRIPS Agreement: compatibility or conflict?', in C. Bellman, G.Dutfield & R. Melendez-Ortiz, *Trading in Knowledge: Development Perspectives on TRIPS, Trade and Sustainability*, Earthscan, London, 2003, p. 77.

of involvement – as reflected in the Hong Kong ministerial declaration.[99] Also the TRIPS committee has been running workshops on the links between TRIPS and the CBD in a bid to raise awareness of the two conventions and possible conflicts.[100] Equally Pascal Lamy, the current Director General of the WTO, addressed the CBD COP in 2006 to emphasise the compatibility of TRIPS and the CBD in a bid to calm concerns of potential conflicts between the agreements.[101]

Potential conflicts are likely to arise in a situation where a signatory to the CBD is also a signatory to the WTO, and a potential benefit under the WTO is lost.[102] Indeed, the fact that the CBD has no dispute resolution system implies that members who are also signatories of the WTO are likely to use the DSB if any TRIPS-related issues come into conflict with the CBD. Specific conflicts between TRIPS and the CBD may require amendments of the CBD, TRIPS, or both.

A meeting of the TRIPS committee in 2002 did review the relationship between the CBD and TRIPS.[103] A group of mainly developing countries (including Brazil and India, and from Europe, Norway) called for negotiations on amendments to the TRIPS text. The particular amendment concerned the requirement for patent applications to disclose the origins of genetic resources and associated traditional knowledge used in their invention, along with evidence of prior informed consent and benefit sharing. Conversely, the USA and Australia disagreed and maintained no change was needed.[104]

The Hong Kong ministerial declaration called for progress on the issue by July 2006.[105] However, the USA and Australia believe that no amendment is necessary and are therefore blocking the negotiations.[106] They contend that TRIPS and the CBD are mutually exclusive and thus can be implemented separately. This is symptomatic of the potential conflicts that exist between TRIPS and the CBD.

99 WTO, Hong Kong ministerial declaration, 2005, para. 39.

100 W. Meier-Ewart, 'The Relationship between TRIPS and the CBD', Presentation at the WTO Symposium on Trade and Sustainable Development, Geneva, 11 October 2005.

101 P. Lamy, Ministerial Segment, Panel on Biodiversity and Trade, CBD, COP 8, 26–29 March 2006.

102 M. Matsushita, T. Schoenbaum & P. Mavroidis, *The World Trade Organisation: Law, Practice and Policy*, Oxford University Press, Oxford, 2004, p. 412.

103 See European Commission website, http://209.85.229.132/search?q=cache:e8T7ZO4-mr8J:trade.ec.europa.eu/doclib/html/122275.htm+Recently+a+meeting+of+the+TRIPS+committee+did+review+the+relationship+between+the+CBD+and+TRIPS&cd=6&hl=en&ct=clnk&client=firefox-a (accessed 28 December 2009).

104 See 'Members Look at TRIPS–CBD Relationship', *Bridges Weekly Trade Review*, ICTSD, 27 March 2006.

105 Hong Kong ministerial declaration, op. cit. 97.

106 See Third World Network website, http://www.twnside.org.sg/title2/twninfo342.htm (accessed 28 December 2009).

4.5.2 The Kyoto Protocol on climate change

Another major environmental multilateral agreement next to which the WTO operates is the United Nations Framework Convention on Climate Change (UNFCCC), the first legally binding global agreement aimed at reducing anthropogenic global warming, and its Kyoto Protocol which sets targets for nations in relation to greenhouse gas emissions.

Global warming is a very controversial issue in the international legal order. Environmentalists have been concerned that the current warming trends have progressed much quicker than in the past.[107] They agree that the Earth does go through heating and cooling periods, but contend that the current phase of warming is much more pronounced than it has been in the past.[108] They hypothesise that the increased warming rate is due to the increased level of carbon dioxide that has been put into the Earth's atmosphere due to the activities of humanity over the last 200 years. The combination of vast deforestation and the increase in burning of fossil fuels has, it is contended, caused a rapid warming of the Earth. It is estimated that in the next 25 years the level of carbon dioxide in the atmosphere will increase by 100 per cent, which could lead to an increase of global average temperatures by as much as 4°C.[109] The consequences of this are as of yet conjecture, but it is contended that sea levels could rise, flooding low-lying countries; desertification could increase in sub-Sahara Africa, and the climate could become more variable and therefore less predictable.[110]

The Kyoto Protocol is seen as a means of global action being taken to avert the worst consequences of the theories outlined above. In 1997 the Kyoto Protocol was agreed by 180 nations as the strategy to combat the effects of global warming.[111] The Protocol essentially aims to provide countries with a meaningful incentive to reduce their emissions of carbon dioxide (and other potential greenhouse gases – global warming is sometimes referred to as the greenhouse effect). In 1997 the signatories agreed that a 5.2 per cent *average* reduction from 1990 global pollution levels was to be achieved by the year 2012, subject to national ratification.[112]

The Kyoto Protocol is set to expire in 2012, when a new framework to tackle climate change will be agreed (at least in theory). The averaging

107 N. Stern, *The Economics of Climate Change: The Stern Review*, Cambridge University Press, Cambridge, 2007.

108 J.T. Houghton, L.G. Meira Filho, B.A. Callender, N. Harris, A. Kattenberg & K. Maskell (eds), *IPCC Second Assessment Report: The Science of Climate Change*, Cambridge University Press, Cambridge, UK, 1995.

109 R. Watson and the core writing team (eds), *IPCC Third Assessment Report: Climate Change 2001*, IPCC, Geneva, 2001.

110 ibid.

111 UN, The Kyoto Protocol to the United Nations Framework Convention on Climate Change, June 1997.

112 UN, Kyoto Protocol, Article 3, June 1997.

approach under Kyoto means that some countries have to reduce their emissions more than others – the US being the largest producer of greenhouse gases is expected to reduce its output of carbon dioxide by 7 per cent below 1990 levels. Conversely, some developing countries have a small or zero burden in the framework as low producers of greenhouse gases.

The Kyoto Protocol has been hampered by the requirement for it to take effect only after ratification by signatories whose emissions make up over 55 per cent of global greenhouse emissions, based on 1990 production levels. The US, the world's biggest polluter, eventually did not sign the Protocol.[113] Being responsible for one quarter of greenhouse gases, mainly carbon dioxide due to the emphasis put on cars and power production, this put a major break on the advancement of the Protocol. The USA has a preference for using voluntary measures or market mechanisms to reduce greenhouse gas production, rather than agreeing an overall reduction strategy. The US government noted that ever increasing energy efficiency and the reduction in availability of cheaper fuels would combine to reduce the level of carbon dioxide emissions in due course. They also provided a number of studies showing that environmentalists' projections were exaggerated, and that the Kyoto Protocol may not reduce emissions significantly anyway.[114] The Obama administration does, however, appear to be more willing to make a credible cut in greenhouse gas production although it has not yet successfully reflected this at an international level.

The motivations behind the original US position can be linked to economic and trade policies. The US government feared the implementation of the Protocol as it was believed that prices for energy and fuel would have to increase sharply – in the case of fuel it was estimated that the increase could be up to 65 cents per gallon. Studies further estimated that the loss of jobs related to this could be as much as 2.5 million in sensitive manufacturing sectors. These studies also predicted the cost to each American family as an average of a reduction of $2,700 per annum to household incomes.[115] Basically, the economic theorists suggested that the Kyoto Protocol would be a disaster for personal wealth in the US, irrespective of other countries

113 See Text of a Letter from the President to Senators Hagel, Helms, Craig, and Roberts, Office of the Press Secretary, 13 March 2001, http://www.gcrio.org/OnLnDoc/pdf/bush_letter010313.pdf (accessed 28 December 2009).

114 See 'The Analysis of Strategies for Reducing Multiple Emissions from Power Plants Report', Report No. SR/OIAF/2000-05, US Department of Energy, 2000; 'The US Environment Protection Agency Analysis of Emissions Reduction Options for the Electric Power Industry', Washington, DC, March 1999; 'Energy-Environment Policy Integration and Co-ordination Study', The Electric Power Research Institute, TR-1000097 (Palo Alto, CA, 2000); and H. Lee & S.K. Verma, 'Coal or Gas: The Cost of Cleaner Power in the Midwest', BCSIA Discussion Paper 2000-08, ENRP Discussion Paper E-2000-08, Kennedy School of Government, Harvard University, June 2000.

115 ibid., Lee & Verma.

making similar commitments. This could exact a large political toll for any US government pursuing the Protocol.

There was also a trade dimension to the fears of the US government. As mentioned above, the Kyoto Protocol does not apply equally to all countries. Developing countries would not be expected to bear such a burden as they are in general low producers of greenhouse gases, with some notable exceptions – including China. This could give them an improved competitive advantage over industrial countries, including the USA. China and India are not under huge reduction pressure through the Kyoto Protocol, and the US with such large trade imbalances feared any measures that could theoretically worsen their trade deficits with these countries. The extra costs of fuel and energy could have made US companies even less competitive. This was seen as too much to give for the environment in the Bush administration's policy circles. Moreover, the Protocol could be seen as unfair for the US, as China and India both have fast growing economies and will therefore contribute to greenhouse gases more and more. As the baseline was set at 1990 these two were not under pressure to make such strong commitments. The US felt that the Protocol failed to take into account their current global economic status, a position reflected to a certain extent by the US administration in the 2009 Copenhagen Climate Change Conference.

These are some of the reasons for the stagnation of the Kyoto Protocol. Nevertheless the Protocol still has effect. All other developed countries have signed the agreement. The Kyoto Protocol was finally ratified in 2005 after the 146th member ratified the Protocol, covering the required amount of greenhouse gas emissions. With the failure of the US to ratify the Protocol, it was the Russian ratification in November 2004 that achieved the ratification threshold (their emissions accounted for 17 per cent of 1990 levels). Nevertheless the Protocol as ratified is only addressing 61.6 per cent of the global 1990 level.[116] The provisions of the Protocol require parties to meet targets for emission reduction by 2012. Where parties fail to do this the Protocol stipulates that an additional 30 per cent reduction will need to take place over the next period.[117]

Each country is allowed to implement the Protocol in its own fashion. The EU has implemented a quota system for 12,000 factories – each factory can buy or sell extra quota capacity as they need to.[118] Essentially the motivation behind this approach is to create a market in carbon emission permits. This is a novel approach and brings in a market economy model to attempt to reduce climate change. Theoretically it could be contended that the US are subsidising their industries by not implementing the Kyoto Protocol, and

116 See 'Climate Change', BBC website, www.bbc.co.uk/climate/policies/kyoto.shtml (accessed 28 December 2009).

117 The Kyoto Protocol, op. cit. 111.

118 BBC, op. cit. 116.

could therefore be challenged under WTO rules.[119] This scenario is perhaps a long way off from being realised. Therefore the terms do have an effect in international law, and indeed some of the provisions are very relevant for the WTO.

At the Montreal Climate Change Conference in 2005 and in Copenhagen in 2009, all the parties to the Kyoto Protocol met and discussed what should happen after 2012 with regard to climate change. Many different views have been put forward and some action has been taken to create partnerships to address climate change.[120] The strategies generally include building on the key Kyoto principles of emission reduction targets and possibly a global trade system in carbon emission permits. Promotion of energy-efficient and carbon low/free technologies, particularly in partnership with the developing countries like India, China and Brazil is also being considered. A road-map has been created out of the Montreal Conference to develop the procedures post-2012, with an aim to also include developing countries and the US.[121]

Political leaders have demonstrated a great deal of commitment to the Kyoto Protocol. Former British Prime Minister, Tony Blair, stated in 2006:

> I don't believe that we can wait five years to conclude a new agreement (on climate change). I think we've got to do it much more quickly than that ... I also believe that such an agreement, if it's going to be successful, has got to include all the major countries of the world and that includes the major developing economies of China and India and also the United States ... I don't want it on the conscience of me or people of my generation that we were told what this problem was and did nothing about it.[122]

Tackling global warming is a top priority for the current British government, and in 2009 at the Copenhagen COP of the UNFCCC the UK Environment Secretary, Hilary Benn, confirmed that the EU was committed to giving $10 billion a year to fight climate change by 2012, as well as encouraging agreement for a post-Kyoto Protocol before the next scheduled climate change meeting in Mexico.[123] This demonstrates a commitment to tackling

119 EU MEPs as quoted in 'Kyoto Protocol Meeting Unable to Reach Agreement on the Future', *Bridges Weekly Trade Digest*, 18 March 2006.

120 See the EU–China partnership agreement on climate change, 2005. In a statement The European Commission stated: 'The two sides were determined to tackle the serious challenges of climate change through practical and results-oriented cooperation. This partnership will fully complement the United Nations Framework Convention for Climate Change and the Kyoto Protocol.'

121 *Bridges Weekly Trade Digest*, op. cit. 119.

122 'Blair Wants Urgent Action on Climate Change', Reuters, 29 March 2006.

123 See DEFRA website, http://www.defra.gov.uk/corporate/about/who/ministers/speeches/hilary-benn/hb091213.htm (accessed 6 February 2010).

this environmental issue, and as mentioned there could be interaction with the WTO.

4.5.3 The Cartagena Protocol on Biosafety (CPB)

Another international environmental agreement with overlapping areas impacting the WTO with global application is the Cartagena Protocol on Biosafety. It also has specific articles relating to trade that bring its provisions very close to the workings of the WTO, and therefore also presents real possibilities in terms of conflict with WTO provisions. This is despite the fact that one of the recitals at the start of the Protocol states:

> Recognising that trade and environment agreements should be mutually supportive with a view to achieving sustainable development.[124]

Nevertheless the provisions have been noted as a possible source of conflict with the Sanitary and Phyto-Sanitary (SPS) Agreement.[125] As one of the protocol conventions to come out of the CBD, this Protocol addresses the issues around living modified organisms (LMOs) or genetically modified organisms (GMOs). The COP of the CBD had set up in 1994 an open-ended group of experts to consider issues such as safe handling, transportation and use of LMOs; this informal group produced the text for the Protocol which was adopted in 2000 by willing parties of the CBD.[126]

The negotiations leading up to the signing of the Protocol had been characterised by a strong split between the US and the EU. The US had wanted the work that is now considered under the Protocol to be put into the remit of the WTO.[127] The US recommended that this should be the case as the trade in such products was being proposed to be part of the Protocol, rather than the WTO. In 1999 the US was positioning to get the work now covered by the Protocol into the WTO through the WTO Seattle Ministerial Conference.

The EU, on the other hand, wanted a separate protocol to be used that had at its basis the precautionary principle – again an issue that the US objected

124 UN, CPB recitals, 'Cartagena Protocol on Biosafety to the Convention on Biological Diversity', 29 January 2000, 39 *I.L.M.* 1027 (2000).

125 See A.H. Qureshi, 'The Cartagena Protocol on Biosafety and the WTO – coexistence or incoherence?', *International and Comparative Law Quarterly*, Vol. 49, pp. 835–55, 2000, p. 854; and S.S. Safrin, 'Treaties in Collision? The Biosafety Protocol and the World Trade Organization Agreements', 96 *The American Journal of International Law*, 3, 2002, pp. 1109–34.

126 UN, 'Cartagena Protocol on Biosafety to the Convention on Biological Diversity', 29 January 2000, 39 *I.L.M.* 1027 (2000).

127 WTO, 'Negotiations on Agriculture, Measures Affecting Trade in Agricultural Biotechnology Products', 4 August 1999, WT/GC/W/365.

to, preferring the basis of proved scientific impact. With the failure of the Seattle Round the US withdrew its objections to the signing of the biosafety Protocol, including the precautionary principle, so that it could be ratified.[128] The use of the precautionary principle is of great significance for environmental regulation, as it operates on the basis that if an action or policy could cause harm to the environment, in the absence of scientific consensus, then the burden of proof falls on those taking the action or policy to prove that it is not harmful. Thus the evidence needs to demonstrate that there will be no negative consequences for the environment from an action. This is a fundamental argument of environmentalists, that no action should be considered unless it is proven that there will be no harm to the environment. This is against the position of most trade agreements which seek only to facilitate trade in the most economic way, with a burden of proof on the importer to demonstrate that a good causes harm before it can limit its import into a territory. The use of the precautionary principle could be considered a major step forward in the defence of the environment through the CPB.

This now means that international trade in LMOs is most significantly addressed outside the context of the WTO. The Protocol governs the trans-boundary movement of most LMOs and therefore has a direct impact upon trade. The overall objectives of the Protocol are to ensure an adequate level of protection in the safe use of LMOs resulting from modern biotechnology, which may have adverse effects on human health, conservation and sustainable use of biodiversity.[129] It specifically focuses on trans-boundary movements of LMOs.

The CPB divides LMOs into two categories for the purpose of international regulatory action subject to different levels of regulation. The trans-boundary movements of LMOs are subject to an Advanced Informed Agreement (AIA) procedure, under which the potential exporter has to gain advance full written consent from the nation through which – or to whom – the export is being made.[130] The AIA procedure involves many steps: notification by the party of export, acknowledgement of receipt of notification by the import party, a decision procedure, and possible review of the decision in light of new scientific information.[131] Decisions are made in accordance with recognised risk assessment procedures; however, lack of scientific certainty can result in the banning of the import on the basis of the precautionary principle.[132]

128 Article 10.6 of the Protocol clearly endorses the precautionary principle; see Indian Department of Trade website, http://commerce.nic.in/trade/international_trade_papers_nextDetail.asp?id=53 (accessed 6 February 2010).

129 UN, CPB Article 1, CBD website, http://www.cbd.int/biosafety/protocol.shtml (accessed 28 December 2009).

130 ibid., CPB Article 10.

131 ibid., CPB Articles 8, 9 and 10.

132 ibid., CPB Article 10.6.

There are several exceptions to the CPB AIA procedures, including LMOs contained in pharmaceuticals, transit LMOs and LMOs intended for direct use as food or feed.[133] In fact LMOs intended for use as food or feed are subject to less rigorous procedures, as it is intended that the SPS Agreement of the WTO should cover the requirements of trade/movement of such goods. Hence it is clear that there is a strong link between the WTO and the CPB.

There could be potential conflict over the food/feed exemption as the CPB allows parties to ban or limit imports of LMOs under its domestic regulatory framework, as long as it is consistent with the objective of the CPB.[134] This could be applied to the food/feed category exemption too. This clearly allows the use of import measures to block trade in these LMOs. A member of the WTO who felt that a right was being impinged could take the case to the DSB. This could mean the provisions of the CPB being scrutinised by the WTO.

Given that the CPB adopts the precautionary principle and the SPS Agreement generally uses the different measure of scientific certainty, such conflict could put the provisions of the WTO and the CPB at loggerheads. It is also clear that a member of the CPB and the WTO who felt that certain rights were being denied in this arena would be likely to attempt to have their case heard at the WTO DSB where the scientific standard is more rigid. As of yet no such cases have arisen. However, it is recognised that the action of the SPS Agreement and the CPB need to be monitored.[135]

Further areas of potential conflict between the CPB and the WTO relate to the labelling and packaging of the LMOs. The CPB subjects LMOs to international standards with regard to transport, packaging and labelling.[136] Negotiations on the content of the labelling requirements have continued since the signing of the Protocol. The original intention was to have a specific labelling requirement for the feed/food LMOs: stating the presence of LMOs if the product 'may contain' LMOs, that LMOs are not intended for intentional introduction to the environment, and providing contact details in the event of a request for further information.[137] The CPB envisages an international labelling system being developed and used.

As mentioned above, the negotiations on this issue have been occurring since the signing of the CPB. In the March 2006 Meeting of the Parties of the CPB (MoP 3) in Curitiba, Brazil, an agreement was reached on how the labelling system would work. Article 18.2(a) of the Protocol, which required that LMOs, specifically feed/food LMOs, must have labels stating that they

133 ibid., CPB Articles 5, 6 and 7.

134 ibid., CPB Article 11.

135 'SPS Agreement module, subsection The Cartagena Protocol on Biosafety', WTO website, http://www.wto.org/english/tratop_e/sps_e/sps_agreement_cbt_e/c8s1p1_e.htm (accessed 6 February 2010).

136 UN, op. cit. 129, CPB Article 18.

137 ibid., CPB Article 18(b).

'may contain' LMOs and are not intended for release into the environment, also mandated parties to the CPB to reach a more detailed agreement on documentation requirements of trade in LMOs.[138]

Much of the discussion at the MoP 3 focused on the issue of the wording 'may contain' as opposed to 'contain' in trade-related documentation. The final decision provides two options, so that in cases where the identity of the LMO is known the shipment should be labelled as containing LMOs. In cases where the identity is unknown, the 'may contain' label would be applicable. In both cases, exporters would be required to provide the importer with the common scientific or commercial names of the LMOs, as well as any information about the specific nature of the LMO.[139]

The decision could be seen as a triumph of vagaries over more strict rules, but it is seen as flexible enough to encourage non-ratifiers such as the USA and Canada to finally take measures to ratify the Protocol in their respective national parliaments. A further decision led to a new paragraph being inserted in the text of the statement to address trade with non-parties. This was at Mexico's behest due to its concerns over trade with its non-ratifying NAFTA partners.[140] The text states that trans-boundary movement of LMOs between parties and non-parties shall be consistent with the objective of the Protocol, but adds that the specific documentation requirements will not apply to such trade.

So again this provision still suggests that there is the possibility for conflict between the CPB and the WTO, especially where there is trade between two WTO members, only one of whom has ratified the CPB. Whilst the MoP 3 has made progress on agreeing the basis for the labelling of LMO goods, the door is still open for challenge under the WTO auspices.

There are further potential conflicts between the CPB and the WTO. Firstly there appears to be some conflict with regard to the status of both treaties in respect of the areas covered. The 10th and 11th recitals in the preamble to the CPB state:

> Emphasizing that this Protocol shall not be interpreted as implying a change in the rights and obligations of a Party under any existing international agreements.
>
> Understanding that the above recital is not intended to subordinate this Protocol to the other international agreements.[141]

138 ibid., CPB Article 18.2(a).

139 See A.H. Qureshi, op cit 125, p. 839; and ICTSD, 'Constructive Ambiguity Saves LMO Labelling Discussions at Cartagena Protocol Summit', International Centre for Trade and Sustainable Development, http://ictsd.org/i/news/biores/9290/ (accessed 6 February 2010).

140 ibid.

141 UN, 10th and 11th recitals in the Preamble to the CPB.

This appears to recognise the legitimacy of the WTO rules before going on to suggest the primacy of the rules of the CPB. Referencing the Vienna Convention on the Law of Treaties it appears that Article 31.3 has the most relevance. This is because the relevant Articles on successive treaties will not apply due to the preamble of the CPB which intends both the WTO and the CPB to be considered on a similar standard. Article 31.3 of the Vienna Convention states:

> There shall be taken into account, together with the context, any subsequent agreement between the parties regarding the interpretation of the treaty or the application of its provisions.[142]

Arguably this can be taken to mean that the CPB's measures supplement the relevant sections of the WTO, like the SPS Agreement. This would mean that the precautionary principle as agreed in the CPB would have effect in the WTO to the same extent and therefore 'supplement' the SPS Agreement requirements for scientific evidence. This could lead to conflict within the WTO where import restrictions would now be allowed on foods containing LMOs or GMOs. This may not be the case at the moment.[143]

The question of who will decide the application of the CPB in relation to any conflicts with the WTO seems rather an open and closed case. The CPB has no dispute settlement provision but refers to the provisions of the CBD.[144] The CBD has no 'real' dispute settlement procedure either; dispute settlement is optional.[145] This is a common problem for environmental treaties and often seen as a norm in international law. The dispute resolution provisions of the CBD read as follows:

> 1 In the event of a dispute between the Contracting Parties concerning the interpretation or application of this convention, the parties concerned shall seek solution by negotiation.
> 2 If the parties concerned cannot reach settlement by negotiation, they may jointly seek the good offices of, or request mediation by, a third party.
> 3 When ratifying, accepting, approving of acceding to this Convention, or at any time thereafter, a State or regional economic integration organisation may declare in writing to the Depository that for a dispute not

142 UN, 'Article 31.3 of the Vienna Convention on the Law of Treaties', UN doc. A/Conf. 39/27 (1969), 8 *I.L.M.* 679 (entered into force 1980).

143 See the WTO, Appellate Body Reasoning in the *EC-Hormones* Case, Appellate Body Report, *EC-Hormones*, paras 179 and 180.

144 UN, 'Biosafety Protocol, Article 34; Convention on Biological Diversity', UNEP/Bio. Div./Conf./L.2, 31 *I.L.M.* 818 (1992).

145 UN, CBD Article 27, op. cit. 94.

resolved in accordance with paragraph 1 or paragraph 2 above, it accepts one or both of the following means of dispute settlement as compulsory.

(a) arbitration in accordance with the procedure laid down in Part 1 of Annex 2;

(b) submission of the dispute to the International Court of Justice.

4 If the parties to the dispute have not, in accordance with paragraph 3 above, accepted the same or any procedure, the dispute shall be submitted to conciliation in accordance with Part II of Annex 2 unless the parties otherwise agree.[146]

This suggests that any dispute under the CBD, CPB with the SPS Agreement is likely to be resolved at the WTO DSB. This is because the diplomatic, arbitrational and finally legalistic approach (through the ICJ) of the CBD is a fairly convoluted process. The issue is also likely to relate to a trade impediment and so the natural and more straightforward option would appear to be the WTO DSB. The WTO DSU, as demonstrated in Chapter 1, is an effective system with greater efficiency and greater certainty of an enforceable outcome.

This of course is a real concern for environmentalists who already fear that environmental issues are being subordinated to trade issues. The solution could lie in the reform of the WTO DSB or the creation of environmental treaties with strong dispute resolution mechanisms. The latter has rarely been found to date; the former may offer some practical realisation of reasoned global environmental rulings.

4.6 Conclusion

This chapter has outlined the various philosophical positions of the free trade and environment schools, the conflicts between them and the flaws in their arguments. This has, as expected, tended to suggest a number of fundamental differences between the two camps, regarding trade and the environment. The brief review of some of the relevant legal international environmental provisions has also shown a number of issues that could lead to conflict between global environmental agreements and the WTO (see Chapter 5 for further analysis of the WTO and its relationship with a number of other MEAs, which use trade measures to enforce their provisions).

Both environmentalists and market economists have relevant arguments and allude to potential conflicts between the competing interests of trade liberalisation and environmental protection. However, the point has been made in the WTO-sponsored trade/environment review that trade liberalisation and environmental protection objectives are not mutually exclusive.[147]

146 ibid.
147 P. Newell, op. cit. 13.

Indeed, it even advocates environmental regulation, stating that the correct national and international environmental laws can support trade liberalisation and environmental protection.[148] Given this, it is important to note that trade and environment is not a zero-sum game. It may be that some environmentalists wish to see a global environmental organisation created to deal with environmental issues, due to perceived failings in the WTO system.[149]

Nevertheless, the practicality of the situation is very much that the WTO will act with regard to the environment when environmental measures have an impact on trade and contracting parties require the WTO to act; not least as some of the protocols and treaties mentioned do not have dispute resolution mechanisms of their own (or they have comparably weak ones). For example, the CPB could have its principles examined at the DSB or AB of the WTO, purely because it does not have a very effective means to address its own disputes. The outcome of such a review would be highly contentious as the WTO may not yet have the best system for dealing with environment-related disputes.

Therefore the reform of the DSB could seem to be highly important in ensuring proper reasoning in cases involving the environment or environmental facets at the WTO. To further support this argument it is prudent to review the WTO's track record with regard to environmental matters. In the next chapters the WTO's environmental record in relation to MEAs will be examined and the contentions of both the environmentalists and free traders, as explained here, will be scrutinised in relation to the WTO's record when dealing with MEAs.

148 ibid.

149 D. Esty, *Greening the GATT: Trade, Environment, and the Future*, Earthscan, Washington D.C., 1994; and F. Macmillan, *WTO and the Environment*, Sweet & Maxwell, London, 2001.

5 The DSB and MEAs

5.1 Introduction

In the context of the debate on trade and its interaction with the environment, of significant importance is the issue of MEAs and the potential conflict that exists between the trade-related provisions contained in MEAs and those of the WTO agreements. The interaction between MEAs and the WTO agreements' provisions has been of considerable concern to the operation of the WTO and its members since the inception of the WTO in 1995.

When the CTE was set up in 1994 one of the main issues under its terms of reference was to review the relationship between the WTO and MEAs.[1] This concern has been reflected at high-level meetings even outside of the WTO. For example, the 1999 G8 meeting in Cologne made the following statement amongst its conclusions:

> We agree that environmental considerations should be taken fully into account in the upcoming round of WTO negotiations. This should include a clarification of the relationship between both multilateral and environmental agreements and key environmental principles, and WTO rules.[2]

This shows the high level of importance that has been attached to this issue in the international community, and also that a real risk of conflict has been identified. This has been reflected in the programme of work that has been given to the CTE by the WTO members.

In the WTO history of the consideration of potential conflicts between MEAs and WTO agreement provisions, the CTE spent much of its time discussing the issue, and indeed many suggestions have been put forward in

1 See 'Items on the CTE's Work Programme', WTO website, http://www.wto.org/english/tratop_e/envir_e/cte00_e.htm (accessed 24 January 2010).

2 Taken from 'G7-G8 Endorse Trade Environment Link', Institute for Trade and Sustainable Development, in *Bridges between Trade and Sustainable Development*, Year 3, No. 5, June 1999.

that forum for how to deal with such potential conflicts.[3] One of the main points of potential conflict lies in the workings of the DSB and its potential consideration of a trade mechanism under a MEA .[4]

Many MEAs contain trade-related actions to support their implementation and effective operation. MEAs such as CITES (much of the agreement is dedicated to the regulation of trade; however Article II lays the fundamental provision that species in danger of extinction will be subject to strict trade regulation),[5] the Montreal Protocol (Article IV of the Protocol concerns regulation of trade with non-parties; the Article stipulates that a year after the Treaty is ratified, all imports of controlled substances as stipulated by the Protocol from any non-party states are banned)[6] and the Basel Convention on the Control of Transboundary Movements of Hazardous Wastes and their Disposal (Article IV of the Convention concerns the right of parties to ban imports of certain hazardous waste on to their territories, again much of the Convention is concerned with trade measures to achieve an environmental goal)[7] all utilise trade means to deliver the desired outcomes of the agreements.[8]

3 See K.P. Ewing & R.D. Tarasofsky, 'The Trade and Environment Agenda: Survey of Major Issues and Proposals, from Marrakesh to Singapore', Environmental Policy and Law Paper No. 33, World Conservation Union-IUCN, Switzerland, 1997.

4 See J. Cameron & I. Robinson, 'The Use of Trade Provisions in International Environmental Agreements and Their Compatibility with the GATT', 2 *Y.B. Int'l Envtl L.* 3, 1991; R.G. Tarasofsky, 'Ensuring Compatibility between Multilateral Environmental Agreements and the GATT/WTO', 7 *Y.B. Int'l Envtl L.* 52, 1996; and D. Brack, 'The Shrimp-Turtle Case: Implications for the Multilateral Environmental Agreement', 9 *Y.B., Int'l Envtl L.* 13, 1998.

5 Text of the Convention, CITES website, http://www.cites.org/eng/disc/text.shtml (accessed 24 January 2010).

6 Text of the Protocol, UNEP Ozone Secretariat website, http://ozone.unep.org/Publications/MP_Handbook/Section_1.1_The_Montreal_Protocol/Article_4.shtml (accessed 24 January 2010).

7 Text of the Basel Convention on the Control of Transboundary Movements of Hazardous Wastes and their Disposal, Basel Convention website, http://www.basel.int/text/documents.html (accessed 24 January 2010).

8 CITES is the longest standing international environmental agreement that has utilised trade measures for environmental ends. Trade measures include the banning of certain listed species – including parts of these animals and dead animals. See D. Edwards, 'Experience with the Use of Trade Measures in CITES', Joint Session of Trade and Environment Experts, OECD/GD(97)106, Paris, 1997.The Montreal Protocol aims to prevent the further erosion of the Earth's ozone layer, which protects the planet from ultraviolet rays. The Protocol calls for signatory countries to ban the production of chloro fluoro carbides (CFCs) and other ozone-depleting substances. The signatories are prohibited from trading in these substances with any country that has not signed the Protocol. See D.M. Goldberg et al., *Effectiveness of Trade and Positive Measures in Multilateral Environmental Agreements: Lessons from the Montreal Protocol*, CIEL, Washington, 1998. The Basel Convention on the Control of Transboundary Movements of Hazardous Wastes and their Disposal controls the trade in hazardous waste. Specifically it bans the trade in hazardous waste between OECD countries and non-OECD countries for final disposal. See J. Krueger, 'The Basel Convention and Transboundary Movements of Hazardous Wastes', Briefing Paper No. 45, Royal Institute of International Affairs, London, 1998.

The means by which the measures are applied and the objectives relating to their use vary according to each agreement. Notwithstanding, each one of these important MEAs utilise trade measures to achieve their ambitions – for example under the Basel Convention, which bans trade in certain hazardous wastes to better control disposal of these substances.[9]

In general, examining the work of the CTE and the DSB, it can be claimed that the WTO favours multilateral approaches to environmental protection. The CTE has given endorsement to MEA approaches to environmental protection: 'multilateral solutions based on international cooperation and consensus are the best and most effective way for governments to tackle environmental problems of a transboundary or global nature'.[10] This has long been the approach of the WTO/GATT dispute resolution body; under the *Tuna-Dolphin I* case.

To date none of the MEAs has been challenged in the WTO, although Zimbabwe did threaten to challenge the banning of trade in elephant ivory under CITES at the WTO.[11] This action was never undertaken. However, the possibility of a trade-related measure under a MEA being contested in the WTO is recognised as a potential issue by the WTO members, and as such the WTO CTE has been instructed to explore the issue.[12] To this extent it has been one of the main tasks of the CTE to map the MEAs with trade provisions and attempt to reconcile in advance any potential areas of conflict through granting observer status to MEA secretariats at the WTO CTE Special Sessions on the environment.[13]

It has also been evident through the working of the CTE that the WTO members view MEAs as the best way to deal with environmental problems of a global nature, preferring MEAs to deal with disputes arising within

9 R. Housman et al., *The Use of Trade Measures in Select Environmental Agreements*, Environment and Trade Series No. 10, UNEP, 1995; and D. Andrews, *Trade Measures in Multilateral Environment Agreements: Synthesis Report of Three Case Studies*, Joint Session of Trade and Environment Experts, OECD, Paris, 1998.

10 WTO CTE Report, 'Report of the Committee on Trade and Environment', WT/CTE/1, 12 November 1996, para. 171.

11 See E.-U. Petersmann, *The GATT/WTO Dispute Settlement System: International Law, International Organisations and Dispute Settlement*, Kluwer Law International, London, 1997, p. 130. In this case the 'Animals Committee' set up by the CITES Convention heard an informal complaint from Zimbabwe on the US import restrictions on elephant ivory. The Zimbabweans believed that the population and stockpile of ivory justified a lifting of the restrictions. See also note 85 in Chapter 4.

12 'The Trade and Environment Committee, and Doha Preparations', WTO website, http://www.wto.org/english/thewto_e/minist_e/min01_e/brief_e/brief11_e.htm (accessed 24 January 2010). This states that exploring the WTO–MEA relationship was one of the first tasks of the CTE after its inception in 1995.

13 See 'WTO Environment Committee Focuses On MEA–WTO Relationship', *Bridges Trade BioRes*, Vol. 2, No. 11, 13 June 2002, ICTSD website, http://ictsd.net/i/news/biores/8794/ (accessed 24 January 2010).

their fora.[14] This would not suffice in the case of one member of the WTO being a member of a MEA and another with whom it is in conflict not being party to that agreement. In this case the role of the WTO and its DSB would be of great importance for resolving the conflict.

This is the area that many scholars have identified as an area of potential threat to the operation of MEAs under the WTO.[15] For a full review of the situation it would be necessary to speculate on the likely outcome of a dispute under an MEA in comparison to the likely outcome of a dispute under the WTO. In this chapter the dispute resolution mechanisms of the MEAs will also be reviewed, to determine whether they have been utilised and are effective at enforcing the requirements of the agreements under which they occur.

5.2 Choosing a forum for dispute settlement

A main issue relating to the dispute settlement procedure in the WTO and MEAs is the choice of a forum for the settlement of trade-related environmental disputes. There are currently over 250 MEAs addressing environmental issues at the international co-operation level. At least 20 of these contain provisions that relate to trade and could therefore come into conflict with the WTO; the CTE has been active in mapping these MEAs.

A potential major problem is one where the trade-related provisions of a MEA could have a negative impact on the trade relationship between members of that particular MEA and non-members of the MEA who are also WTO members. The provisions of the MEA could technically be incompatible with WTO rules if the non-discrimination principle of the most favoured nation is compromised, even though many countries have undertaken to observe the principles of the MEA. The non-discrimination principle requires like products to be granted similar treatment from any country that is a WTO member.[16] Of course, as demonstrated, there are exceptions under Article XX that allow derogations from this principle, including on the grounds of conservation of natural resources and protection of plant/animal life and health. Notwithstanding, there is no guarantee that these exceptions would prevail if they were to be tested in relation to a MEA.

At the present time the WTO, through the work of the CTE, is yet to issue any particular guidance on the issue of resolving trade-related disputes

14 G.P. Sampson, *Trade, Environment and the WTO: The Post-Seattle Agenda*, Overseas Development Council, Washington, DC, 2000, p. 83.

15 Among others see, S. Bajwa, 'The World Trade Organization and the Environment', 12 *Gonzaga Journal of International Law*, 1, 2008–2009, http://www.gonzagajil.org/content/view/181/26/ (accessed 24 January 2010).

16 Article 3 of the GATT contains this fundamental principle. For elaboration on its importance, see 'Principles of the Trading System', WTO website, http://www.wto.org/english/theWTO_e/whatis_e/tif_e/fact2_e.htm (accessed 24 January 2010).

between WTO members who are not both signatories to the MEA in question, especially in relation to MEAs that rely on trade measures to be successful. In this regard there are three particularly successful environmental treaties that rely on trade-related measures to achieve international environmental protection goals. Many other MEAs use such measures, including the Kyoto Protocol, but for the purposes of this investigation the following high profile MEAs, as mentioned earlier, will be considered, due to their length of existence and relative success in meeting their aims: CITES, the Basel Convention and the Montreal Protocol as examined in Chapter 2.

Since the inception of CITES no species that appears on the protection lists of the Convention have become extinct due to trade;[17] large-scale dumping of hazardous waste in developing countries has been significantly reduced under the Basel Convention;[18] and the Montreal Protocol has been successful in reducing the trade in – and use of – ozone-depleting substances.[19] If a non-member of one of these treaties were to choose the WTO as a forum to challenge a particular measure in the respective treaty it is not clear whether the WTO would accept to rule on the issue. It appears at this time that it would, despite the party's undertaking in the MEA. This fundamentally threatens to undermine the workings of such MEAs (depending upon the outcome of the dispute – which is not necessarily clear cut).

As yet no parties have resorted to the WTO dispute settlement mechanism to undermine their obligations accepted in becoming a member of the relevant MEA.[20] However, it is also not clear that the DSB would not rule on an issue that had been dealt with under a MEA's own dispute resolution procedure – again a threat to the legitimacy of the agreements. The CTE, for its part, considers it unlikely that such a conflict with a MEA would arise, even

17 'Managing Wildlife Trade & Conservation: CITES at 30', UNEP website, http://www.unep.org/Documents.Multilingual/Default.asp?DocumentID=443&ArticleID=4827&l=en (accessed 24 January 2010).

18 'The Basel Convention at a Glance...', UNEP, Basel Convention website, http://www.basel.int/convention/bc_glance.pdf (accessed 24 January 2010). This explains how many seizures of hazardous waste have been made under the auspices of the Convention reducing the amount of hazardous waste shipped for dumping in developing countries. However, it is worth noting that there is a serious attempt to tighten the rules of the Basel Convention to ban the shipment of hazardous waste entirely. This is being led by the Basel Action Network and is in response to continuing dumping of hazardous waste in developing countries. The incident in 2006 in the Ivory Coast where dumping of 500 tonnes of toxic waste led to deaths and injury resulted in the prosecution of two individuals and repeated calls for a ban on the trade. See 'Toxic Colonies', EHP website, http://www.cieh.org/ehp/ehp3.aspx?id=8312 for further details (accessed 24 January 2010).

19 J. Cameron & K. Campbell, 'A Reluctant Global Policy Maker', in O. Perez, *Ecological Sensitivity and Global Legal Pluralism: Rethinking the Trade and Environment Debate*, Hart Publishers, Oxford, 2003.

20 No party to a MEA has used the WTO to contest a trade measure in the MEA.

though parties have the right to bring such matters to the attention of the DSB.[21]

The position of the CTE can be explained in the sense that parties to a MEA should use the mechanisms available under the MEA first, before trying to use the dispute resolution mechanisms of the WTO.[22] Therefore, the MEA should be the forum for the resolution of any disputes arising over its own provisions; the WTO would only be involved if no resolution was found and the parties considered it necessary to continue the dispute through WTO channels. In some ways this could make the WTO DSB look like an appeal court for MEA disputes that have not been resolved; and it is arguable whether many environmental campaigners would accept such a status quo. Nevertheless, this is how the situation appears.

The CITES Secretariat did not issue any statements or guidance during the *Shrimp-Turtle* dispute at the WTO, which suggests that the MEA secretariats are not likely – at the present time – to try to influence the outcome of such debates on trade and environment conflicts at the WTO. This is probably due to the need not to offend their own member state governments, as much as due to the fact that they have no status in such disputes at the WTO. Yet, the complexity of the relationship between MEAs and the WTO should not be underestimated. For example, the *Chile Swordfish* case[23] highlighted the difficulty that can be encompassed in addressing the correct forum for dispute resolution in an international context.

Given this situation it seems imperative that the CTE delivers some authoritative position on MEAs in relation to the working of the DSB in *all* circumstances. Nations are now naturally drawn to the WTO to resolve cases involving economic issues, because of the efficient and effective dispute settlement procedure.[24] MEA dispute settlement procedures have not been

21 CTE report, WT/CTE 1, 1996, para. 178.

22 ibid.

23 See M. Orellana, 'The EU and Chile Suspend the Swordfish Case Proceedings at the WTO and the International Tribunal of the Law of the Sea', *ASIL Insights*, The American Society of International Law, February 2001, http://www.asil.org/insigh60.cfm (accessed 24 January 2010). The case concerned swordfish fisheries in the South Pacific. Chile claimed that the EU did not co-operate over the protection of the fish, and the EU countered that Chile did not allow access to its ports for the EU fishing fleet. Chile used the UNCLOS (United Nations Convention on the Law of the Sea) regime to defend its point; the EU preferred to use the WTO dispute resolution system to advance its arguments. Chile, for its part, invited the EU for formal dispute resolution under the UNCLOS system. Eventually in 2001 the parties agreed to suspend both proceedings and to work together bilaterally to resolve the issue outside of the dispute settlement proceedings. It is not clear what the outcome of the cases would have been if the two different dispute resolution systems had been required to rule on the case. Nevertheless, it highlights the possible situation of one issue being dealt with by different international law forums and the potential conflict that such a situation would generate.

24 See J.H. Jackson, 'Designing and Implementing Effective Dispute Settlement Procedures: WTO Dispute Settlement, Appraisal and Prospects', in A.O. Krueger & C. Aturupane, *The WTO as an International Organisation*, University of Chicago Press, Chicago, 2001, p. 161.

developed in such a thorough and authoritative way.[25] So there is a real possibility that a MEA measure could end up having its legality contested at the WTO DSB. The real context for this could be a challenge to a MEA measure that relates to trade, and a dispute arises between a MEA member and a non-member. It could also be the case that if it is a serious trade/economic issue the aggrieved nation may choose the WTO DSB as it could perceive a more favourable hearing for its economic concerns.

A number of suggestions have been made to improve the current situation of trade–environment disputes at the WTO. One of these is to create an international court for the environment, under the auspices of the UN.[26] Other suggestions include amending GATT Article XX on General Exceptions to the WTO rules to include specific exceptions for undertakings that members may have signed up to in MEAs. There is a precedent for this; for example the NAFTA states explicitly that MEAs take precedence over NAFTA obligations.[27] The WTO could adopt such a policy.

In early negotiations in the CTE on the issue of the relationship between MEA provisions and the rules of the WTO, the EU put forward this very solution, suggesting that an amendment to Article XX be made for MEAs.[28] Conversely, many developing countries favoured maintaining the text as it was rather than making specific changes, suggesting that waivers could be given when disputes around the text of the GATT arose.[29] In this context certain commentators have argued that the developing countries had a more realistic approach to the issue, as they state that 'it is virtually impossible to amend Article XX of the GATT'.[30] This is hypothetical, and, as argued earlier in this book, it entirely depends upon the will of the parties involved in the WTO.[31]

25 J. Cameron & K. Campbell, op. cit. 19.

26 See International Court for the Environment Coalition website, http://www.environment-court.com/ (accessed 24 January 2010).

27 See NAFTA text, Article 104: Relation to Environmental and Conservation Agreements, SICE website, http://www.sice.oas.org/trade/nafta/chap-01.asp#An104.1 (accessed 24 January 2010); which provides that where inconsistency exists between the NAFTA agreement and the provisions of the Montreal Protocol, the Basel Convention or CITES, the obligations under those three MEAs will prevail (as long as the measure implemented is the least inconsistent with NAFTA's free trade provisions). See also M. Tiemann, 'NAFTA: Related Environmental Issues and Initiatives', US Department of State website, 1 March 2000, http://www.fpc.state.gov/6143.htm (accessed 24 January 2010).

28 WTO CTE, Report (1996) of the Committee on Trade and Environment, WT/CTE/W/40, 12 November 1996, para. 17, p. 5; see also Y. Harashima, *Trade and Environment Negotiations in the WTO: Asian Perspectives, International Environmental Agreements: Politics, Law and Economics*, Springer, Netherlands, Vol. 8, No. 1, March 2008, p. 22.

29 ibid., Harashima.

30 ibid.

31 See Chapter 1 which examines the development of the WTO legal system, showing that the contracting parties have had the will to make major changes.

It would also be possible to use the Vienna Convention on the Law of Treaties, specifically Article 31.3 that requires certain previous standing agreements between parties to be taken into account.[32] This author would consider a more organic approach using the semi-formal precedent of the WTO DSB decisions in a slightly modified DSU to deliver the required compromise between MEAs and the DSU. The general principles of environmental protection and sustainable development are already enshrined in the WTO; the working of the DSB needs to be more proactive in advancing them. This seems the most likely way to get MEA legitimacy recognised in the DSB. It is also unlikely that the WTO would choose to disrupt a MEA through the dispute process, a position given more credence by the AB report in the *Shrimp-Turtle* case.[33]

5.3 Dispute resolution mechanisms of Multilateral Environmental Agreements

In order to gain a full understanding of why the WTO's DSB can be perceived as a more powerful body than the systems operated under MEAs, it is necessary to review the provisions available to parties in dispute under a MEA. As argued previously in Chapter 1, the WTO DSB has evolved into a quasi-court with strong powers of decision, appeal and enforcement. The process of dispute resolution is entirely self-contained within the framework of the rules of the WTO; this represents a strong apparatus for dispute resolution within the confines of international law. Examining the dispute resolution systems of MEAs will provide an insight into the operation of these international agreements and allow a comparison with the WTO DSB system.

5.3.1 CITES

Firstly, the dispute resolution system of CITES will be analysed. As mentioned in Chapter 2, the CITES Treaty is one of the oldest MEAs currently in existence and it is often described as a successful treaty in terms of protecting the species contained within its lists.[34] The Treaty has 25 articles and one of these is devoted to the issue of dispute resolution, Article XVIII.

The article describes the dispute resolution process as follows:

> Article XVIII
> Resolution of Disputes

32 M. Matsushita, T.J. Schoenbaum & P.C. Mavroidis, *The World Trade Organization: Law, Practice and Policy*, Oxford University Press, Oxford, 2004, pp. 458–9.

33 WTO, *United States – Import Prohibition of Certain Shrimp and Shrimp Products*, Report of the Appellate Body, WT/DS58/AB/R, 12 October 1998, para. 185, p. 75.

34 CITES, op. cit. 8.

> 1. Any dispute which may arise between two or more Parties with respect to the interpretation or application of the provisions of the present Convention shall be subject to negotiation between the Parties involved in the dispute.
>
> 2. If the dispute can not be resolved in accordance with paragraph 1 of this Article, the Parties may, by mutual consent, submit the dispute to arbitration, in particular that of the Permanent Court of Arbitration at The Hague, and the Parties submitting the dispute shall be bound by the arbitral decision.[35]

The Article offers only bilateral negotiation or referral to the Permanent Court of Arbitration under the condition of mutual consent. This is a relatively soft form of dispute resolution and the initial stage bears the hallmark of an alternative dispute resolution mechanism, rather than a formal legal system. The measures under paragraph 2 allow a more formal resolution to be sought, but only under mutual consent, which could be difficult if the respondent does not agree to attend the Permanent Court of Arbitration.

Another aspect of CITES that reflects its rather soft focus on dispute resolution is the fact that there is not one article dedicated to the issue of compliance within the terms of the Convention.[36] Measures relating to compliance can be inferred from the text contained in the articles and there is a focus on monitoring and promoting compliance – and identifying cases of non-compliance.[37] The practice of CITES requires that member states submit a biennial report to explain what actions they have undertaken to enforce CITES's requirements.[38]

There has been a relatively poor compliance rate with this requirement under CITES, resulting in the Convention producing many guidelines to help parties comply better with the requirement.[39] Nevertheless, the CITES system has, as of yet, failed to result in a referral to the Permanent Court of Arbitration; no issue of non-compliance has been dealt with in a judicial proceeding – instead the CITES Secretariat encourages a more negotiated form of dispute resolution.[40] To improve the effectiveness of compliance with the important reporting procedures, and to the Convention in general, there

35 Text of the Convention, CITES website, http://www.cites.org/eng/disc/text.shtml#XVIII (accessed 24 January 2010).

36 ibid.

37 L. Kurukulasuriya & N.A. Robinson, *Training Manual on International Environmental Law*, UNEP, Earthprint, November 2007, para. 88, p. 181.

38 CITES, op. cit. 35, Article VIII.

39 C.E. Bruch & E. Mrema, *Manual on Compliance with and Enforcement of Multilateral Environmental Agreements*, UNEP, 23 February 2007, p. 139.

40 L. Kurukulasuriya & N.A. Robinson, op. cit. 37.

should be more use of the threat of trade suspension, particularly in the case of persistent non-compliance.[41]

At the moment recommendations to suspend trade are made, but only as a means of last resort – as mentioned above the CITES Secretariat puts more emphasis on inducing parties into compliance using the informal methods of consultation, advice or assistance. Equally, the use of trade suspensions are only likely to be considered where there is significant volumes of trade and there is no national enforcement.[42] Any trade measure enacted by CITES's parties is withdrawn as soon as the party at fault returns to compliance.[43]

In general CITES is seen as a successful MEA and none of the species included in its category A lists have become extinct.[44] Nevertheless, the compliance and enforcement mechanisms are relatively weak – the CITES Secretariat does not have a strong means of controlling disputes, with only a resort to move to the Permanent Court of Arbitration if both sides agree to such a move.

The fact that no disputes have been heard there could be considered as a success of the more informal compliance regime, but is more likely to be due to the requirements of the procedure: mutual consent of the disputing parties. There is little that can be done by the parties if another party persistently ignores a trade suspension. Hence, it is probable that in comparison to the WTO DSB the CITES resolution of disputes mechanism can be considered to be weaker. This is why the WTO DSB can be seen to be more effective and in some ways more of a threat to CITES than the other way around.

5.3.2 The Montreal Protocol on Substances that Deplete the Ozone Layer

Article 8 of the Montreal Protocol lays down that the parties should determine the means and institutional mechanisms for dealing with non-compliance with the requirements of the Protocol.[45] This process was to be agreed at the first meeting of the parties after the ratification of the Protocol. The parties thereafter agreed to set up an Implementation Committee to monitor and assist states in non-compliance.[46] This Committee produced a series of

41 L. Kurukulasuriya & N.A. Robinson, op cit. 37; see also M. Yeater, 'Compliance and Enforcement Indicators' in CITES, Legislation and Enforcement Unit CITES, CITES Secretariat, 2004, p. 1, http://www.inece.org/indicators/proceedings/04s_other_cites.pdf (accessed 24 January 2010).

42 ibid., Yeater, p. 2.

43 ibid.

44 'Managing Wildlife Trade & Conservation: CITES at 30', op. cit. 17.

45 'Article 8, The Montreal Protocol on Substances that Deplete the Ozone Layer', 2000, UNEP website, http://www.unep.org/OZONE/pdfs/Montreal-Protocol2000.pdf (accessed 24 January 2010).

46 C.E. Bruch & E. Mrema, op. cit. 39, p. 117.

recommendations for operating a non-compliance scheme that was adopted by the 4th Meeting of the Parties in 1992, including suggestions for actions to take in the instance of non-compliance by a party.[47]

The measures that were adopted included the following provisions:

- The Implementation Committee consists of ten member states' representatives, who are responsible for reviewing any accusation of non-compliance from one member against another. It also reviews cases where member states declare that they cannot meet the requirements under the Protocol; or where the Secretariat itself suspects that a member state may not be in compliance with the Protocol's requirements.
- The Implementation Committee, once referred to, gathers information 'with a view to securing an amicable solution of the matter on the basis of respect for the provisions of the Protocol'.[48] It produces a report for submission to the Meeting of the Parties (MoP) for approval, including recommendations for how to resolve the issue. The MoP then has to decide the best way to take the case forward, based on the recommendations of the Implementation Committee. The Implementation Committee can support this work.
- To date the MoP has accepted all the recommendations of the Implementation Committee in relation to disputes regarding non-compliance.[49]

The Implementation Committee has adopted a review and report approach to resolving disputes, and trade sanctions have never been suggested.[50] Trade sanctions are provided for under the Protocol to be applied against parties not in conformity with the Protocol's provisions.[51] However, the use of the soft measures has been considered to be the best approach by the Implementation Committee, perhaps because the use of hard measures, such as sanctions, may, in the case of the Montreal Protocol, be more ineffective.[52]

It is worth noting that the Protocol is a legal instrument based on the 1985 Vienna Convention for the Protection of the Ozone Layer,[53] and as such the dispute resolution mechanism outlined in Article 11 of that Convention is

47 UNEP Secretariat, 'Decisions of the Parties Related to the Non-Compliance Procedure of the Montreal Protocol on Substances that Deplete the Ozone Layer', October 2007, UNEP website, http://ozone.unep.org/Meeting_Documents/impcom/MOP_decisions_on_NCP.pdf (accessed 24 January 2010).

48 ibid.

49 C.E. Bruch & E. Mrema, op. cit. 39, p. 147.

50 ibid.

51 D.G. Victor, *The Early Operation and Effectiveness of the Montreal Protocol's Non-Compliance Procedure*, ER-96-02, International Institute for Applied Systems Analysis (IIASA), Austria, May 1996, p. 17.

52 ibid., p. 23.

53 Text of the 1985 Vienna Convention for the Protection of the Ozone Layer, 1985, UNEP website, http://www.unep.org/ozone/vc-text.shtml (accessed 24 January 2010).

open to parties of the Montreal Protocol. This allows appeals to the ICJ. Yet no case has been referred from the Montreal Protocol to the Vienna Convention, let alone the ICJ.[54] The rules under Article 11 allow access to the ICJ only in the circumstances that both of the parties to a dispute agree to the referral.[55]

This is similar to the CITES dispute resolution mechanism, and again it can be argued that the need for joint agreement for a legal intervention acts as a deterrent to seeking such a forum for arbitration. Perhaps, in recognition of this, the Convention also provides for a conciliation procedure under Article 11, paragraphs 4 and 5.[56] This conciliation procedure can be instigated by one of the parties of a dispute, through submission of a request to the Secretariat. The procedure creates a conciliation commission made up of an equal number of members appointed by the parties to the dispute, who then appoint a chairman.[57]

But the conciliation committee can only render a final report that the parties 'shall consider in good faith'.[58] This falls far short of the standard of the WTO DSB: the wide-ranging powers for enforcement and the members' rights of initiation of disputes. Therefore it is possible to conclude that the dispute resolution procedure under the Montreal Protocol and its umbrella Vienna Convention lacks the semi-formal legal proceeding aspects that are associated with the WTO DSB.

Nevertheless, it is important to consider that the non-compliance procedure under the Montreal Protocol is considered as relatively successful.[59] However, this is 'relative'. For example, the Russians were long in non-compliance over the provision of data relating to the use of substances banned under the Convention – even when the Implementation Committee asked for the provision of estimate statistics on the use of the substances the Russians did not comply.[60] Compliance was only ensured later after Russia had itself come to terms with its obligations. The Implementation Committee did not act to try and enforce compliance with suggestions to the MoP.

The activities of the Committee in relation to exposing countries who are not meeting the commitments of the Protocol could also be argued to be a means of encouraging compliance, a sort of 'name and shame' approach. However, there is no evidence that this approach really delivers results. The fact remains that the success of the Protocol's dispute resolution mechanisms and compliance procedures comes down to the will of the parties rather than

54 D.G. Victor, op. cit. 51, p. 1.
55 Vienna Convention, op. cit. 53, Article 11, para. 3, p. 12.
56 ibid., Article 11, paras 4 and 5, p. 12.
57 ibid., Article 11, para. 5, p. 12.
58 ibid.
59 See D.G. Victor, op. cit. 51, for a review of the Montreal Protocol and its compliance and dispute resolution regimes.
60 D.G. Victor, op. cit. 51, p. 18.

to the enforcement of decisions, which generally does not happen. This is a clear example of a soft law approach and one which is considerably less legalistic than the WTO's own DSB.

It is for this reason that the Montreal Protocol could be seen to be less legalistic than the WTO in its dispute operations. If the WTO were to rule on a trade-related sanction under the Montreal Protocol, due to its stronger enforcement mechanisms the WTO's ruling could possibly be more effective. If this ruling would be against the Montreal Protocol decision, the WTO could have an impact on the operation of this MEA. This potential occurrence can be considered in the knowledge that this situation has never arisen to date and that the premise is full of '*ifs*'. In spite of that, it is quite clear that the WTO has a more legalistic and effective dispute settlement regime than the one under the Montreal Protocol.

5.3.3 The Basel Convention on the Control of Transboundary Movements of Hazardous Wastes and Their Disposals

The dispute resolution procedures under the Basel Convention can be found in Article 20 and also reflect a soft law approach to dispute resolution. The parties are encouraged to resolve disputes through peaceful means, and negotiation is the recommended means: only if no agreement can be reached will the process refer to the ICJ as a means of last resort. The relevant section of the Basel Convention reads as follows:[61]

> ARTICLE 20
> Settlement of Disputes
>
> 1. In case of a dispute between Parties as to the interpretation or application of, or compliance with, this Convention or any protocol thereto, they shall seek a settlement of the dispute through negotiation or any other peaceful means of their own choice.
>
> 2. If the Parties concerned cannot settle their dispute through the means mentioned in the preceding paragraph, the dispute, if the Parties to the dispute agree, shall be submitted to the International Court of Justice or to arbitration under the conditions set out in Annex VI on Arbitration. However, failure to reach common agreement on submission of the dispute to the International Court of Justice or to arbitration shall not absolve the Parties from the responsibility of continuing to seek to resolve it by the means referred to in paragraph 1.

61 Text of the Basel Convention on the Control of Transboundary Movements of Hazardous Wastes and their Disposal, Basel Convention website, http://www.basel.int/text/documents.html (accessed 24 January 2010).

Article 20 provides for a basic negotiation settlement for disputes that arise between the parties in relation to interpretation or compliance. It leaves the make-up of the dispute forum to the choice of the parties and final sanction to the ICJ – if both parties agree. This again is an example of the 'soft law' approach common to many international agreements, and MEAs in particular.

The Basel Convention has also been consumed with the discussion of the parties around the possibility of creating a stricter compliance mechanism.[62] However, this took a lot of effort, mainly due to the reluctance of the majority of the parties to set up a formal dispute agency/body.[63] This led commentators to conclude that the Basel Convention had a weak enforcement mechanism and that much work was needed to improve compliance and enforcement within the Convention.[64]

So eventually in 2002 the parties to the Convention agreed to set up a compliance committee – at the sixth conference of the parties.[65] The main purpose of the committee is to help avoid disputes arising in a preventative manner, supporting parties to meet obligations and avoid infractions. The Committee can also review submissions from one party regarding the non-compliance of other members, or from the Secretariat.[66] In this regard this is similar to the Montreal Protocol.

The Compliance Committee can either reject the notification or it can offer support to the party under scrutiny – through technical support or through a cautionary statement, including advice.[67] The Committee does not enact any sanctions per se and its recommendations must be approved by the COP – even then these are only recommendations. Again this procedure reflects some of the processes of the Montreal Protocol. The Committee, in dealing with a complaint, has the power to gather evidence and conduct research in the territories of the alleged offence, but the recommendations of the Committee fall short of any binding action or remediation.

62 K. Kummer, 'The Basel Convention: Ten Years On', 7 *Reciel*, 3, pp. 227–36, 1998, p. 233.

63 ibid.; see also UNEP, 'Analysis of the Dispute Settlements Mechanism under Article 20 of the Basel Convention', Note by the Secretariat, UNEP/CHW/LWG/2/6, 24 August 2000. This confirms that only six parties responded to the questionnaire on the dispute resolution mechanism under the Convention and that none particularly prioritised a stronger dispute resolution mechanism.

64 I. Rummel-Bulska, 'Compliance with and Enforcement of the Basel Convention on Control Transboundary Movements of Hazardous Wastes and their Disposal', Paper at the Fifth International Conference on Environmental Compliance and Enforcement, 1998, http://www.inece.org/5thvol2/rummel-bulska.pdf (accessed 24 January 2010).

65 C.E. Bruch & E. Mrema, *Manual on Compliance with and Enforcement of Multilateral Environmental Agreements*, UNEP, Nairobi, 23 February 2007, p. 151.

66 Earth Negotiations Bulletin, 'Summary of the 6th Convention of the Parties to the Basel Convention: 9–14 December 2002', 20 *IISD*, 12, Monday 16 December 2002.

67 C.E. Bruch & E. Mrema, op. cit. 65.

As mentioned in note 18, the recent dumping of hazardous waste in the Ivory Coast has re-ignited the debate on the Basel Convention and the need for a proper compliance mechanism and a strengthened enforcement mechanism.[68] The dumping of tonnes of toxic waste in Abidjan resulted in deaths and injury to tens of thousands of people in 2006, and led the Executive Secretary of the Basel Convention, Sachiko Kuwabara-Yamamoto, to state:

> One of the important lessons from the situation in Abidjan is that we have a serious problem with enforcement. National and international laws are in place to regulate these exports, but problems arise because of the lack of legal and technical institutional capacity in many developing countries to monitor traffic across their borders. Strengthening the enforcement capacity of the Parties will therefore remain a priority for the Basel Convention in years to come.[69]

The key to her statement was her recognition that the Basel Convention did not have a strong enforcement mechanism. In this case only local charges were brought, there was no international litigation, and no action taken against the countries from where the toxic waste had come.[70] This clearly shows the weakness in the enforcement and compliance mechanisms of the Basel Convention. Again, in comparison to the WTO DSB, the Basel Convention is comparably soft and not as legalistic in its mechanism to deal with disputes and non-compliance.

It would therefore not be unrealistic to conclude that in comparison to the dispute resolution systems of these MEAs, the WTO DSB is a far more legalistic system for dispute resolution. The argument about whether it is more effective is for another study, as the number of cases handled by a dispute function is not necessarily a measure of effectiveness, especially if other forums are able to avoid full-scale disputes.

However, what is for certain is that the practice and rulings of the WTO have a greater impact on the development of international legal norms than the non-result focused methods of the MEAs. Therefore the WTO dispute resolution can be seen to be legalistic and a driver of international law to a further extent than MEAs; this too may cause some concern to MEA secretariats who could see the WTO overruling their decisions. The WTO to its credit has realised this and has dedicated much of its work in relation to the environment to the issue of the relationship between the WTO and MEAs.

68 See E. Chukwukan, 'The Probo Koala Incident in Abidjan Cote D'Ivoire: A Critique of the Basel Convention Compliance Mechanism', International Network for Environmental Compliance and Enforcement (INECE) 8th International Conference, Cape Town, South Africa, April 2008.

69 Reported on BBC News website, 24 November 2006, http://news.bbc.co.uk/2/hi/science/nature/6180604.stm (accessed 24 January 2010).

70 E. Chukwukan, op. cit. 68.

5.4 The Doha agenda and the MEA/WTO relationship

The 2001 WTO Doha Ministerial Conference continued the discussion of the relationship between MEA and WTO rules.[71] The mandate that the member states agreed to directed the CTE to lead on the negotiations concerning WTO rules and MEAs that contain 'specific trade obligations' (STOs). These negotiations are conducted in Special Sessions of the CTE and are aimed at providing guidance on the issue of the applicability of WTO rules to WTO members that have signed a MEA that is under consideration in relation to the WTO and its rules. Figure 5.1 shows the work of the WTO and its CTE under the Doha ministerial agenda.[72] This clearly shows the areas that the CTE Special Sessions (CTESS) and CTE are addressing under the Doha agenda in relation to the trade and environment debate.[73] The diagram shows that the CTESS are singularly responsible for dealing with the issue of WTO and MEA compatibility. This demonstrates the importance that has been placed on the resolution of potential conflicts between the WTO and MEAs by the members through the work of the CTE. The issue is worthy of an entire CTESS to consider it.

Alongside the work on the relationship between MEAs and WTO rules, the CTE has also been working in its normal sessions on the issue of eco-labelling. In 2001, the Doha Ministerial Conference made this an issue of special focus for the regular CTE.[74] This work is currently moving forward with many discussions in issues around the phenomenon of eco-labelling, including the issue of labels for production and process methods which have

71 See 'The Doha Mandate on Multilateral Environmental Agreements (MEAs)', WTO website, http://www.wto.org/english/tratop_e/envir_e/envir_neg_mea_e.htm (accessed 24 January 2010). This official WTO information outlines the main points of negotiation on the relationship between the WTO and MEA trade provisions that were agreed in Doha. See also the 'WTO Ministerial Conference Doha Declaration', para. 31(i), WTO website, http://www.wto.org/english/thewto_e/minist_e/min01_e/mindecl_e.htm#tradeenvironment (accessed 24 January 2010).

72 ibid., WTO Ministerial Conference Doha Declaration.

73 The paragraphs referred to in Figure 5.1 relate to the WTO Ministerial Meeting of 2001 and the subsequent Doha Declaration. The CTE was tasked with examining the effect of environmental measures on market access, the impact of the measures in the Agreement on TRIPS in relation to trade and the environment, labelling for environmental purposes, providing technical assistance to developing countries in the field of trade, and the environment and support national reviews of environmental laws related to trade. Under para. 51 the CTE was to work with the Committee on Trade and Development to ensure that sustainable development is reflected in the Doha negotiations. The CTESS was tasked with examining the relationship between the WTO and MEAs with trade-related aspects, as well as examining the issue of market access for 'environmental goods'.

74 'WTO Ministerial Conference Doha Declaration', op. cit. 71.

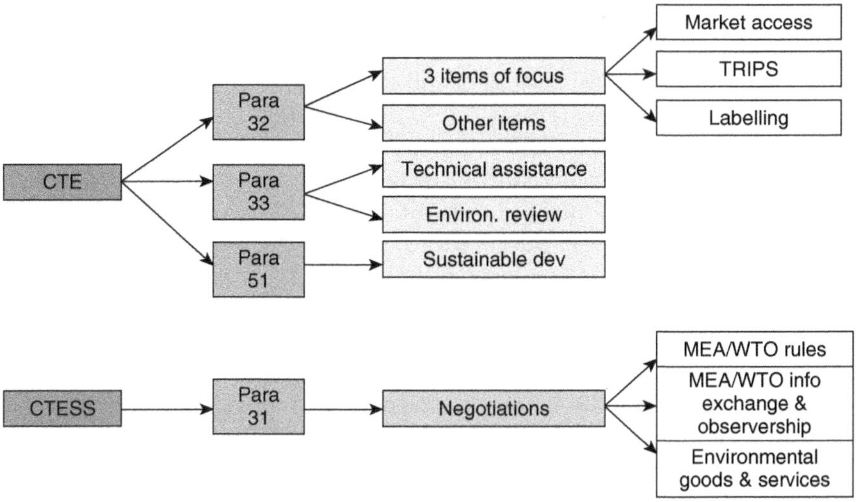

Figure 5.1 The work of the CTE under the Doha development agenda in relation to the environment and MEAs particularly

Source: WTO website, http://www.wto.org/english/tratop_E/envir_e/cte_doha_e.htm, last accessed 18 February 2010.

caused some concern among certain WTO members.[75] Recent meetings have focused on practices in the USA and Australia.[76] As with many trade–environment debates the discussions around eco-labelling have moved forward, but are far from complete.

Returning to the question of the interaction of WTO rules and trade-related provisions in MEAs, to date the negotiations in the CTESS have focused on the scope of the mandate for the negotiations – specifically on the definition of STOs and the desired outcomes of the negotiations. In this negotiation it has also been interesting to note the continued disagreement between different groups of the members. The EU and Switzerland have focused on conceptual approaches to the discussion on developing a common understanding on the terms in para. 31(i) of the Doha Declaration,[77] whereas the US and some developing countries have been more concerned with the identification of terms such as STOs and MEAs in the Doha Declaration more generally.[78] Australia was the country that looked to adopt a practical way

75 'Labelling', WTO website, http://www.wto.org/english/tratop_e/envir_e/labelling_e.htm (accessed 24 January 2010).

76 ibid.

77 See WTO, Compilation of Submissions under Paragraph 31(i) of the Doha Declaration, CTESS, TN/TE/S/3, 31 January 2003, pp. 6 and 7 inter alia.

78 Y. Harashima, op. cit. 28.

forward and therefore proposed that the CTESS work in a formulaic approach with members identifying STOs in MEAs and whether they had caused implementation issues; this would be followed by a process of addressing the issues that arose from this review.[79]

Since the Cancun Ministerial Conference of 2003, further submissions have been made by a number of countries to move the discussions on the means for negotiations forward, including the EU's proposal for consideration of the WTO–MEA relationship in the context of the global governance system, and the Australian proposal for national co-ordination.[80] However, the CTESS is yet to complete the process of setting its own mandate and therefore most of the discussions are theoretical – negotiations have not yet begun on the actual substance of the proposals.

This has meant that the CTESS has been slow to move, but the reason for the relative tardiness of the process must lie with the members who have yet to come to accommodations even on the issue of what the mandate of the CTESS should be. This crucial work needs to be moved forward to enhance the reputation of the WTO in general, and especially in regard to the competency of the WTO to address environmental issues. The conflict, or potential conflict, between the rules of the WTO and many MEAs is a highly emotive issue, and the members would do well to recognise the need to address the issue in a timely and considered way. Time limiting the negotiations would be one way to ensure that some progress is made, even if deadlines have been hard to enforce in the WTO system.[81]

At the same time the member states have also been undertaking an exercise to share their experiences of negotiating and implementing MEAs that involve the use of trade measures. This is aimed at sharing good practice and reducing the chances of highly variable methods being used to implement such measures under MEAs. The negotiations have also gone beyond the issues of STOs and WTO rules, and have examined ways for information to be shared between MEA secretariats and the WTO – specifically, how information can be exchanged more effectively between those secretariats and the WTO's relevant committees, such as the CTE. The discussions so far

79 WTO, 'Compilation of Submissions under Paragraph 31(i) of the Doha Declaration', CTESS, TN/TE/S/03, 31 January 2003, p. 4.

80 See the European Commission, 'Paragraph 31(i) of the Doha Declaration: Putting MEA/WTO Governance into Practice: the EC Experience in the Negotiation and Implementation of MEAs', DG Trade, 27 June 2005, Brussels. See also WTO, 'Proposal for an Outcome on Trade and Environment Concerning Paragraph 31(i) of the Doha Ministerial Declaration', CTESS submission from Australia, TN/TE/W/72, 3 May 2007.

81 The ongoing Doha development agenda negotiations have been an example of how the WTO members have found it very difficult to come to agreement on substantive changes. The negotiations have been ongoing for eight years and a number of WTO Director Generals, including Pascal Lamy and Supachai Panitchpakdi, have set deadlines for the conclusion of the Doha negotiations. None have yet been met.

have resulted in an agreement on procedures for regular information exchange. It is apparent that this is a necessary step to ensure that the trade and MEA regimes using trade measures develop coherently. This is undoubtedly a good way to ensure that the chances of conflicts between MEAs and the WTO are sufficiently reduced.

Again, this has been recognised at high level forums outside of the WTO. For example, in its plan of implementation, the 2002 World Summit on Sustainable Development (WSSD) called for efforts to 'strengthen cooperation among UNEP and other United Nations bodies and specialised agencies, the Bretton Woods institutions and WTO, within their mandates'.[82] This statement acknowledges the need for closer co-operation between the institutions charged with international environmental protection and those responsible for the global economic order. This has led to more co-operation and information exchange between WTO and MEA secretariats, including more formal communication between the UNEP and the WTO.[83]

This has led to the creation of information sessions held by the CTE with MEA secretariats, the exchange of documents, collaboration between the WTO and UNEP/MEAs on the provision of technical and capacity assistance to developing countries on trade and the environment, and the organisation of events by the WTO in the margins of MEA meetings and their parties. The negotiations have supported the driving forward of this process so that relationships have been built between major MEA secretariats and the WTO. This demonstrates that the WTO through its CTE has been highly active in attempting to reduce the chances of a lack of information leading to a conflict arising between its requirements and those of an MEA. Whilst this is commendable it is still not clear exactly what the WTO would do if it was presented with a challenge that related to a trade measure under a MEA from a WTO member not actively participating in that MEA.

A further reason for caution relates to the status of MEA secretariats in the CTE negotiations. At the present time there are several MEA secretariats that are given observer status in the negotiations, and also those that have observer status for the CTE. However, as observers they have no powers beyond those to 'observe'. It would be a more satisfactory situation if the MEA secretariats were 'actively' involved in the negotiations and discussions, as this would improve the synergies and understandings between the MEAs and the WTO.

This is an unfortunate detail, as it is not clear what the MEAs can do if they disagree with the direction the negotiations are going in, in the CTESS or the CTE. Other than lobbying from the outside the options are limited. It would be better for all parties concerned if the MEAs had the power to participate

82 WSSD, Plan of Implementation, Johannesburg, 2002.

83 See the WTO, 'Existing Forms of Cooperation and Information Exchange Between UNEP/MEAs and the WTO', TN/TE/S/2/Rev.2, 16 January 2007.

effectively in the negotiations. This could then be further enhanced with more participation of MEA secretariats within various WTO committees of relevance. This would be the most effective means to reduce the risk of conflict between MEA provisions and the WTO.

5.5 Commentaries on the WTO and its interaction with MEAs

There are a number of criticisms that have been made concerning the operation of the WTO with regard to its interactions with MEAs – some commentators have suggested that the WTO is a threat to the operation of MEAs.[84] In a particularly scathing attack, Buckman, in *Global Trade: Past Mistakes, Future Choices*, cites the example of the Johannesburg World Summit on Sustainable Development in 2002 where serious negotiation took place over the content of the report of the conference.[85] The concerns arise over the attempts of some high-income countries to insert text into the report to state that the purpose of the summit was to 'continue to enhance the mutual supportiveness of trade, environment and development in a manner consistent with WTO rights and obligations'.[86]

This was picked up by certain NGOs who asked the EU and other countries to intervene and remove the phrase from the report. What had been so offensive for them was the term 'consistent with WTO rights and obligations', which they felt made other forums such as the UN subservient to the WTO. It is after all in the UN where most MEAs are based. The final text did state that there would be mutual supportiveness between the UN and WTO systems.[87] Nevertheless, the positions of these commentators and the NGOs on the content of the report of the UN World Summit on Sustainable Development, with regard to the relationship between the WTO and the environment, demonstrates the perceived lack of environmental credentials of

84 G. Buckman, *Global Trade: Past Mistakes, Future Choices*, Zed Books, London, 2005, p. 168; see also S. Retallack, J. Mander & E. Koohan Paik (eds), *Intrinsic Consequences of Economic Globalisation and the Environment: Interim Report*, International Forum on Globalisation, San Francisco, 2002, p. 28; F. Jawara & A. Kwa, *Behind the Scenes at the WTO: The Real World of International Trade Negotiations*, Zed Books, London, 2003, p. 127; and L. Wallach & P. Woodall/Public Citizen, *Whose Trade Organisation?: A Comprehensive Guide to the WTO*, The New Press, New York, 2004, p. 25.

85 G. Buckman, *Global Trade: Past Mistakes, Future Choices*, Zed Books, London, 2005, p. 169; see also United Nations, Report of the World Summit on Sustainable Development, Johannesburg, South Africa, 26 August to 4 September 2002, A/CONF.199/20, United Nations, New York, 2002, para. 98, p. 57.

86 ibid., Buckman.

87 'The Doha Mandate on Multilateral Environmental Agreements', op. cit. 71.

the WTO with these stakeholders. This is particularly true of environmental NGOs' (ENGOs') positions.[88]

The major problem for the WTO in this regard is that the ENGOs perceive the WTO as a self-serving organisation that pursues its own ambitions rather than perceiving it as an organisation run by the desires of its members. It is the members who after all drive the WTO, rather than the very small Secretariat of the WTO driving the members. This can be clearly seen in the failure to draw the Doha negotiations to a conclusion, an outcome highly desired by the Secretariat. The positions of ENGOs have been built up by their perception that the WTO has failed to address environmental issues adequately, in its text and in the disputes that have been resolved under the DSB relating to environmental matters.[89]

This view has developed an overall mistrust by ENGOs and their members, and some commentators have queried the structure of the Doha Declaration in relation to resolving the situation of potential conflict between the WTO and MEAs.[90] The statement in the declaration relating to the MEA/WTO negotiations – which included 'negotiations shall be limited in scope to the applicability of such existing WTO rules as among parties to the MEA in question' – was considered to be a get-out clause for countries that had not signed a MEA, certainly among ENGOs, as it suggested an exemption for them.[91]

This appears to be a strong view of the WTO and it must be recalled that it is not the WTO that determines whether nation states sign MEAs. In these terms the WTO is being criticised for something it does not control, as competency for MEA adherence belongs with the signatories. Equally it appears perverse to enforce standards in MEAs through the WTO on MEA non-signatories as a norm – this issue needs clear guidance and a position from the WTO members to resolve the speculation. This is clearly a matter

88 See Dr S. Pfahl, S. Lovera & K. Bizzarri, 'Is the WTO the only Way?: Safeguarding Multilateral Environmental Agreements from International Trade Rules and Settling Trade and Environment Disputes outside the WTO', Greenpeace Briefing Paper, Greenpeace, Adelphi Consult and Friends of the Earth Europe, Belgium, December 2005. See also 'Trade Campaign', Friends of the Earth Europe website, http://www.foeeurope.org/trade/about.htm (accessed 24 January 2010). This calls for a new global trading system to replace the WTO to protect the environment.

89 ibid. Greenpeace; see also Sierra Club, 'Letter to President Clinton on the *Shrimp-Turtle* case', 1998, http://www.sierraclub.org/trade/environment/turtles.asp (accessed 11 July 2009).

90 See M. Khor, *The WTO, the Post-Doha Agenda and the Future of the Trade System: A Development Perspective*, Third World Network, 2002; see also S. Charnovitz, 'Expanding the MEA Mandate in the Doha Agenda', Global Environment & Trade Study, Yale, 2002, http://www.ppl.nl/bibliographies/wto/files/1553.pdf (accessed 24 January 2010).

91 F. Jawara & A. Kwa, *Behind the Scenes at the WTO: The Real World of International Trade Negotiations*, Zed Books, London, 2003, p. 127.

for the members to determine and then enact the necessary policy to reflect their will.

Other accusations of the ENGO community against the so-called 'WTO comes first approach' involve the notion that certain nation states have been trying to insert terms into MEAs with the aim of making them subordinate to the WTO. It has been claimed that the final negotiations of the Basel Convention on the Trade in Hazardous Waste was an example of just such behaviour.

The US had asked for text that recognised the role of the WTO in moderating global trade, and this was seen as an attempt to give the WTO precedence over the convention.[92] In the end the text that was adopted gave credit to both the WTO and the importance of the Convention in its own right.[93] The same criticism is made with regard to the negotiations on the Cartagena Biosafety Protocol in 1999 and 2000. Again, the US has been accused of trying to assert the influence of the WTO over the text of the Protocol, so that the WTO rules of trade would have to be adhered to before safety considerations for the trade in genetically modified organisms.[94] The outcome was once again described as a compromise between the desires of those countries promoting the WTO and those resisting its ascendancy, to the extent that the text has no clear guidance on the issue of prevalence of one forum or the other.[95]

It is also of interest to note that certain trade agreements do give precedence to environmental trade regulations in MEAs. For example, NAFTA gives precedence to some aspects of MEAs that relate to trade in Chapter 1.[96] Treaties such as CITES are recognised as having precedence over NAFTA, and as such this is an approach to reconciling trade with environmental measures that the WTO could consider. The only footnote to this argument would be to point out that NAFTA has not been the choice for dispute resolution of Mexico in relation to the ongoing tuna labelling dispute with the USA.[97] This is perhaps a consequence of the NAFTA provisions and potentially that Mexico may believe that it has a better chance of success in the WTO system where there are more partners – as opposed to the NAFTA which is dominated by the USA. Nevertheless, this is an example of how a trade agreement does give precedence to certain MEAs' trade-related provisions.

92 L. Wallach & P. Woodall/Public Citizen, op. cit. 84, p. 24.

93 ibid.

94 See L. Rajamani, 'The Cartagena Protocol – a Battle over Trade or Biosafety?', 1999, Third World Network website, http://www.twnside.org.sg/title/lavanya-cn.htm (accessed 24 January 2010).

95 ibid.

96 NAFTA, Article 104 and 104.1 which lists the MEAs that take precedence over the provisions of NAFTA.

97 WTO, United States – Measures Concerning the Importation, Marketing and Sale of Tuna and Tuna Products, WT/DS381/11, 27 January 2012.

Another interesting argument about the interaction of MEAs and the WTO relates to the Vienna Convention on the Law of Treaties.[98] This position argues that the efforts of countries, such as the USA, to insert WTO-dominant clauses in the MEAs is due to the fact that the Vienna Convention often gives prevalence to new agreements over older ones.[99] This is unless there are specific clauses to state otherwise.[100] For example, Article 31.1 of the Vienna Convention on the Law of Treaties requires certain issues to be taken into account when determining the meaning of any treaty, including (i) any subsequent agreement between the parties; (ii) any relevant rules of international law; and (iii) subsequent practice. This would bring the provisions of most MEAs into the WTO remit (assuming that the start date of the WTO is related to GATT).

Therefore the WTO under the Convention has to consider the provisions of MEAs when reviewing disputes if the terms of the Vienna Convention are applied. So the suspicions of some of the ENGOs and commentators, regarding inclusion of WTO-favourable language in MEAs, could be justified on the basis that to protect the meanings that were intended under the WTO it is necessary for members to request such provisions be included in MEAs.

5.6 Conclusion

As yet there has been no conflict between the WTO DSB and a MEA, but it is possible such a situation could arise. The WTO could be described as making a concerted effort to avoid such a situation.[101] Notwithstanding, fears exist that the WTO DSB, backed by the application of powerful enforcement mechanisms in the case of non-compliance,[102] will eventually rule on a MEA that uses trade restrictions for effectiveness. Certainly the GATT made contentious broad-scale trade–environment decisions to unpopular effect (with ENGOs), but few of these panel rulings were adopted.[103] The WTO – with its recognition of environmental protection and sustainable development – must tread a fine line to avoid such repeats. Yet, with just slight reforms of the WTO DSU, the fear of any WTO–MEA conflict could

98 United Nations, Vienna Convention on the Law of Treaties, Treaty Series, Vol. 1155, p. 331, done on 23 May 1969, 2005.

99 M. Matsushita, T.J. Schoenbaum & P.C. Mavroidis, *The World Trade Organisation: Law, Practice, and Policy*, Oxford University Press, Oxford, 2004, p. 459.

100 UN, op. cit. 98.

101 See N. Singh, 'Trade Related Environmental Measures in Multilateral Environmental Agreements and the WTO: Irreconcilable Differences?', 1 *American Journal of Economics and Business Administration*, 3: 2009, 249–54.

102 Enforcement mechanisms are highlighted in Chapter 1, but include high financial penalties and reciprocal actions from member states.

103 The classic *Tuna-Dolphin* case is an example of this.

be assuaged. The crux of the issue seems to lie in the interpretation of the meanings of Article XX of the GATT.

The WTO members have been working hard to try to avoid the situation where a MEA measure would be brought under the scrutiny of the WTO DSB; the CTE has been engaged in much work to establish a mechanism for solving possible contentious issues before they arrive. This work has to some extent been stifled by the members themselves being unable to agree on the way forward over relatively technical issues, rather than addressing the big questions on the inter-relationship. It would be beneficial to all the members of both MEAs and the WTO if further progress were made in this area. The Secretariat of the CTE and the members bear responsibility for pushing this agenda forward.

Finally, it is worth recalling that the MEAs themselves have only soft dispute resolution mechanisms, especially as in practice getting a dispute to the ICJ can be a very arduous process under a MEA. The WTO is therefore in a position that its rulings could impact on the operation of a MEA if it were to rule on the undertakings in such a treaty. This is not desirous unless the WTO has fully developed the capacity to rule on MEAs effectively. A possible answer to this conundrum is to use the MEAs' systems first, before any referral to the WTO. The CTE in its work could push such an agenda. In the next chapter the role of the CTE in addressing the trade–environment question will be examined.

6 Environment under the WTO and the CTE

6.1 Introduction

> While the World Trade Organization does not have rules that are specific to the environment, to energy or to Climate Change per se, there is no doubt that the rules of the multilateral trading system – as a whole (i.e. the WTO 'rule book') – are indeed relevant to Climate Change. In fact the Preamble to the WTO Agreement explicitly mentions 'sustainable development' as one of its fundamental objectives. Moreover the WTO rule book authorises its Members to give priority to environmental concerns, provided this is done in a non-protectionist manner. It is therefore not a case of trade 'trumping' the environment.[1]

This is what Pascal Lamy, the current WTO Director-General, said in his speech to the European Parliament in 2008. The statement shows that at the highest levels of the WTO Secretariat the operation of the WTO is not deliberately aimed to place trade above the environment in the international policy-making arena. It does reiterate the notion that the objective of the WTO is to ensure that trade and other concerns can interact as long as measures undertaken by member states are not discriminatory against other members. This excerpt from Pascal Lamy's speech shows the ongoing relevance of the direct interaction between international trade and the environment, and sets the context for the following chapter.

This chapter will examine the interaction of environmental concerns with the WTO, with a strong focus on the operations of the WTO Committee on Trade and Environment (CTE) in particular. Having reviewed the context of the global debate on trade and environment, and the interaction of the WTO with MEAs, it is prudent to take a closer look at the operations of the WTO with a direct focus on the environment. The CTE is the main body that the

1 Pascal Lamy, 'A Consensual International Accord on Climate Change is Needed', speech to Climate Change Committee of the European Parliament, 29 May 2008, WTO website http://www.wto.org/english/news_e/sppl_e/sppl91_e.htm (accessed 24 January 2010).

WTO has established to monitor the relationship between MEAs, sustainable development issues and the environment in relation to the global trading system. This review will throw some light on the question of whether the WTO could be more effective in accommodating environmental concerns into the fabric of its decision-making process.

Reflecting on the operations of the CTE to date will support an assessment of the commitment that exists in the WTO to treat environmental concerns on a fair and equal footing with other concerns that the WTO addresses. The broader themes of the work of the CTE will be examined and the areas assessed for their relevance to the context of the trade and environment debate. A thorough examination of the WTO and its areas that address environmental concerns will also support the generation of an overall picture of the workings of the WTO in the environmental field. The agreements that make up the WTO often refer to the environment, and therefore it is necessary to determine to what extent the agreements also reflect a conscious effort to include the environment in WTO decision making.

The competence of the WTO in environmental matters is crucial in determining whether it has a constructive future role to play in international environmental regulation. There are arguments that suggest that given the overriding trade focus of the WTO, it is too one-sided to be unbiased in its assessment of trade and environment interactions.[2] This will be analysed against current WTO practice, and measures that already exist in the WTO and its agreements.

Having examined the ongoing current debate on trade and the environment in Chapter 4, it is pertinent to review the record and the commitment to the environment in the WTO. This chapter will focus on the current practice of the WTO, with a brief overview of the historical development of the incorporation of environmental issues into the fabric of the WTO. This will include a short review relating to the operation of the GATT pre-1995 – this will be useful to determine the historical progression of the relationship with trade and the environment in the GATT/WTO in relation to the ongoing debate on trade and environment, and also in respect of WTO current practice and philosophy.

6.2 The environment under the WTO

At a basic fundamental level, the WTO has a clear commitment to the principles of sustainable development, which directly relate to the environment

2 The major critics of the WTO and its trade bias are a number of environmental NGOs and organisations such as Greenpeace, Friends of the Earth, the World Wildlife Fund, etc. For an example see http://www.greenpeace.org/international/campaigns/trade-and-the-environment (accessed 24 January 2010).

and its conservation. This is clearly stated in the opening recitals of the preamble to the 1994 Marrakesh Protocol founding the WTO:

> ... the optimal use of the worlds [sic] resources in accordance with the objective of sustainable development, seeking both to protect and preserve the environment and to enhance the means for doing so in a manner consistent with their respective needs and concerns at different levels of economic development.[3]

This demonstrates a real commitment to the environment in the principles of the founding of the WTO; that the WTO should be operated in a manner that reconciles environmental concerns with global trade. In Chapter 4 the environmentalist arguments suggest that the preamble is not evidence enough of a commitment to balancing trade and environment concerns in the WTO.[4] Although the preamble has no legal standing per se, the Vienna Convention on the Law of Treaties under Article 31 suggests that the wording of treaties should be given their natural meaning.[5]

This should be applicable to the preamble and therefore the WTO members have made a formal commitment to the principles of sustainable development, the environment and environmental protection. So the preamble has some value and supports the notion that environmental protection and sustainable development can be considered in WTO DSU decisions, as it is a fundamental principle of the WTO. This is reinforced by the comments made by Pascal Lamy in his speech to the European Parliament in May 2008, as noted above.[6] He clearly states that trade does not trump environmental concerns.[7] There follows an examination of the development of commitment to environmental principles in the WTO, through reference to the active work of the CTE.

The CTE fulfils a role mandated to it – to monitor trade and environment issues – the mandate being agreed in 1995 and its standing made permanent after the Doha Ministerial in 2001.[8] After a brief recap of the development of environmental competence in the GATT/WTO system, it is to the CTE that attention will first be turned to assess its role with regard to environmental issues in the WTO.

3 WTO Agreement 1995, first recital in the preamble.

4 C.A.R. Robb et al., *Trade and Environment, International Environmental Law Reports*, Vol. 2, University of Cambridge, Cambridge, 2001, p. 285.

5 United Nations, *Vienna Convention on the Law of Treaties 1969*, United Nations Treaty Series, Vol. 1155, 2005, p. 331.

6 Pascal Lamy, op. cit. 1.

7 ibid.

8 WTO, Ministerial Conference, Fourth Session, Doha, 9–14 November 2001, Ministerial Declaration, WT/MIN(01)/DEC/1, 20 November 2001, paras 31–33.

6.2.1 The historical context

The development of the consideration of the environment in the global trading system has a long history. In the 1970s growing international concern about the state of the environment led to a call for an international conference on how to manage the human environment.[9] This awareness led to the staging of the 1972 United Nations Stockholm Conference on the Human Environment. The GATT contracting parties were asked to contribute a paper to the conference, as the link between trade and environmental protection – both the impact of environmental policies on trade, and the impact of trade on the environment had been recognised.[10]

This shows that in the first decades of the operation of the GATT an awareness of the synergies and potential conflicts that existed between trade and environmental policy were already being mapped by the parties and the GATT Secretariat, as well as in the UN. Therefore, it can be maintained that the environment has been an active part of the international trade law regime since the 1970s.

In 1971 the GATT Secretariat prepared the study: this was under its own auspices, not the auspices of the contracting parties. The paper was presented at the Stockholm Convention and was entitled 'Industrial Pollution Control and International Trade'.[11] The study focused on the implications of environmental protection policies on international trade. It was mostly concerned with the trade effects of environmental protection, and fears of a new form of 'green' protectionism.[12] This has been a concern during the past four decades, and the issue of environmental protection as a barrier to free trade is an issue that remains alive and well today.[13] The GATT and WTO have reviewed a number of cases where the environmental integrity of a policy measure has been cast against its nature as a barrier to trade.[14]

Going back briefly to those early trade–environment discussions, in 1971 the GATT contracting parties reviewed the study and a number of members suggested that a body be set up within the GATT to further examine the relationship of trade and environment.[15] It was suggested that a similar body

9 WTO, 'Early Years: Emerging Environment Debate in GATT/WTO', WTO website, http://www.wto.org/english/tratop_e/envir_e/hist1_e.htm#EMIT (accessed 24 January 2010).

10 ibid.

11 GATT, *Industrial Pollution Control and International Trade*, Studies in International Trade No. 1, Unipub, December 2001.

12 ibid.

13 'Environmental Requirements and Market Access: Preventing "Green Protectionism"', WTO website, http://www.wto.org/english/tratop_e/envir_e/envir_req_e.htm (accessed 24 January 2010).

14 See Chapter 7 for a full review of the WTO DSB consideration of environmental measures in relation to international trade.

15 'Early Years: Emerging Environment Debate in GATT/WTO', op. cit. 9.

to the environment committee of the Organization for Economic Co-operation and Development (OECD) be established.[16] This again highlights the early recognition of the need for environmental concerns to be reflected in the operation of the global trading system by the GATT Secretariat and the contracting parties.

Enhancing the links between trade and the environment has been a long-standing concern of experts in the field of trade law – the relationship between trade and the environment is a clear and well-established phenomenon.[17] When the GATT set up the Group on Environmental Measures and International Trade (EMIT), agreed in November 1971,[18] the first institutional trade and environment body had been founded. This was under the auspices of the GATT and before any global environmental organisation had been established.[19]

The fact that the contracting parties set up a body concerned with the environment in 1971, prior to the 1972 Stockholm Convention on the Human Environment, demonstrates a commitment to understanding and reconciling trade and environment issues within the GATT. This was perhaps before many campaigners for the environment and nature conservation were even aware of the issues relating to trade and the environment. The establishment of EMIT in 1971 means that there has been a long-standing interest in environmental matters and their relation to trade within the GATT/WTO system.

This historical aspect is important in the context of the current debate on trade inter-relations with the environment, as it is clear that the need to reconcile environmental concerns with the international trading system has long been recognised as a necessary building block for an effective global trading regime. The fact remains that many environmental commentators may not have appreciated the long-standing nature of the relationship between international environmental law and international trade law, as underlined by the creation of EMIT under GATT.

Nevertheless, there were drawbacks with EMIT. One particular stumbling block of the EMIT system was that the group would only convene at the

16 See F. Weiss, 'The GATT 1994: Environmental Sustainability of Trade or Environmental Protection Sustainable by Trade', in K. Ginther et al., *Sustainable Development and Good Governance*, Kluwer, Deventer, 1995, p. 382; and F. Weiss et al., *International Economic Law with a Human Face*, Kluwer Law International, Dordrecht, 1998, p. 204.

17 There is a large amount of literature on this topic. See, inter alia, D.C. Esty, *Greening the GATT: Trade, Environment and the Future*, Institute for International Economics, Washington, 1994; K.V. Thai et al., *Handbook of Globalisation and the Environment*, CRC Press, Boca Raton, 2007.

18 GATT, The GATT Council of Representatives Decision, Geneva, November 1971.

19 UNEP was not founded until after the 1972 Conference on the Human Environment; see 'UNEP Milestones', UNEP website, http://www.unep.org/Documents.multilingual/Default.asp?DocumentID=287 (accessed 24 January 2010).

request of a GATT member.[20] No contracting party asked for EMIT to convene until 1991, with the forthcoming 1992 United Nations Conference on Environment and Development (UNCED).[21] Therefore EMIT was inactive for 20 years. So despite the mechanism being available, it was badly underutilised by the parties to the GATT.

When EMIT did meet prior to UNCED in 1991, it focused on some of the more pressing matters regarding trade and environment, including issues that are still being discussed in the WTO today.[22] The EMIT group examined the effects of environmental measures (including eco-labelling schemes) on international trade; the relationship between the GATT rules and the trade provisions contained in MEAs; and the transparency of national environmental regulations that could have an impact on trade.[23] These remain some of the main contentious issues in the trade and environment debate, which the CTE continues to address through its work.

So when EMIT finally did come into action, its work was highly relevant both in terms of the trade–environment agenda in 1991 and now. Such issues and their handling under the WTO remain contentious and closely scrutinised. Indeed, as noted in Chapter 5, the CTE has been devoting much of its resources to analysing the MEAs that have trade aspects, while attempting to ensure that there is no conflict between the workings of the WTO and such MEAs. EMIT may have been a poorly utilised body, but its existence and eventual operation show that the GATT/WTO system has been engaging with environmental issues for a long period of time. Reconciling differences between the needs of the global trading system and protection of the natural environment are in-built factors of the GATT/WTO system. But does this infer competence?

Following the EMIT meeting of 1991, the 1992 UNCED meeting drew further attention to the links between international trade and the environment. Agenda 21, the programme of action adopted at the conference, addressed the importance of promoting sustainable development through, amongst other means, international trade.[24] This can be seen as the catalyst for driving the trade and environment debate – certainly interest in the

20 In G.P. Sampson, *The WTO and Sustainable Development*, TERI Press, Delhi, United Nations University Press, 2005, p. 18; the mandate of the EMIT group is described thus 'to examine upon request any specific matters relevant to trade policy aspects of measures to control pollution and protect the human environment, especially with regard to the application of the provisions of the General Agreement taking into account the particular problems of developing countries'.

21 In 1991 the members of the European Free Trade Association (EFTA) asked the Director General of GATT to convene the EMIT group.

22 G.P. Sampson, op. cit. 20, p. 22.

23 C.A.R. Robb et al., op. cit. 4.

24 See Principle 12 of the Rio Declaration, UNCED, June 1992.

interaction between trade and environment grew in the 1990s.[25] However, the GATT through EMIT played an important role in driving this agenda and in trying to develop a common understanding of how the interaction between trade and the environment could be best managed.

The need for the WTO to include environmental considerations in its undertakings has a long history of development. The formal linkage of trade and environment at UNCED was only the precursor to more explicit linkage following the negotiations for the inception of the WTO. These historical developments show that there is a pedigree within the GATT/WTO system for the consideration of environmental issues relating directly to the international trading regime, suggesting some form of competence.

The preamble to the Marrakesh Agreement Establishing the WTO places environmental protection, the conservation of scarce resources and sustainable development firmly among the WTO's core principles.[26] The fact that the first paragraph of the preamble recognises sustainable development as an integral part of the multilateral trading system demonstrates the importance placed by WTO members on environmental protection, and clearly presents the case that trade is not exclusive of environmental concerns. In Marrakesh, in April 1994, the WTO members also signed a Decision on Trade and Environment which states that:

> There should not be, nor need be, any policy contradiction between upholding and safeguarding an open, non-discriminatory and equitable multilateral trading system on the one hand, and acting for the protection of the environment, and the promotion of sustainable development on the other.[27]

This also demonstrates that the linkage between the operations of the WTO and environmental protection is clearly recognised by the members of the WTO. These early developments in the conception of the WTO demonstrate a commitment to environmental protection under the WTO and how such thinking entered the WTO/GATT system during the last decades of the previous GATT 1947 regime.

25 See M. Matsushita, T.J. Schoenbaum & P.C. Mavroidis, *The World Trade Organisation Law Practice and Policy*, Oxford University Press, Oxford, 2004, p. 448, which states that prior to 1991 the relationship between trade and the environment was an arcane speciality that attracted little attention.

26 'Marrakesh Agreement Establishing the World Trade Organisation', in WTO, *The Legal Texts: The Results of the Uruguay Round of Multilateral Trade Negotiations*, Cambridge University Press, Cambridge, 2004, p. 4.

27 WTO Trade and Environment Ministerial Decision, adopted April 14, 1994, GATT Doc MTN.TNC/MIN (94)/1/Rev.1, (1994) 33 I.L.M. 1267, WTO website, http://www.wto.org/english/tratop_e/envir_e/issu5_e.htm (accessed 24 January 2010).

To demonstrate the value of the words of the opening of the Marrakesh Agreement, it is worth noting the importance of the preamble of the WTO, as stressed in the AB's ruling on the *Sea Turtles* case:

> As this preambular language reflects the intentions of negotiators of the WTO Agreement, we believe it must add colour, texture and shading to our interpretation of the agreements annexed to the WTO Agreement.[28]

This statement clearly shows that the operators of the WTO dispute resolution system see their remit as broader than simple trade issues. The panel members will consider other factors in determining the outcomes of cases depending upon their relevance to all parts of the WTO Agreement, including the preamble.

Further to this, in recognition of the importance of environmental issues and their relationship with trade, the member states set up the CTE under the WTO Agreement.[29] This important body is part of the machinery of the WTO's commitment to the environment. The operations of the CTE are a good starting point to review the relationship between the WTO and the environment. Commitments are being made to the environment in the WTO, but the question of competency to deal with certain environment measures remains an illusive question. The WTO's record on environmental protection and its competence to deal with environmental issues will now be considered, specifically looking at the work of the CTE to date.

6.3 The WTO CTE terms of reference

The CTE was established in 1994 by ministerial decision.[30] Basically the CTE was originally charged with adopting the work that had begun under the EMIT, but to ensure that the work would have a new higher profile. Certainly the terms of reference of the CTE reflected the work of EMIT, whilst also embracing a broader collection of themes to review.[31] The main aim of the CTE could be seen as the attempt to bring environment and sustainable development concerns into the WTO policy setting on a more formal basis, developing a further understanding of the relationship between trade and the environment within the WTO and the wider international trade and environment policy field.

28 *United States – Import Prohibition of Certain Shrimp and Shrimp Products*, Appellate Body Report: WT/DS58/AB/R, Oct 12, 1998.

29 WTO Trade and Environment Ministerial Decision, adopted 14 April 1994, GATT Doc MTN.TNC/MIN (94)/1/Rev.1, (1994) 33 I.L.M. 1267.

30 WTO Trade and Environment Ministerial Decision, adopted 14 April 1994, GATT Doc MTN.TNC/MIN (94)/1/Rev.1, (1994) 33 I.L.M. 1267.

31 G.P. Sampson, op. cit. 20 and C.A.R. Robb et al., op. cit. 4.

The terms of reference given to the CTE included the following remit:

(a) To identify the relationship between trade measures and environmental measures, in order to promote sustainable development;
(b) To make appropriate recommendations on whether any modifications of the provisions of the multilateral trading system are required, compatible with the open, equitable and non-discriminatory nature of the system, as regards, in particular:
  (i) The need for rules to enhance positive interaction between trade and environmental measures ... with special consideration to the needs of developing countries ...
  (ii) the avoidance of protectionist trade measures, and the adherence to effective multilateral disciplines to ensure responsiveness of the multilateral trading system to environmental objectives set forth in Agenda 21 and the Rio Declaration, in particular Principle 12;
  (iii) surveillance of trade measures used for environmental purposes, of trade-related aspects of environmental measures which have significant trade effects, and of effective implementation of the multilateral disciplines governing those measures.[32]

The terms of reference are clearly designed to allow the integration of environmental/sustainable development issues within the WTO framework, as point (b) requires the CTE to recommend any modifications that might be needed of the multilateral trading system in relation to general environmental concerns.

Specifics for the CTE include the relationship between trade and environment rules and any recommendations that may need to be made to enhance a positive relationship; responsiveness to environmental measures and objectives deriving from the UNCED and Agenda 21 – Principle 12 being particularly mentioned which concerns the development of open trading systems with due attention for environmental protection;[33] and to survey

32 GATT, Uruguay Round Agreement – Decision on Trade and Environment, done at Marrakesh on 15 April 1994, WTO, Geneva, 1994, WTO website, http://www.wto.org/english/docs_e/legal_e/56-dtenv_e.htm (accessed 24 January 2010).

33 Principle 12 of Agenda 21 reads as follows: 'States should cooperate to promote a supportive and open international economic system that would lead to economic growth and sustainable development in all countries, to better address the problems of environmental degradation. Trade policy measures for environmental purposes should not constitute a means of arbitrary or unjustifiable discrimination or a disguised restriction on international trade. Unilateral actions to deal with environmental challenges outside the jurisdiction of the importing country should be avoided. Environmental measures addressing transboundary or global environmental problems should, as far as possible, be based on an international consensus.' See the Rio Declaration on Environment and Development, UNEP website, 1992, http://www.unep.org/Documents.multilingual/Default.asp?DocumentID=78&ArticleID=1163 (accessed 24 January 2010).

trade measures that are used for environmental purposes, and the multilateral agreements that govern the use of such measures.[34] These terms of reference form the clear outline of the work of the CTE and include a significant aspect on the review of trade-related measures in MEAs.

As discussed in Chapter 5, the WTO under the auspices of the CTE has been very active in this particular sphere, and the work of the CTE in this area is still ongoing and a current issue in the WTO today. The terms of reference became the basis for the work of the CTE and resulted in a mandate being given to the CTE to examine many distinct areas of interaction between the multilateral trading system and the environment.

In all, there are ten areas that the CTE has been mandated to explore.[35] With this broad-based mandate the CTE has been working over the past ten years to bring environment and sustainable development considerations into the mainstream of the WTO's work. Certainly the CTE has been active and has worked on all the areas of its mandated programme since its inception. The formation of the CTE immediately led to an upsurge in a belief that trade and environment conflicts could be reconciled.[36]

However, the CTE's work has been somewhat constrained, given that it has very broad terms of reference, and the work has focused on specific areas, such as the relationship between the WTO and MEAs. This does not mean that the CTE has been unsuccessful in its endeavours, merely that it has a wide remit and through necessity has focused its energies on specific pressing issues of our time.

6.3.1 *The ten areas of work of the CTE*

As mentioned above, the CTE has ten distinct areas upon which it is mandated to work. At the first WTO ministerial meeting in Singapore, the CTE produced a report covering all of the areas in its mandate, suggesting further work and making recommendations.[37]

Table 6.1 outlines the main areas that the CTE is working on in the WTO.[38]

34 ibid.

35 WTO Trade and Environment Ministerial Decision, adopted 14 April 1994, GATT Doc MTN.TNC/MIN (94)/1/Rev.1, (1994) 33 I.L.M. 1267.

36 See J. Schultz, 'The GATT/WTO Committee on Trade and the Environment – Toward Environmental Reform', *American Journal of International Law* 423, 1995.

37 WTO CTE, Report (1996) of the Committee on Trade and Environment, WT/CTE/1, (96-4808), 12 November 1996.

38 Items on the CTE Work programme, WTO website, http://www.wto.org/english/tratop_e/envir_e/cte00_e.htm (accessed 24 January 2010).

Table 6.1 Areas of work of the CTE

Number	*Area of focus*
1	The relationship between the provisions of the multilateral trading system and trade measures for environmental purposes, including those pursuant to multilateral environmental agreements;
2	The relationship between environmental policies relevant to trade and environmental measures with significant trade effects and the provisions of the multilateral trading system;
3	The relationship between the provisions of the multilateral trading system and: (a) charges and taxes for environmental purposes; (b) requirements for environmental purposes relating to products, including standards and technical regulations, packaging, labelling and recycling;
4	The provisions of the multilateral trading system with respect to the transparency of trade measures used for environmental purposes and environmental measures and requirements which have significant trade effects;
5	The relationship between the dispute settlement mechanisms in the multilateral trading system and those found in multilateral environmental agreements;
6	The effect of environmental measures on market access, especially in relation to developing countries, in particular to the least developed among them, and environmental benefits of removing trade restrictions and distortions;
7	The issue of exports of domestically prohibited goods;
8	That the Committee on Trade and Environment will consider the work programme envisaged in the Decision on Trade in Services and the Environment and the relevant provisions of the Agreement on Trade-Related Aspects of Intellectual Property Rights as an integral part of its work, within the above terms of reference;
9	That, pending the first meeting of the General Council of the WTO, the work of the Committee on Trade and Environment should be carried out by a Sub-Committee of the Preparatory Committee of the World Trade Organization (PCWTO), open to all members of the PCWTO;
10	To invite the Sub-Committee of the Preparatory Committee, and the Committee on Trade and Environment when it is established, to provide input to the relevant bodies in respect of appropriate arrangements for relations with inter-governmental and non-governmental organizations referred to in Article V of the WTO.

The CTE is working on the following issues and has been mandated under the Doha development agenda (DDA) to focus on some of these as a matter of priority:

1 Trade rules, environment agreements and disputes (covered under actions 1 and 5): under this function the CTE is mandated to examine the relationship between MEAs and the operation of the WTO. This is with particular

regard to the possible interaction of the dispute resolution mechanisms contained within the MEAs and its relationship to the WTO DSU. This is a current work area of the CTE with parties engaged in negotiations on the issue, and has been examined previously in detail in Chapter 5.

2 Environmental taxes and other national environmental requirements: the CTE is examining the link between taxes for environmental purposes and requirements for product labelling relating to environmental practices, such as standards and technical regulations. This is a current focus of the work of the CTE under the DDA mandate.
3 Environment and trade liberalisation: the CTE is exploring how environmental measures affect market access, especially in relation to developing countries and the least developed countries, while at the same time exploring any potential benefits of removing trade restrictions and distortions. This is also a current area of focus for the CTE under the DDA mandate.
4 Intellectual property: the CTE is reviewing the relevant provisions of the TRIPS Agreement in relation to the CBD. This is also being considered under the mandate of the DDA.
5 Interaction with other relevant instruments' secretariats: the means of effectively doing this is currently being negotiated by the parties in the CTE.

These areas are the main focus of the CTE at the present time, and have been since its inception. The DDA has driven work on certain areas forward, and these will be examined below. As examined previously, points 1 and 5 above have been an area of major negotiation in the CTE, and the form of co-operation with MEA secretariats and provisions continues to be dominated in the CTE negotiations. Therefore the focus of the following analysis will be on the areas of the CTE's agenda that the DDA is driving forward.

6.4 The Doha Development Agenda and the work of the Committee on Trade and Environment

In 2001 the DDA negotiations were launched by the WTO members. The discussions focused on a new round of tariff reductions and multilateral trade rules. However, of relevance for the trade and environment debate, the DDA negotiations identified areas of importance for the CTE to work on in its ministerial declaration. The DDA focuses on the CTE's regular work and in three paragraphs outlines the main issues that need to be prioritised for the CTE:

> 31 With a view to enhancing the mutual supportiveness of trade and environment, we agree to negotiations, without prejudging their outcome, on:
>
> (i) the relationship between existing WTO rules and specific trade obligations set out in multilateral environmental agreements (MEAs). The negotiations shall be limited in scope to the

applicability of such existing WTO rules as among parties to the MEA in question. The negotiations shall not prejudice the WTO rights of any Member that is not a party to the MEA in question;

(ii) procedures for regular information exchange between MEA Secretariats and the relevant WTO committees, and the criteria for the granting of observer status;

(iii) the reduction or, as appropriate, elimination of tariff and non-tariff barriers to environmental goods and services.

We note that fisheries subsidies form part of the negotiations provided for in paragraph 28.

32 We instruct the Committee on Trade and Environment, in pursuing work on all items on its agenda within its current terms of reference, to give particular attention to:

(i) the effect of environmental measures on market access, especially in relation to developing countries, in particular the least-developed among them, and those situations in which the elimination or reduction of trade restrictions and distortions would benefit trade, the environment and development;

(ii) the relevant provisions of the Agreement on Trade-Related Aspects of Intellectual Property Rights; and

(iii) labelling requirements for environmental purposes.

Work on these issues should include the identification of any need to clarify relevant WTO rules. The Committee shall report to the Fifth Session of the Ministerial Conference, and make recommendations, where appropriate, with respect to future action, including the desirability of negotiations. The outcome of this work as well as the negotiations carried out under paragraph 31(i) and (ii) shall be compatible with the open and non-discriminatory nature of the multilateral trading system, shall not add to or diminish the rights and obligations of members under existing WTO agreements, in particular the Agreement on the Application of Sanitary and Phytosanitary Measures, nor alter the balance of these rights and obligations, and will take into account the needs of developing and least-developed countries.

33 We recognize the importance of technical assistance and capacity building in the field of trade and environment to developing countries, in particular the least-developed among them. We also encourage that expertise and experience be shared with members wishing to perform environmental reviews at the national level. A report shall be prepared on these activities for the Fifth Session.[39]

39 Doha WTO Ministerial Declaration, 14 November 2001, WTO website, http://www.wto.org/english/thewto_e/minist_e/min01_e/mindecl_e.htm#tradeenvironment (accessed 24 January 2010).

From examining the above paragraphs of the Doha ministerial proclamation it is clear to note that the focus of the work of the CTE is directed towards specific controversial areas in the trade and environment agenda under paragraph 32. These can be summarised as follows:

- the effect of environmental measures on market access;
- the relationship between the WTO and MEAs;
- the sections of TRIPS relating to the environment; and
- labelling for environmental purposes.

The declaration requires the CTE to specifically identify any areas of WTO rules that need to be clarified in relation to these issues. This was supported with the requirement for the CTE to make recommendations to the fifth Ministerial Conference held in Hong Kong in 2005.[40] Most of the work of the CTE under the DDA has been focused on the three points outlined under paragraph 31, with much work going on regarding MEAs (as seen in Chapter 5) and environmental goods and services.[41] These negotiations will be considered in this chapter. Finally, the CTE was mandated to carry out the work and negotiations in a way compatible with the multilateral trading system, such that the rights and obligations of WTO members would not be adversely impacted.

The CTE has been active in addressing these issues since 2001. However, the progress that has been required by some actors has not been made.[42] The UK House of Commons Environmental Audit Committee produced a number of recommendations in 2006 for the UK government to drive forward the agenda of the CTE in relation to the DDA and the associated work themes.[43] In these recommendations the Audit Committee raised a concern that the CTE was in fact hindering a holistic discussion of the issues of trade, environment and development, rather than driving such debate forward.[44] This could be attributed to the fact that the CTE focuses mainly on the environmental aspects of trade rules.

Nevertheless, it is interesting to note the types of criticism that the CTE has faced in the pursuit of its mandate, especially when from a group of honourable MPs. The recommendation in question directs concern at the work of the CTE; however, it is of course the member states who set up the

40 ibid.

41 WTO, 'Negotiations on Trade and the Environment', WTO website, http://www.wto.org/english/tratop_e/envir_e/envir_negotiations_e.htm (accessed 24 January 2010).

42 House of Commons Environmental Audit Committee, *Government Response to the Committee's Eleventh Report of Session 2005–06: Outflanked: The World Trade Organisation, International Trade and Sustainable Development, Fourth Special Report of Session 2006–07*, The Stationery Office, London, 13 March 2007.

43 ibid.

44 ibid., Recommendation 9, p. 5.

work programme of the Committee. This criticism of the Committee may be slightly unfair in its tone and content. Clearly, the work of the CTE is of great importance and the fact that it attracts high-level criticism is telling of the demanding nature of the work it undertakes.

The work of the CTE on the DDA has focused to a large extent on the questions of liberalisation of trade in environmental goods under paragraph 31 (iii) of the Doha Declaration – to the extent that the CTE Chair has in the past suggested that work in other areas be suspended so that full attention can be given to this issue.[45] Toufiq Ali, as Chair of the CTE Special Session on the DDA issues, suggested this course of action in the run up to the Hong Kong ministerial meeting in 2005.[46]

The suggestion reflected the nature of the difficulty within the CTE Special Sessions (CTESS) in approaching this issue, namely that the different groups of countries had different needs. For example, the Swiss and Canadians proposed a list of goods to be liberalised, whereas the Indians proposed a project-based means to determine which products should be considered as environmental goods and liberalised. Brazil finally proposed the request offer approach that is used to liberalise services under the GATS agreement.[47]

It is worth noting that at the Hong Kong ministerial meeting in 2005 the report of the CTESS working on paragraph 31 (iii) of the Doha Declaration stated that the CTESS had not yet reached an agreement among the parties in how it should agree on moving work on to the next stage with regard to environmental goods and services.[48] The report went on to note the difficulty it was facing in trying to redress the differences between the approaches suggested by the different parties and the challenge faced in trying to find a way forward.[49] No one reading this document can be in any doubt of the serious nature of the challenge in moving forward on the issue in the CTESS. Neither can anyone deny the importance the CTESS have put on ensuring that the negotiations would result in a win-win-win scenario for trade, environment and development.[50] Since the ministerial meeting the work of the CTESS on this issue has been ongoing, and still the negotiations are incomplete.

The main issue that can be detected in the work of the CTESS on this subject is the ongoing disagreement between developing and developed nations.

45 'CTE Gets Down to Details on Environmental Goods', 5 *Bridges Trade BioRes*, 16, 16 September 2005, ICTSD website, http://ictsd.net/i/news/biores/8989/ (accessed 24 January 2010).

46 ibid.

47 'A Doha Round Deliverable for Climate Change?', 1 *News and Analysis*, 2, December 2007, ICTSD website, http://ictsd.net/i/news/bioresreview/10631/ (accessed 24 January 2010).

48 WTO, Committee on Trade and Environment Special Session, Report by the Chairperson of the Special Session of the Committee on Trade and Environment to the Trade Negotiations Committee, TN/TE/14, WTO, 28 November 2005, para.16, p. 3.

49 ibid., para. 17, p. 3.

50 ibid., para. 23, p. 4.

The arguments have been portrayed as a win–lose scenario, with the developed country producers of environmental goods set to gain from the liberalisation at the expense of developing country border tariffs.[51] This is of course an over-simplification of the situation, and win–win scenarios can easily be foreseen. Increasing access to environmental goods and services (EGS) can bring benefits for all societies. The approach to the liberalisation of trade in such EGS is the crucial element in determining the success of the policy; gradual trade liberalisation with careful monitoring of impact and suitable redress mechanisms would be an option for making market opening potentially successful.[52]

The liberalisation of trade in such goods would lead to broad economic development and also the extremely useful exchange of knowledge around the utilisation of such technologies.[53] Such argumentation also holds that a highly managed trade liberalisation policy around these EGS would help developing countries reach the Millennium Development Goals and the objectives of the Johannesburg implementation plan, and the desired outcomes of many MEAs.[54]

However, it is acknowledged that the failure in the progress of negotiations on this issue is due to the scepticism of the many developing countries to the coverage of EGS and the impact of a too broad definition on their employment, industries and general economic growth. The collated lists of environmental goods submitted to the WTO in 2005 include many more goods that are produced in developed countries rather than developing countries.[55] Whilst the lists of EGS have now been reduced, they still incorporate more developing country imports than exports.[56] Figure 6.1 shows the relevant levels of exports of EGS in 2007 (as defined under the 153 suggestions made to the CTESS in 2007). It is clear that the main exporters of EGS are the developed nations.

The fact remains that tariff revenue is a major income earner for most developing countries' governments, as few have a sophisticated income tax or corporation tax system, relying heavily on the income generated in the form of cross-border tariffs. Finally, it is worth noting that an analysis of the lists of EGS as submitted in 2007 (and it is this list that has formed the basis for most negotiations on the issue since) at the WTO demonstrates that not all

51 'CTE Gets Down to Details on Environmental Goods', op. cit. 45.

52 V. Jha, 'Environmental Priorities and Trade Policy for Environmental Goods: A Reality Check', Environmental Goods and Services Series, Issue Paper 7, ICTSD, Switzerland, September 2008, http://ictsd.net/downloads/2008/11/ictsd-veena-jha_final-integrated-cover.pdf (accessed 24 January 2010).

53 ibid.

54 ibid.

55 WTO, Synthesis of Submissions on Environmental Goods, TN/TE/W/63, WTO, Geneva, 2005.

56 V. Jha, op. cit. 52.

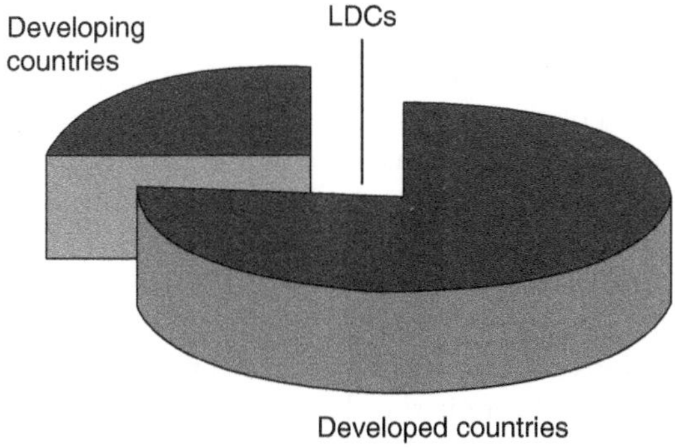

Figure 6.1 Global exporters of EGS in 2007
Source: ITC Trade Map[57]

developing countries are in the same position on EGS.[58] China, Malaysia, Mexico and Korea appear amongst the leading top ten countries of exporters of these EGS (the list has 153 goods) on a global scale in 2006. Therefore, there are clear benefits for some developing countries from increased liberalised trade in EGS.

Progress in the negotiations has been hard and slow, but in July 2009 the Chair of the CTESS dealing with paragraph 31 (iii) of the Doha Declaration gave formal instruction to the parties to draw up further lists of EGS of interest that could be used as a negotiation mandate, without prejudice to the current offers on the table.[59] There is flexibility in the approach that the members may use: either in terms of lists across as many sectors as possible, or the EGS that are identified could also be part of a request-offer form of negotiation.[60] The members were also asked to identify cross-cutting issues

57 Reprinted from F. Khatun, 'Trade Negotiations on Environmental Goods and Services in the LDCs Context', Centre for Policy Dialogue, Presentation at the Informal Discussions on Environmental Goods and Services: The LDC Perspective, UNDP & ICTSD, Geneva, 24 September 2009.

58 WTO, Continued Work under Paragraph 31 (iii) of the Doha Ministerial Declaration, JOB (07) 54, WTO, Geneva, 2007.

59 Ambassador M.A.J. Teehankee, 'State of Play in the Environmental Goods Negotiations', Speech at the ICTSD/Japan Informal Roundtable on Trade in Energy Efficient Products: Implications for Environmental Goods Negotiations, Geneva, 23 September 2009.

60 WTO News, 'Lamy Presents Road Map for the Autumn Negotiations', Trade Negotiations Committee, WTO, Geneva, 24 July 2009, WTO website, http://www.wto.org/english/news_e/news09_e/tnc_dg_stat_24jul09_e.htm (accessed 24 January 2010).

and development-related issues under the mandate for negotiations on this subject.[61]

The plan for the next phase of work for the CTESS in this area is to undertake a more substantive examination of the EGS in certain sectors, including air pollution control, renewable energy, waste management and environmental technologies.[62] Proposals that come forward on these areas will form the basis of substantive negotiations in 2010.

It is these issues that the CTE, through its Special Sessions on the DDA paragraph 31 (iii), needs to clearly address to deliver a meaningful and useful outcome to these specific negotiations on EGS. To date the CTESS have not been able to drive the member states through the door of co-operation on EGS – better co-ordination with other committees, such as the Trade and Development Committee, may support a settlement of the issue. The CTESS is now driving forward the programme in this crucial aspect of the trade and environment debate. A win here for the CTE in terms of improving trade in EGS could enhance its reputation as a key body in the promotion of environmental principles.

6.5 Other areas of work of the CTE

As noted previously, the DDA contained a number of areas for work on the relationship between the environment and trade rules. Two other major areas of activity for the CTE, both under its original ten-point mandate and the DDA, are the interaction of TRIPS with environmental concerns and the concept of environmental labelling of goods. These activities were explicitly covered under paragraph 32 of the DDA.[63] Work has been moving forward in these areas, although they could be considered to be secondary to the focus on the EGS issue – neither are considered under the CTESS.

At the Hong Kong Ministerial Conference the report of the CTE informed the members that work had been carried out in the Committee under the terms of paragraph 32 of the Doha Declaration.[64] The report outlined that meetings had reviewed the main issues under paragraph 32, with a focus on the impact of environmental measures on market access (paragraph 32 (i)), the relationship between TRIPS and the environment (paragraph 32 (ii)), and the issue of labelling for environmental purposes (paragraph 32 (iii)).[65] Under paragraph 32 (i) the report stated that the CTE had, through its meetings, addressed the need to move forward, using national and sectoral experiences

61 ibid.

62 V. Jha, op. cit. 52.

63 Doha WTO Ministerial Declaration, op. cit. 39.

64 WTO, Report (2005) of the Committee on Trade and Environment, WT/CTE/12, WTO, 14 October 2005.

65 ibid., para. 2, p. 1.

as a means to encourage an advancement. This issue remains an active area of work of the CTE, but for the purposes of this study attention shall be turned to the work of the CTE on the items under paragraph 32 (ii) and 32 (iii).

6.5.1 TRIPS and the Committee on Trade and the Environment

That same report at the Hong Kong Ministerial Conference outlined that the CTE had also been reviewing the work of the Committee in relation to the TRIPS agreement.[66] The work of the TRIPS council on this issue is also mandated under paragraph 19 of the Doha Ministerial Declaration, whereby the main area of concern is the relationship between TRIPS and the CBD.[67] As examined previously in Chapter 4, there are a number of concerns around the operation of the TRIPS and its impact on the CBD.

The potential for conflict between the CBD and the WTO exists in the sense that a member of the CBD who is also a member of the WTO could challenge a CBD-compatible measure under the WTO, whereby the measure could be incompatible.[68] The CTE is to lead on the study into the relationship between the two international instruments and has been active in working on the issue since the Hong Kong Ministerial Conference.[69]

The CTE, in reviewing the relationship between the CBD and TRIPS, has been working with the TRIPS council, which, as noted, also has a mandate to address the issue of compatibility of the WTO TRIPS agreement with the CBD. The CTE has not been the main forum for discussion on this dossier, but nevertheless there have been developments in the consideration of the issue therein.[70] Three main proposals have been put forward in the CTE on the issue of improving the relationship between the TRIPS agreement and the CBD.

As noted in Chapter 4, a group of mainly developing countries have put forward a detailed proposal calling for the mandatory requirement for patent applications to divulge the source of their biological material – this, in their opinion, will help reduce the number of erroneous patents that are filed and also ensure that such patent requests comply with the laws from which the products come. This position is opposed by a number of developed countries who believe that the argument is not made and that there is no need to change the patent system.[71] The third view seeks a common ground between the two opposing positions, suggesting a limited patent disclosure system at

66 ibid., para. 5, p. 2.

67 Doha WTO Ministerial Declaration, op. cit. 39.

68 See Chapters 4 and 5.

69 See 'Members Look at TRIPS–CBD Relationship', *Bridges Weekly Trade Review*, 27 March 2006.

70 WTO, 'Intellectual Property and the Environment', Geneva, WTO website, http://www.wto.org/english/tratop_e/envir_e/trips_e.htm (accessed 24 January 2010).

71 See Chapter 4; and ibid.

the international level, outlining the sources of genetic material without making implications for the patent system.[72]

The interesting aspect of this work stream is that a number of members wished to have the discussions on the inter-relationship between the TRIPS agreement and the CBD held under the TRIPS council rather than under the CTE.[73] Brazil, India and Pakistan all made it clear that they wished the substantive part of the negotiations on this issue to take place in the TRIPS council.[74] This demonstrates that the CTE, whilst mandated to deal with the issue, was not perceived as a 'strong' enough forum for gaining the desired outcomes that the developing countries wished.

The discussions on the TRIPS agreement and the CBD have been limited in the CTE because of this very issue, with countries preferring to deal with the questions in the TRIPS council.[75] The CBD Secretariat submits its observations to both the CTE and the TRIPS council.[76] However, there are frustrations at the lack of co-operation between the CTE and the CBD Secretariat from some member states, and the role of the CTE on this topical issue appears to be subordinate to the TRIPS council.[77]

In terms of the discussions under paragraph 32 (ii) of the Doha Declaration, it seems that the work of the CTE has been trumped by the TRIPS council, with most of the activity around the issue being undertaken therein. In a brief on the issue to WTO members, WTO Director General, Pascal Lamy, did not even mention the work of the CTE on the issue, referring only to the TRIPS council.[78] This clearly shows that whilst the CTE should be the key place for discussions on issues of an environmental nature, it has not yet asserted itself over the TRIPS council on this issue.

Perhaps the failure of the CTE to really engage with the Secretariat of the CBD is a contributing factor, but it seems that the WTO members themselves prefer to have the discussion under the acting body for intellectual property rights. The CTE therefore faces a challenge to gain greater recognition in this area and to make its contribution to a successful outcome under paragraphs 19 and 32 (ii) of the Doha Declaration.

72 ibid.

73 IISD & ICTSD, 'Developments since the Fourth WTO Ministerial Conference: Trade and Environment', *Doha Round Briefing Series*, Vol. 1, No. 9, February 2003.

74 ibid., p. 3.

75 N. Bernasconi-Osterwalder, *Environment and Trade: A Guide to WTO Jurisprudence*, Earthscan, London, 2006, p. 312.

76 ibid.

77 J.A. McNeely, 'Commentary on the Convention on Biological Diversity (CBD) COP-8', 6 *Bridges Trade BioRes*, 7, ICTSD, 14 April 2006.

78 WTO News, 'Lamy Briefs Members on his Intellectual Property Consultations', 27 July 2009, WTO website, http://www.wto.org/english/news_e/news09_e/trip_27jul09_e.htm (accessed 24 January 2010).

6.5.2 Environmental labelling and the CTE

Labelling for environmental purposes is also one of the CTE's original ten work areas, which the Doha Declaration identified (under paragraph 32 (iii)) as an area for further work under the normal meetings of the CTE.[79] The fact of the matter is that environmental labelling is an activity that has been increasing considerably in the past two decades. This is both driven by consumer demand and government intervention.

Of interest in the WTO is the concern that the use of such labels in a particular country could be a disguised restriction on trade. Concerns have been raised regarding the growing complexity of the labels and the impact this can have on developing countries' industries.[80] Recently, both the US and Australia have presented case studies to the CTE meetings outlining the operation of their main labelling schemes in the environmental field – this is aimed at increasing understanding of the operations of such schemes.[81] The concern around the issue of environmental labelling has encouraged some member states to take the action outlined above to better clarify the situation of their systems, so that they are less likely to be considered as disguised restrictions on trade.

The reason why environmental labelling can be considered to be controversial relates to the question of processes and production methods (PPMs). In this case the particular issue relates to the way in which PPMs are used to apply labels to products. Given that many labels used to indicate environmental qualities cover the whole life cycle of the product, it is clear that they also relate to the way a good is produced or the methods used to develop the good. The labels therefore are fundamentally concerned with reflecting this particular aspect of a product.

The debate on the issue in the WTO is further complicated by another distinction drawn between the PPMs that have an impact on the physical aspect of the good and those that have no discernible impact on the physical quality of the good (nprPPMs).[82] In the WTO the members are in general agreement that PPMs that leave an impact on the product are covered by the WTO agreements. They do not, however, agree that the nprPPMs are compatible with the WTO provisions.[83] Many developing countries believe

79 Doha WTO Ministerial Declaration, op. cit. 39.

80 WTO Environment, 'Environment Issues: Labelling', WTO website, http://www.wto.org/english/tratop_e/envir_e/labelling_e.htm (accessed 24 January 2010).

81 ibid.

82 T. Rotherham, 'Labelling for Environmental Purposes: A Review of the State of the Debate in the World Trade Organisation', Trade Knowledge Network Thematic Paper, IISD/ICTSD, Geneva, January 2003, p. 7.

83 WTO, 'Environment Issues: Labelling', op. cit. 80.

that eco-labels that discriminate on the basis of nprPPMs are incompatible with the Technical Barriers to Trade (TBT) and the WTO agreements.[84]

Once again a major problem for the CTE is the lack of authority it has on the issue of labelling, despite being the body in which negotiations have been requested on the subject in the mandate of the CTE and under the DDA. The issue of labelling falls under two specific areas of the WTO agreements: the Sanitary and Phyto-sanitary (SPS) agreement, and the TBT agreement.[85] The CTE can only make recommendations that can be adopted by the committees responsible for the operation of the SPS and TBT agreements.

In the case of labelling the more relevant agreement has been the TBT agreement, and its committee (CTBT) has been active on the issue of labelling too. It is thus the case that the CTBT is considered to be the best place to discuss this issue by many member states, and as such the CTBT has been active in holding debates and workshops on the issue of environmental labelling.[86] The TBT contains most of the rules on labelling and also has a code of good practice for the preparation, adoption and application of standards. It is not surprising that most member states see the CTBT as the place to negotiate on this issue.

Therefore if the CTE decides a way forward in the discussions on how to treat environmental labelling it would still need to be adopted by the relevant committees. This makes its power somewhat limited on the issue and this is reflected in the fact that the CTBT also works on the issue. Commentators have also expressed that the CTE is unlikely to be the body that will resolve the questions around the use of labels for environmental purposes, in the main due to the fact that the issue is so inter-related with other areas of the WTO agreements that the CTE cannot possibly achieve a cover-all solution.[87]

Equally the drive of some member states, such as the EU, has become more muted over the period of the negotiations, as other issues have dominated their attention. Without such member state drivers many states will be satisfied to leave the dispute resolution panels to determine what is acceptable under the TBT agreement, which as of yet is unclear given the limited jurisprudence in this area.[88] This situation for the CTE is not dissimilar to the discussion on intellectual property rights, where the TRIPS council has run much more of the substantive negotiations on the relevant issues. The CTE

84 WTO, 'Environment Issues: Labelling', op. cit. 80; and T. Rotherham, op. cit. 82, p. 8.

85 T. Rotherham, op. cit. 82, p. 3.

86 The CTBT held a labelling workshop in 2003 to provide members with a better understanding of the issues around preparing, adopting and applying labelling requirements. Accordingly the workshop focused on case studies and areas of concern for developing countries; see also WTO, 'Environment Issues: Labelling', op. cit. 80.

87 T. Rotherham, op. cit. 82, p. 28.

88 T. Rotherham, op. cit. 82, p. 29.

needs to gain more authority on these issues if it is to be seen as a legitimate negotiation forum for trade and environment issues.

6.5.3 CTE work in relation to Article XX GATT

The CTE has also briefly considered its role in the process of dispute resolution where cases before the DSB have an environmental concern. The CTE has stated that Article 13 and Appendix 4 of the Understanding on Rules and Procedures Governing the Settlement of Disputes give the panel the opportunity to request information and technical advice from any relevant individual or body that it believes can support the case, and also to consult experts and set up expert groups to provide a review of the issue under consideration.[89] This facility is open to the panel in environmental–trade disputes and therefore it can be used at the panel's discretion.

However, the CTE to date has not advanced the theory that it should be a standing body of knowledge that could be consulted by the panel in the event of a trade–environment dispute. Instead the CTE has merely announced that the function outlined in Article 13 and Appendix 4 of the Understanding on Dispute Resolution exists, and has not advanced its cause to play such a role. These clauses are enough for the CTE to have confidence in the WTO DSU, and no calls have been made for further involvement of the CTE on dispute settlement resolution.[90]

The CTE did attempt to review the decision of the AB in the 1998 case regarding the *US – Import Prohibition of Certain Shrimp and Shrimp Products* (*Shrimp-Turtle* case).[91] However, notably, India and Hong Kong opposed the step to take any consideration of the decision in the CTE as they claimed the DSB had not made a full discussion of the issue,[92] despite the fact that the EU, Australia and Canada all broadly welcomed the outcome of the case and the discussion in the CTE – the implications set in the jurisprudence of the outcome appeared to give more strength to MEA negotiations for environmental protection in the WTO.[93]

89 WTO, 'Understanding on Rules and Procedures Governing the Settlement of Disputes', WTO Legal Texts, Geneva, 1995, WTO website, http://www.wto.org/english/docs_e/legal_e/28-dsu_e.htm (accessed 24 January 2010); see also WTO CTE, Report (1996) of the Committee on Trade and Environment, WT/CTE/W/40, 12 November 1996, para. 39.

90 Committee on Trade and Environment, Report of the Committee on Trade and Environment to the Singapore Ministerial Conference, WT/CTE/1, WTO, 1996; see also WTO, Trade and Environment Division, High Level Symposium on Trade and the Environment: Background Document, WTO, Geneva, 1999.

91 R.G. Tarasofsky, *The WTO Committee on Trade and Environment: Is it Making a Difference?*, Max Planck Institute, UNYB 3, Heidelberg, 1999, p. 479.

92 Committee on the Environment, Report of the Meeting held on 26–27 October 1998, WT/CTE/M/19, WTO, Geneva, 1998, paras 68 and 72.

93 ibid.

This was, however, one of the only examples of the WTO DSB activities under Article XX being discussed in the CTE.[94] The CTE has not therefore been a forum that has closely followed the outcomes of cases on trade and environment issues in the WTO DSB. Instead it is considered political in nature and so has not been active in considering its position in relation to the DSB.

Nevertheless the CTE was the forum that on one occasion saw a request for a review of a potential dispute. In 1998 the Chileans raised concerns over the EC's agricultural subsidies on peaches in a comment at the CTE, and called for negotiations on the issue with the EC.[95] This was not responded to by the EC and the issue was not raised again in the CTE.[96] This one occasion where a potential dispute was raised in the CTE does not necessarily prove that members feel the CTE is a forum that can be used to resolve such issues, but it does show that it has the potential to become such a forum should members grow confidence in its operations.

It is worth noting that the CTE has not discussed issues relating to Article XX to any great extent since the Doha agenda has diverted its activities into specific areas.[97] So at this time the relationship between Article XX and the activities of the CTE remains somewhat remote, even though some members have expressed an interest in discussing cases and potential conflicts therein.

6.6 Impact of the CTE on the trade and environment debate

As expected at the time of its formation, the CTE has had an impact on the debate concerning the inclusion of environmental concerns within the WTO. Some of the aspects of its work have been somewhat successful – there is in general a more positive relationship between environmental issues and trade developing, and this is in part due to the activity of the CTE.[98]

A recent study has shown that a number of leading experts on WTO systems and interaction with the environment believe that the CTE has successfully increased awareness and reduced cynicism regarding the

94 There were brief mentions of the *US Gasoline* case in the CTE: see WTO CTE document, WT/CTE/M/11, 22 August 1996, paras 10, 13, 14, 15, 18, 48, 52, 57; and the AB's findings on *Hormones* in WTO CTE document, WT/CTE/M/18, 10 August 1998, para. 16.

95 WTO CTE document, WT/CTE/M/I9, 1998, para. 27.

96 E. da Silva, 'Trade and Environment Conflicts in the WTO', Paper presented at the annual meeting of the Law Society Association, Montreal, 27 May 2008, p. 27.

97 ibid., p. 28.

98 D. Brack and T. Branczik, 'Trade and Environment in the WTO: After Cancun', The Royal Institute of Foreign Affairs: Sustainable Development Programme, Briefing Paper No. 9, London, February 2004, p. 9.

potential compatibility of trade and environment measures.[99] This is a move from what the experts described as a historical antagonism towards environmental issues being included in the WTO/GATT towards a more objective approach to environmental issues.[100] The study quotes the experts as stating that there is now greater acceptance that the environment could be a common element of WTO discussions.[101]

This demonstrates that there is a greater understanding of the possibility to reconcile environmental measures with trade concerns. In the study the respondent experts quoted the examples of fisheries subsidies and trade in environmental goods as two distinct areas where the work of the CTE had led to a greater understanding of the need for inclusion of environmental principles in the WTO.[102] This work of the CTE can be seen as instrumental in improving the member states' understanding of the need to reconcile trade and environment measures in the WTO.

However, the study also showed that there were still a number of caveats that the experts felt needed to be addressed before the role of the CTE could be entirely seen as positive, including the need to examine the outcome of the current ongoing Doha negotiations.[103] In general, the experts with a bias towards including environment in the WTO discussions stated that the current Doha mandate was not sufficiently wide to provide a clear role for environmental concerns in the WTO, as, for example, the precautionary principle is not being discussed for inclusion in the WTO as a principle.[104]

However, those experts familiar with the SPS agreement under the WTO may argue that the precautionary principle is already given some support by the wording and practical application of Article XX under that agreement.[105] The CTE has its mandate set by the parties and therefore is somewhat constrained in what it can do and address. Nevertheless, with the mandate that it is given, there is a strong case for the CTE being able to drive the reconciliation of trade and environment issues in the WTO forums.

The broad consensus of opinion appears to be that the instigation of the CTE has had some benefit for consideration of environmental issues in

99 R. McCormick, 'A Qualitative Analysis of the WTO's Role in Trade and Environmental Issues', 6 *Global Environmental Politics*, MIT Press, 1, February 2006, p. 121.

100 ibid., p. 107.

101 ibid.

102 ibid.

103 ibid., p. 103.

104 ibid., p. 107.

105 International Institute for Sustainable Development and the United Nations Environment Programme, *Environment and Trade: A Handbook*, IISD, Winnipeg, 2000.

the WTO, but has itself not gone far enough in its work.[106] The main criticisms circle around the fact that as a political body the CTE should have made recommendations on issues assigned to it, such as how to treat MEAs in relation to the WTO, but that it has instead been satisfied to consider itself a negotiating forum and prefer to engage in deep technical analysis of issues rather than statements on what needs to be done in other implementing committees to reconcile trade and environmental concerns.[107]

However, even in the task of negotiating, the prevailing view is that the only achievement is to map members' disagreements.[108] Thus, a major challenge that can be seen is one of a political nature in the CTE. To effectively influence the WTO agenda and the deliberations of other implementing committees the CTE needs to give recommendations and statements – something that it has failed to do sufficiently to date.

Returning briefly to the study of expert opinions on the WTO and trade and comments made on the CTE, it was also reported that some experts felt that the progress of integrating environmental concerns into the WTO would be a slow one.[109] Among the reasons listed for this slow development of the integration of environmental concerns in the WTO agenda the experts cited the approach of the CTE to the issue.[110] This is reflected in a number of

106 See inter alia: V.P.B. Yu III, 'Briefing Paper on the WTO Committee on Trade and Environment', Friends of the Earth International, Geneva, 2002, http://www.iatp.org/tradeobservatory/library.cfm?refID=25583 (accessed 24 January 2010); K. Gnath, 'The WTO and Environment: ... More Words than Deeds?', *DGAP*, 19 February 2009, Aussenpolitik.net website, http://aussenpolitik.net/themen/weltwirtschaft/the_wto_and_environment---smore_words_than_deeds/ (accessed 24 January 2010); F. Yamin & J. Depledge, *The International Climate Change Regime: A Guide to Rules Institutions and Procedures*, Cambridge University Press, Cambridge, 2004; E. Neumayer, 'The WTO and the Environment: Its Past Record is Better than Critics Believe, but the Future Outlook is Bleak', 4 *Global Environmental Politics*, 4, Project Muse, MIT Press, August 2004; G.C. Schaffer, 'The World Organisation under Challenge: Democracy and the Law and Politics of the WTO's Treatment of Trade and Environment Matters', 25 *Harvard Environmental Law Journal*, 1, 2001; G.P. Sampson, *Trade, Environment and the WTO: The Post-Seattle Agenda*, Policy Essay 27, Overseas Development Council, Washington, 2000; C.F. Runge, 'The Climate Commons and a Global Environmental Organisation', Brookings Trade Forum 2008/2009, Project Muse, MIT Press, 2009, p. 139.

107 R.G. Tarasofsky, op. cit. 91, p. 485; and D. Brack and T. Branczik, op. cit. 98.

108 E. Neumayer, 'The WTO and the Environment: Its Past Record is Better than Critics Believe, but the Future Outlook is Bleak', 4 *Global Environmental Politics*, 4, Project Muse, MIT Press, August 2004, p. 6.

109 R. McCormick, op. cit. 99, p. 120.

110 ibid., p. 121.

sources that reflect a concern for environmental issues and their consideration in the WTO.[111]

It is important to recall that the negotiations in the CTE and the work that it has been mandated to complete were agreed by all the parties to the WTO. Logistically it is very difficult to balance the needs of such a wide variety of national administrations and the various stakeholders they represent. Indeed, it is on this issue that the main differences between developing and developed countries can be seen. Developing countries can perceive that the protection of the environment can be misused for environmental protection; on the part of the developed countries the environment is a low-level priority in the WTO negotiations so can be easily given up to secure a benefit in another part of the negotiations.

It is not clear if this happens in practice, but there is speculation on the part of NGOs and academics that this could be the case.[112] However, there is clear evidence to support the notion that developing countries do have concerns over 'green protectionism', whereby standards on production and process methods could be used as disguised restrictions on trade.[113] The CTE has been working to address this issue and to drive forward win-win-win scenarios, whilst noting concerns over the plethora of standards that exist in northern markets and the difficulty experienced by developing countries in meeting them. However, more needs to be done in terms of technical and capacity support for developing countries – as agreed under the Rio Bargain – before this question will be resolved.[114]

6.7 Conclusion

In this chapter the work of the CTE has been reviewed and the impact that it has had on driving forward the rules of the WTO and their synthesis with environmental concerns. The CTE has an ambitious and broad-ranging remit.

111 See G.P. Sampson & W Bradnee Chambers, *Trade, Environment and the Millennium*, UN University Press, Tokyo, 2002. The book considers that the CTE has been given a wide-reaching remit, but that political influences of the member states have influenced the content of its reporting; and although the reporting remains full and accurate it has fallen short in fulfilling expectations of those who saw the CTE as a means to resolve the issues of concern to environmentalists. (See page 4, Introduction.) The book does, however, include an appendix that calls for the CTE to maintain a key role in issues such as reconciling MEAs with the needs of the trade agenda in the WTO.

112 R. McCormick, 'A Qualitative Analysis of the WTO's Role in Trade and Environmental Issues', 6 *Global Environmental Politics*, 1, February 2006, MIT Press; and R.G. Tarasofsky, op. cit. 91, p. 485.

113 WTO, 'Environmental Requirements and Market Access: Preventing "Green Protectionism"', WTO website, http://www.wto.org/english/tratop_e/envir_e/envir_req_e.htm (accessed 24 January 2010).

114 D. Runnalls, *Shall We Dance: What the North Needs to Do to Fully Engage the South in the Trade and Sustainable Development Debate*, IISD, Geneva, 1996.

It is, however, hampered due to the fact that it is a political committee rather than an implementing committee. It has therefore not achieved as much as would have been possible if it had been the implementing committee of a WTO agreement on trade and environment.

Nevertheless, the CTE could have done more if the members had shown more commitment to create recommendations under the framework of the CTE for the implementing committees. This is clearly one of the main areas that the CTE needs to be more active in, if it is to gain a greater role in the consideration of environmental issues in the WTO. As things stand the DSB and the AB appear to have had more impact on how environmental rules at a global level interface with the WTO.

The CTE should look to gain an increased role in the WTO. To do this it needs to make recommendations on trade–environment syntheses in the WTO to the implementing committees. The CTE should also consider how it can better interface with the dispute resolution mechanism of the WTO: as noted, only once a dispute has been raised in the CTE and only on a relatively few occasions have DSB decisions been considered in the CTE.

The CTE has the possibility of defining itself a new role in the post-Doha WTO era. One area that should be considered is its role in dispute resolution when environmental issues are considered in the WTO. The Doha agenda has given the CTE the possibility to exert influence on the consideration of major environmental issues in the WTO. This opportunity should have seen the secretariat of the Committee galvanised to deliver a greater profile of its work rather than to shy away into technical analyses and noting of members' differences.

The CTE has had some influence on the trade–environment debate, but it has not achieved major outcomes in the majority of areas of its work. To better include environmental issues in the WTO the activity of the CTE will need to be more dynamic and potentially more controversial, but only then will legitimacy questions be resolved for the consideration of environmental concerns in the WTO.

7 Application of Article XX in the trade–environment context

7.1 Introduction

Having reviewed the interaction of the WTO with global environmental measures and its own internal mechanisms for considering the environment, it is important to consider the actual interface of environmental measures with WTO provisions and the disputes that arise there out of – and the actions of the DSB in response to these disputes. In essence, the purpose of this chapter is to determine the capacity of the WTO to be an authoritative arbiter in the trade–environment arena at an international level.

Equally, this analysis can be used to assess the activities of the WTO DSB and the level of competence it has in dealing with disputes arising around environmental laws enacted by member states. To do this adequately it is necessary to consider the case law of the WTO DSB as it relates to trade–environment disputes, and also to review some of the challenges that could arise in the near future due to member states' activities.

A thorough examination of the WTO and its areas that address environ mental concerns will also support the generation of an overall picture of the workings of the WTO in the environmental field. The agreements that make up the WTO often refer to the environment and therefore it is necessary to determine to what extent the agreements also reflect a conscious effort to include the environment in WTO decision making. This will involve a review of the areas of the WTO agreements that have particular inference to the environment, including the following:

1 The Sanitary and Phyto-sanitary Agreement (SPS);
2 The Technical Barriers to Trade agreement (TBT); and
3 The General Agreement on Trade in Services (GATS).

All of these agreements have reference to the environment or environmental-related issues, or contain clauses of relevance for the principles of sustainable development or environmental protection. Other agreements also have relevance for the environment, but for the purposes of this study the focus will be on the three agreements mentioned above. Other aspects such as TRIPS, the Agriculture agreement and the SCM agreement have certain relevance, but have not been invoked in Article XX proceedings. Therefore for the purpose of this study the main focus will be on the agreements that have been referred to in cases considered at the WTO relating to trade and the environment.

This investigation will review the dispute resolution system of the WTO and examine whether it can, through its operations in settling cases, drive environmental policies and their interaction with trade both in terms of the international sphere and the national arena. It will also examine the suitability of the dispute resolution system (DSU) in the WTO with regard to resolving trade–environment disputes.

There is a certain degree of flexibility in the WTO articles and the panels are able to refer to the broad principles of the preamble and wider public international law when determining cases. Thus, there is capacity for environmental concerns to be considered in the WTO, and indeed for their relevance to be incorporated into the operations of the organisation. However, it is the specific WTO treaty rules relating to the environment that have caused the most controversy, or rather it should be considered that the rules that have been used to reflect broader environmental concerns by member states are those that have resulted in most criticism, for their alleged inadequacy to offer real environmental protection in the situation of dispute resolution.

7.2 Treaty rules of relevance to the trade–environment debate

The treaty rules of most relevance to the trade and environment debate can be found in Article XX of the GATT (and to a lesser extent in the SPS agreement, the TBT agreement, the TRIPS agreement and the GATS, which also contain provisions relating to the environment, but until now have proved to be less controversial). The provisions of Article XX give the impression to some parties that non-WTO conforming trade measures can be taken if they are to protect the environment.[1] This is despite the fact that Article XX does not mention the environment per se.[2]

The Article is concerned with exceptions to the general rules of non-discrimination in the GATT. Article XX provides exceptions to Article I, 'the Most Favoured Nation' principle (that all trade partners should be treated the same as the most favoured) and Article III on national treatment (that trading partners should be treated the same as domestic producers). Article XX can

1 See B.G. Jansen, 'Climate Change, Emissions Caps and Carbon Leakage: Cracking a Tough Policy Nut', Presentation for Copenhagen and Beyond Panel, ABA Section of International Law, 2009 Spring Meeting, Washington DC, April 2009, p. 6.

2 WTO, *The Legal Texts: The Results of the Uruguay Round of Multilateral Trade Negotiations*, Cambridge University Press, Cambridge, 2004, p. 455.

also provide exceptions to other articles' general application, such as Article XI that bans import prohibitions and quantitative restrictions.[3] Article XX states:

> Subject to the requirement that such measures are not applied in a manner which would constitute a means of arbitrary or unjustifiable discrimination between countries where the same conditions prevail, or a disguised restriction on international trade, nothing in this agreement shall be construed to prevent the adoption or enforcement by any contracting party of measures: (inter alia)
>
> (b) necessary to protect human, animal or plant life or health
>
> (g) relating to the conservation of exhaustible natural resources if such measures are made effective in conjunction with restrictions on domestic production or consumption.[4]

There are ten listed exception clauses under Article XX. However, the two listed above are the clauses that have been used for environmental protection measures by member states.

These two are the most relied upon in disputes regarding environmental protection and trade, so they are considered the key exceptions for environmentalists.[5] This is because the Article does not mention the environment directly and therefore environmental protection under the GATT exemptions is somewhat limited. In this respect member states try to protect potentially discriminatory environmental measures under Article XX (b) and (g) as a best available defence. In relation to the trade–environment paradigm, the failure to allow specific exemptions to the GATT's fundamental principles for environment protection could be seen as a weakness in the GATT.[6] This would be one of the main requests of the environmental lobby, which has been keen to point out the weaknesses of the WTO system, especially as related to defending environmental measures under Article XX.[7] Confusion regarding the use of Article XX and its apparent lack of clear relation to protecting the environment can be examined through a reasonable assessment of the overall meaning of Article XX.

3 F. Francioni, *Environment, Human Rights and International Trade*, Hart Publishing, Oxford, 2001, p. 9.

4 WTO, *The Legal Texts*, op. cit. 2.

5 J. Cameron & K. Campbell, 'A Reluctant Global Policy Maker', in O. Perez, *Ecological Sensitivity and Global Legal Pluralism, Rethinking the Trade and Environment Debate*, Hart, Oxford, 2003.

6 J. Cameron, 'Dispute Settlement and Conflicting Trade and Environment Regimes', in G.P. Sampson & J. Whalley, *WTO, Trade and the Environment*, Edward Elgar Publishing Ltd, Cheltenham, 2005, p. 464.

7 D.C. Esty, *Greening the GATT: Trade, Environment, and the Future*, Institute for International Economics, Washington, 1994, pp. 221–2.

The chapeaux to Article XX lays out how these exemptions to the general principles of the WTO are to be used (as does the chapeaux to GATS Article XIV). The chapeaux states that the measures must not be disguised restrictions on international trade or a means of arbitrary or unjustifiable discrimination by one party against another.[8] During a dispute between members based on Article XX it is the panel/AB that makes the decision as to whether or not the exemption is justified.

7.2.1 The environment in other WTO agreements

The exemptions as listed under the GATS agreement Article XIV read in a similar vein as the general exemptions under GATT Article XX.[9] There are fewer exemptions and GATS does not contain a clause relating to the conservation of exhaustible natural resources, though it does have a similar provision to Article XX (b).[10] This may have implications in circumstances where there may be a crossover between services and environmental protection – such as the provision of water supplies, activities such as damming of rivers, etc. In this context it could be more difficult to protect broader environmental concerns under the GATS.[11]

To some extent it seems slightly illogical that there are variations in the wording of the general exemptions of the GATS in comparison to the GATT. It would be more consistent for the wording in the agreements to reflect similar principles and issues. Indeed, other agreements (see below) mention the environment or environmental protection in general as a cause for derogation from the principles of the agreements concerned. Consistency would better serve the cause of value-neutral justice throughout the operations of the WTO.

Before considering the TBT agreement, it is worth examining other areas of the GATT/WTO system that also include exceptions to the general rules of the WTO. Both the SPS and TBT agreements recognise exemptions to the general duties of the agreements. The SPS agreement specifically states under Article 2.1:

> Members have the right to take sanitary and phyto-sanitary measures necessary for the protection of human, animal, plant life or health,

8 WTO, *The Legal Texts*, op. cit. 2.

9 Article XIV, 'GATS', in WTO, *The Legal Texts: The Results of the Uruguay Round of Multilateral Trade Negotiations*, Cambridge University Press, Cambridge, 2004, p. 296.

10 ibid.; and GATS Article XIV (b) states 'necessary to protect human, animal or plant life or health'.

11 See N. Bernasconi-Osterwalder et al., *Environment and Trade: A Guide to WTO Jurisprudence*, Earthscan, London, 2006, p. 78 for a review of the relevance of Article XX (g) in environmental disputes.

> provided that such measures are not inconsistent with the provision of this agreement.[12]

Article 2.3 does provide some conditions similar to those of the chapeaux of GATT Article XX, though with the footnote that:

> To successfully challenge an import restriction, the challenging party must show that another measure that would achieve the same level of protection is *reasonably* available and would be *significantly* less restrictive to trade.[13] (emphasis added by the author)

This footnote provides clear and unambiguous guidance regarding the type of measure that could be reasonably applied by one party, whilst also providing the clarity to another party that may feel its privileges have been impaired by a measure. In this case the injured party would be in a certain position to know whether there could be an alternative action that was available to the other party that could gain the same level of protection as the measure implemented and in controversy.

The question then must be asked: Could such a footnote also be added to the requirements of disavowing exemptions under Article XX of the GATT? This would seem to strengthen the framework in the provisions of Article XX (b) and (g) for environmental protection. This would improve the operation of the DSU as member states would be able to calculate the likelihood of a successful intervention more easily. Such guidance could be a requisite for improving the overall operation of the WTO DSU in relation to the environment.

Again, there is precedent in the WTO agreements to suggest a change in the text of the general agreement could be possible. This would depend upon member state will, and that may be a more difficult aspect to obtain. Nevertheless the SPS agreement shows that the WTO can devise rules that relate to environmental protection measures that guide and indicate to countries how they should conduct their extra-jurisdictional environment policy. It also demonstrates a willingness to devise rules that relate to the environment within the SPS; this too can be found in the TBT agreement.

The TBT agreement preamble recognises the right of members to adopt such measures at the level they consider appropriate, relating in Article 2.2 of the agreement to the protection of human, animal or plant life or health

12 Article 2.1, 'SPS Agreement', in WTO, *The Legal Texts: The Results of the Uruguay Round of Multilateral Trade Negotiations*, Cambridge University Press, Cambridge, 2004.

13 ibid., SPS Agreement, footnote 3.

and the protection of the environment.[14] These are legitimate objectives for a member to pursue, as stated under the terms of the preamble. This seems to give a much greater role to the *environment* as such, than is found in other agreements within the WTO and the GATT agreement itself.

This wording gives the environment a clear and specific legal standing in the TBT agreement, so the question arises as to why the TBT agreement includes specific reference to the environment as such, and that other agreements do not. Perhaps it was by chance and that the TBT drafting team had decided to give the environment a higher profile, or rather it may be because the TBT agreement in many ways has less relationship to the environment in general than say SPS.

Nevertheless, it is important to note the use of the term in the context of the TBT agreement, and perhaps argue that this explicit mention demonstrates the development of a desire in the WTO to move out of the competence of trade into broader legal fields. It is also important to note that again the use of the term 'environment' in the field of derogations from the principles in the TBT can be argued to show a willingness to improve the profile of environmental protection in the WTO, and also to suggest that such wording should also be extended to all aspects of the WTO, including the GATT itself. Indeed, some of the work and rulings under the TBT has given optimism that the TBT agreement can drive the adoption of voluntary and non-consensus standards at an international level.[15]

However, the TBT agreement also contains the requirements that such measures (those taken with regard to the protection of the environment) are not a disguise on international trade nor a means of arbitrary discrimination.[16] Both the SPS and TBT agreements overtly state that they are attempting to avoid the use of environmental standards or protection measures as unnecessary obstacles to trade.[17] This is natural given the overarching aim of the WTO to improve global trade regulation and facilitate trade flows.

14 Article 2.2, 'Agreement on Technical Barriers to Trade', in WTO, *The Legal Texts: The Results of the Uruguay Round of Multilateral Trade Negotiations*, Cambridge University Press, Cambridge, 2004, p. 122.

15 See WTO Appellate Body Report, European Communities – Trade Description of Sardines, WT/DS231/AB/R, adopted 23 October 2002, paras 221–2. The AB decided that the TBT agreement does apply to non-consensus standards bringing them into its remit and giving the opportunity to legitimise them under the WTO.

16 Article 2.1 & 2.2, 'TBT Agreement', in *The Legal Texts: The Results of the Uruguay Round of Multilateral Trade Negotiations*, Cambridge University Press, 2004, Cambridge, p. 122.

17 ibid.; and Article 5.6 SPS Agreement, p. 62.

In 2011 the issues around Articles 2.1 and 2.2 of the TBT were put to the test in a dispute involving the US and Mexico, regarding the labelling of tuna cans for sale in the US.[18] The provisions of the Articles are as follows:

> **Article 2**
> Preparation, Adoption and Application of Technical Regulations by Central Government Bodies. With respect to their central government bodies:
>
> 2.1 Members shall ensure that in respect of technical regulations, products imported from the territory of any Member shall be accorded treatment no less favourable than that accorded to like products of national origin and to like products originating in any other country.
>
> 2.2 Members shall ensure that technical regulations are not prepared, adopted or applied with a view to or with the effect of creating unnecessary obstacles to international trade. For this purpose, technical regulations shall not be more trade-restrictive than necessary to fulfil a legitimate objective, taking account of the risks non-fulfilment would create. Such legitimate objectives are, inter alia: national security requirements; the prevention of deceptive practices; protection of human health or safety, animal or plant life or health, or the environment. In assessing such risks, relevant elements of consideration are, inter alia: available scientific and technical information, related processing technology or intended end-uses of products.[19]

The Mexicans had raised concerns that the 'dolphin safe' labelling requirements for tuna sold in the US discriminated against their rights under the TBT. Essentially the problem related to the US policy of refusing to award such labels for tuna caught using purse-seine nets in the eastern Pacific Ocean. The US argued that such a fishing method resulted in the unnecessary deaths of marine animal life such as dolphins. Importantly, the Mexicans pointed out that using purse-seine nets was compliant with the Agreement on the International Dolphin Conservation Program (AIDCP). The AIDCP had been negotiated as a result of the previous US-Mexico disputes relating to tuna. The case is a continuation of the *Tuna-Dolphin* cases that were heard under the GATT in the 1990s and which lead to scrutiny of the GATT in relation to environmental protection.

The Mexicans argued that the labelling requirements were discriminating against their products and that their rights under the TBT were being infringed. Conversely the US argued that the measure applied to all tuna

18 WTO, *United States – Measures Concerning the Importation, Marketing and Sale of Tuna and Tuna Products*, WT/DS381/R, 15 September 2011.

19 WTO, Article 2, 'TBT Agreement', in *The Legal Texts: The Results of the Uruguay Round of Multilateral Trade Negotiations*, Cambridge University Press, Cambridge, 2004.

products irrespective of origin and was therefore non-discriminatory. Of relevance under the TBT, Mexico also claimed that the labelling measures were mandatory and not voluntary, based on the fact that the US refused to recognise any standards other than their own for setting what was dolphin safe. This particular aspect is of great importance for the Mexicans as they claim that their methods are also dolphin safe under the AIDCP. Mexico requested a Panel hearing to determine the case and relied, among other points, on Articles 2.1, 2.2, and 2.4 of the TBT Agreement. This is the first time that such reliance had been made on these articles in a case relating to environmental protection objectives.

In determining the case, the Panel assessed whether the US dolphin-safe labelling provisions could actually be considered to be a technical regulation under the TBT Agreement. This would establish if the measures were mandatory or voluntary as claimed by the US. In making this decision the Panel decided that the measures were mandatory and therefore within the meaning of Annex 1.1 of the TBT Agreement. Highly unusually, one of the members of the Panel opposed the decision and a dissenting opinion was recorded on this particular issue. The panellist believed that the measures did not constitute a mandatory requirement for labelling, stating:

> the measures do not impose a general requirement to label or not to label tuna products as 'dolphin-safe'. It remains a voluntary and discretionary decision of operators on the market to fulfil or not fulfil the conditions that give access to the label, and whether to make any claim in relation to the dolphin-safe status of the tuna contained in the product.[20]

The panellist felt strongly that the labelling requirements were not mandatory and therefore that the panel should not have considered the argumentation under the TBT agreement. Nevertheless they agreed to consider the rest of Mexico's argument, having lodged their dissenting opinion.

Examining the claims under Article 2.1 of the TBT the Panel found that the labelling requirements were not discriminatory and therefore were in accordance with the requirements of the Article. The Mexican tuna products were like products in the meaning of Article 2.1 of the TBT. The issue of being 'like' products is key to determining whether the labelling requirements would be discriminatory. The Panel found that the products were indeed like and that Mexican tuna products were not afforded less favourable treatment than US tuna or tuna from other countries. To do so the Panel turned to the ruling in the *EC-Asbestos* case which stated:

> As products that are in a competitive relationship in the marketplace could be affected through treatment of *imports* 'less favourable' than the

20 Op cit 18. p. 154.

> treatment accorded to *domestic* products, it follows that the word 'like' in Article III:4 is to be interpreted to apply to products that are in such a competitive relationship. Thus, a determination of 'likeness' under Article III:4 is, fundamentally, a determination about the nature and extent of a competitive relationship between and among products.[21]

The Panel went on to decide that the relationship between the products was comparable and that no less favourable treatment had occurred. This decision is interesting as it demonstrates that the Panels clearly use the decisions of previous Appellate Bodies and Panels to inform their thinking, even when there is no direct precedent to take note of – as this is the first case dealing with the TBT Article 2.1 in a dispute.

Despite the finding under Article 2.1 the Panel went on to reason that under Article 2.2 Mexico had demonstrated that the labelling provisions were more trade restrictive than necessary to fulfil the objectives of the labelling: (i) ensuring that consumers are not misled about practices used for catching tuna and (ii) contributing to the protection of dolphins. The Panel stated that the labelling requirements only partly addressed the legitimate objectives of the US, as it did not address the observed mortality existing in areas outside the eastern Pacific Ocean caused by other tuna methods. It could therefore be seen to be too specific geographically, a wider remit for the labelling might have resulted in a different outcome.

Secondly, Article 2.2 requires that technical regulations shall not be more trade-restrictive than necessary to fulfil a legitimate objective. In this case Mexico provided the Panel with a less restrictive alternative that could achieve the same level of protection of dolphins desired under the US labelling requirements. In this respect the labelling requirements were not specifically able to guarantee that no dolphins were injured or killed in the fishing of tuna from outside of the eastern Pacific Ocean. The labels only applied to tuna fishing in this area, and thus the Mexicans were able to successfully argue that the labelling requirements did not in fact protect dolphins in general, only those from the Eastern Pacific. This is perhaps an oversight of the US labelling requirements, but it is clear from the Panel that having one standard for tuna in one geographic area is not consistent with Article 2.2 of the TBT. This is indeed a logical outcome, even if it is not a pleasing outcome to environmentalists.[22]

The case is still in consideration at the WTO at the time of writing; both the US and Mexico have appealed against the ruling. Nevertheless the TBT remains to be one of the most interesting agreements under the WTO given its overt mention of the environment as a legitimate objective for derogation

21 Appellate Body Report, *EC-Asbestos*, para. 99.

22 ICTSD, 'Panel Rules US "Dolphin Safe" Label Too Trade Restrictive', 15 *Bridges Weekly Trade News Digest*, 31, 21 September 2011.

of the rules. The forthcoming Appellate Body report will be of great significance in determining the value the environment can be seen to have under the TBT.

The recognition of the environment in the TBT agreement as a means to derogate from the provisions shows an attempt to reconcile general trade rules with the need for environmental protection. Both the SPS and TBT agreements are also deeply concerned with the creation of international standards relating to their subject matters, and in the SPS agreement specifically in the field of risk assessment in relation to the production of goods.[23] Under the SPS agreement a measure taken to protect human, plant or animal life or health can be deemed to be an exception to the general WTO rules if it is supported by sufficient scientific evidence to warrant its continuation.[24]

The issue of risk assessment is a very important one and relates to the internationally recognised precautionary principle.[25] The precautionary principle has been used in international environmental law for over 20 years, and espouses the virtue of caution when dealing with substances/practices that could have a negative impact on the environment.[26] The European Union define the precautionary principle as follows:

> The precautionary principle is not defined in the Treaty, which prescribes it only once – to protect the environment. But in practice, its scope is much wider, and specifically where preliminary objective scientific evaluation, indicates that there are reasonable grounds for concern that the potentially dangerous effects on the environment, human, animal or plant health may be inconsistent with the high level of protection chosen for the Community.[27]

This statement by the Commission is also followed by a statement recognising the importance for WTO members to be free to pursue the levels of environmental protection that they deem suitable.[28] Clearly the precautionary principle is an important environmental principle that has been given

23 See Article 5 of the SPS Agreement.

24 G.P. Sampson, *Trade, Environment, and the WTO: The Post-Seattle Agenda*, Overseas Development Council, Washington, 2000, p. 68.

25 Principle 15 of the Rio Declaration on Environment and Development recalls that states should apply the precautionary approach when seeking to protect the environment: see the UNEP website, http://www.unep.org/Documents.Multilingual/Default.asp?documentid=78&articleid=1163 (accessed 24 January 2010).

26 The UN Charter for Nature of 1982 contains a rudimentary form of the precautionary principle: see UN, World Charter for Nature, A/RES/37/7, 28 October 1982, Article 11 (b).

27 European Commission, Communication from the Commission on the Precautionary Principle, 2000, para. 3, available at: http://eur-lex.europa.eu/smartapi/cgi/sga_doc?smartapi!celexplus!prod!DocNumber&lg=en&type_doc=COMfinal&an_doc=2000&nu_doc=1 (accessed 24 January 2010).

28 ibid.

support in international law. The interaction of the WTO with this principle also sheds some light on the influences of environmental norms on WTO practice.

7.2.2 The precautionary principle in the WTO agreements

Under both the SPS and TBT agreements members may provisionally prohibit the importation of goods whilst national control measures are being employed.[29] This is a limited expression of the precautionary principle familiar to environmentalists, and focus has especially been directed at this notion under the SPS agreement.[30] The application of the measures is explained under Article 5.7 of the SPS agreement, which states that where relevant scientific evidence is insufficient, a member may adopt SPS measures on the basis of available pertinent information.[31] There is a requirement that this should only be for a relevant period of time.[32] This basically means that a member state may introduce trade controls on imports, whilst investigating the potential danger associated with an import to its territory. This is limited to scenarios where the broader health and safety of the domestic population could be at risk, but it clearly links to the precautionary principle as there is no evidence of harm from the imports at the time of instigation of the measures.[33]

However, in the workings of the DSU the principle has been given a very narrow interpretation by the AB, thus limiting its use for environmental protection measures.[34] In fact in the *EC-Hormones* case the AB also stated that they did not accept that the status of the precautionary principle was part of customary international law. It stated:

> that while the precautionary principle might have crystallised into a general principle of customary international environmental law, it was less clear whether it had been widely accepted as a principle of general or customary international law.[35]

29 Article 5, 'SPS Agreement', 1994, Articles 2–4. 'TBT Agreement', in *The Legal Texts: The Results of the Uruguay Round of Multilateral Trade Negotiations*, Cambridge University Press, Cambridge, 2004.

30 International Institute for Sustainable Development and the United Nations Environment Programme, *Environment and Trade: A Handbook*, IISD, Winnipeg, 2000.

31 Article 5.7, 'SPS Agreement', in *The Legal Texts: The Results of the Uruguay Round of Multilateral Trade Negotiations*, Cambridge University Press, Cambridge, 2004, p. 62.

32 ibid. No time limit is put on these measures; only that they should be reviewed in a reasonable period of time.

33 *Environment and Trade: A Handbook*, op. cit. 30.

34 WTO, *EC – Measures Concerning Meat and Meat Products* (*EC-Hormones*), complaint by Canada – report of the panel, WT/DS48/R, 18 August 1997.

35 Appellate Body report, *EC-Hormones* case, para. 123.

To some extent this ruling of the AB is in line with the expectations of a ruling under the WTO, looking at the broader international context rather than simply at trade or environment customary practice. It is interesting to note that a distinction was drawn between general and environmental customary, international law. It could also be expected given that the panellists would not have been environmental experts and that an overriding motivation would have been to protect the enshrined principles of free trade as expressed in the WTO agreement. Therefore, it is notable that such a principle as the precautionary principle finds any place in the WTO agreement at all.

Nevertheless, the precautionary principle has been given potential in the body of the SPS agreement under Article 5.7, and it is applicable as long as it is time-bound and not an alternative to risk assessment or scientific evidence for a definitive standard.[36] It would be hoped that in the future, if further cases and disputes arise in this area, the DSB panels/AB decisions may be more inclined to recognise the precautionary principle as formal customary international law. This could be possible with a greater formally recognised remit for the WTO in the field of environmental regulation, if it were recognised as having such a competence in a more stated manner.

Given that its agreements contain principles as understood in international environmental law, there is some evidence that the WTO has shown more understanding of environmental principles that go beyond the trade regulation origins from whence it came. Steps such as recognising the precautionary principle under the WTO SPS would move the authority of the WTO further in the direction of broad trade–environment competence by demonstrating a multidisciplinary nature to its dispute resolution system.

7.3 Article XX and 'like' products

To return to an examination of the general exemptions of Article XX of the GATT, another major point of contention relates to the treatment of 'like' products under the GATT. The exceptions as allowed under Article XX only apply to the product and not the process of production.[37] For measures to be WTO consistent, products that have the same physical form are to be considered like products even if they haven't been subject to the same production process rules.[38] For example, a member state may have a national requirement for a product requiring certain production processes. However, a tariff may not be applicable on imported goods that are like, but have no

36 WTO, *The Legal Texts*, op. cit. 31.

37 See N. Perdikis & R. Read, *The WTO and Regulation of International Trade: Recent Trade Disputes between the European Union and the United States*, Edward Elgar Publishing, Cheltenham, 2005, p. 244.

38 ibid.

such production process tax. In this instance it could be the requirement for certain processes to be subject to a carbon tax or a specific environmental tax. The reason for this is that the measure should not be applied extra-jurisdictionally, or have an extra-territoriality effect.[39]

Like products should be treated in the same way, and therefore if there is no production tax on the imported good during its production process the good should not be subject to any taxes that are not applied to finished goods of like substance in another territory. This is an important rule as it suggests that it could be very hard to apply environmental measures on a national basis if they are of a fiscal nature.[40]

If a member state does this it risks making its products uncompetitive in the international trade arena, unless similar taxes are placed on all competing goods. This again reflects the concern of the WTO to allow the market to operate in an unfettered manner and uphold principles of non-distortion of markets. However, from an environmental protection perspective it is possible to see that the WTO can be construed as an impediment to using a broader set of tools for environmental protection.[41]

This has current application in the working of the EU's Emissions Trading System (ETS). The ETS is a system that requires industries to purchase their carbon dioxide (CO^2) emissions from a European-wide fund of CO^2 emission certificates. It is a form of taxation on industries, as it requires the industries to modernise and reduce emissions to reduce the cost of purchasing certificates. The ETS has been set up to fight climate change, but it is only applicable to EU-based industries. In the present economic crisis some interests, including the former French President, have called for a border adjustment tax on imports from territories that do not have an ETS or equivalent. Whether this would be legal under the WTO would depend much on the type of mechanism that was used, but is a question open to scrutiny.[42]

39 In a WTO paper by M. Jansen and A. Keck it is speculated that a national tax on more fuel-inefficient cars that negatively impacted cars entering a territory due to the fact that they were also more inefficient could be considered contrary to WTO rules: see M. Jansen & A. Keck, 'National Environmental Policies and Multilateral Trade Rules', WTO Economic Research and Statistics Division, Staff Working Paper ERSD-2004-01, January 2004, p. 4.

40 ibid., p. 20. The paper cites the ruling in the *Japan – Taxes on Alcoholic Beverages* case as an example of this principle.

41 See G.P. Sampson, *The WTO and Sustainable Development*, TERI Press, New Delhi, United Nations University Press, 2005, p. 89.

42 See 'Sarkozy Renews Pressure for CO_2 Border Tax', Monday September 14, 2009, EurActiv website, http://www.euractiv.com/en/climate-change/sarkozy-renews-pressure-co2-border-tax/article-185387 (accessed 24 January 2010).

7.4 The operation of the dispute resolution system and environmental measures

The rulings of the AB and panels have been considered as narrow in their interpretation of the exemptions under Article XX.[43] The use of Article XX for environmental protection measures under these circumstances has therefore had varied fortunes.[44] Historically it has been the case that national measures taken and relied upon as exemptions to the general principles of GATT, on the grounds of environmental protection, have been 'successfully' challenged through the dispute resolution system.[45]

Albeit that the reasoning of the panels has been sound in the main, the outcome of the disputes has left a particularly one-sided view of the dispute resolution process, especially by environmental groups. Under the GATT (pre-1995), six cases can be identified. Under the WTO, a further three cases relating to directly employed environmental protection measures have been identified that have been the subject of dispute resolution in the WTO, although it appears that in the future there could be more such cases on the horizon.[46] The number of environmentally-related cases is relatively small in comparison to the large number of cases that are now being considered by the WTO DSB; nevertheless, the outcome of the cases is crucial for national/international environmental law and its interaction with global trade rules.

Under the GATT (pre-1995) none of the national measures taken for environmental protection were successfully defended in the dispute resolution process, with the interests of trade being well reflected in the outcomes of the decisions.[47] The panels did recognise some useful points, such as the extra-territoriality of the provisions of Article XX (g).[48] It is also worth noting that three of the panel decisions under GATT were not adopted, so their outcomes

43 See J. Cameron & K.R. Gray, 'Principles of International Law in the WTO Dispute Settlement Body', 50m *International and Comparative Law Quarterly*, 2, Cambridge University Press, April 2001, p. 279.

44 G.P. Sampson, *Trade, Environment and the WTO: The Post-Seattle Agenda*, Overseas Development Council, Washington, DC, 2000, p. 108.

45 See C. Wofford, 'A Greener Future at the WTO: The Refinement of WTO Jurisprudence on Environmental Exceptions to GATT', Vol. 24, *Harvard Environmental Law Review*, 2000, p. 563; and R. Howse, 'The Appellate Body Rulings in the Shrimp-Turtle Case: A New Legal Baseline for the Trade and Environment Debate', 27 *Columbia Journal of Environmental Law*, 2002, p. 491.

46 The recent seal product ban in the EU is threatening to blow up into a full dispute with Canada: see CBC News, 'Seal Product Ban will Withstand WTO Challenge: EU', 28 July 2009, CBC website http://www.cbc.ca/world/story/2009/07/28/eu-seal-ban-wto876.html (accessed 24 January 2010).

47 See S. Charnovitz, 'The WTO's Environmental Progress', 10 *Journal of International Economic Law*, 3, Advance Access Publication, 9 August 2007, p. 695.

48 *Tuna/Dolphin II* US restrictions of imports of tuna, DS29/R, 16 June 1994, para. 5.20.

do not represent formal jurisprudence in terms of future disputes.[49] Neither did the GATT panels question the environmental policy choices underlying the national measure; no value judgments were placed on the measures that had been enacted.

In relation to the outcomes of the panel deliberations, from the perspective of environmentalists, there have been some benefits.[50] Having access to an effective means to ensure the extra-territoriality application of minimum standards is a key to ensuring sound global environmental practice.[51] The outcome of the panels to allow extra-jurisdictional application under the exemption of Article XX (g) is a boon in this respect.

Few environmentally-related cases have been brought to the attention of the DSB. The WTO AB has been fashioning its own interpretation of Article XX, which arguably can be said to be significantly improving the allowance for legitimate measures of environmental protection.[52] In fact much of the reasoning in the previous GATT cases has been overruled.[53] The AB in two cases (the *US-Reformulated Gasoline* case and the *Shrimp-Turtle* case) has advanced a consistent theory and approach to environmental protection issues.[54]

In the *US Shrimp-Turtle* case of 2001 the panel addressed the issue of the US prohibiting shrimp products from its market that had not been fished for using turtle excluding devices (TEDs). The concern of the US administration had been to protect turtles from being threatened by fishing methods that were responsible for a large number of turtle deaths as a by-catch in shrimp gathering practices in other countries.[55] In this case the main complainant had been Malaysia, with a number of third parties interested in the outcome including Thailand, Hong Kong, Ecuador, Australia and the EU. The US had sought to protect the turtles due to concerns regarding

49 The rulings in *Tuna-Dolphin I*, *Tuna-Dolphin II* and the *US Taxes on Automobiles* cases were not adopted under the GATT.

50 See ICTSD, 'Tuna-Dolphin Update', 13 *News and Analysis*, 1, March 2009, ICTSD website, http://ictsd.net/i/news/bridges/44208/ (accessed 24 January 2010); the article recalls that the Tuna-Dolphin original dispute in 1994 led to the panel declaring that labelling for dolphin-friendly tuna was not against the principles of GATT.

51 J. Salzman, 'Free Trade and National Environmental Policy: Lessons from the Tuna-Dolphin Conflict', Proceedings of the Second Annual Free Trade in the Hemisphere Conference, UNAM, 1996.

52 M. Matsushita, T.J. Schoenbaum & P.C. Mavroidis, *The World Trade Organization: Law, Practice and Policy*, Oxford University Press, Oxford, 2004. p. 451.

53 S. Charnovitz, op. cit. 47, p. 696.

54 ibid.

55 R. Howse, 'The Appellate Body Rulings in the Shrimp-Turtle Case: A New Legal Baseline for the Trade and Environment Debate', 27 *Columbia Journal of Environmental Law*, 491, 2002, p. 3.

the dwindling population of sea turtles, and therefore invoked a defence under Article XX (g) in particular.[56]

In addressing the case the AB reviewed the consistency of the US-implementing measure for their policy to protect turtles (i.e. the requirement to use TEDs) against the contents of Article XX. The AB adopted a methodology to determine if the measure was provisionally justifiable under Article XX (g) and would then determine whether the measure had been applied in conformity with the chapeau of Article XX.[57] This reflects the methodology of the AB panel in the 1996 *US-Reformulated Gasoline* case.[58] In doing so it appears that the AB has adopted a dual test in relation to Article XX, so that the implementing measure will be judged firstly against the paragraph which is being relied on (for example b or g) and then against the fundamental provisions of the chapeau of Article XX. This process will be further explored later in this chapter.

The adoption of this methodology lends weight to the argument that the WTO DSU is now operating beyond the competencies of trade, as it has set down a mechanism for how to proceed on cases relying on Article XX exceptions with application to the environment under Article XX (b) and (g).

7.4.1 The role of the panel in trade–environment dispute resolution

It is the panel that reviews the measure taken and determines whether it conforms to the requirements of the chapeau of Article XX; this would be the main test of the measure's applicability.[59] The role of the panellists and their expertise is crucial in gaining a reasoned outcome for a dispute. Here it is important to note the make-up of the panel, especially in relation to cases involving environmental measures. There is no permanent group of panellists at the WTO DSU; each panel is determined on the nature of the case concerned.[60]

The panel is formed of trade experts appointed to a register by member states and then selected by the secretariat and the disputing parties.

56 ibid., p. 2.

57 J.P. Kelly, 'The Seduction of the Appellate Body: Shrimp/Sea Turtle I and II and the Proper Role of States in WTO Governance', 38 *Cornell International Law Journal*, 2005, p. 461.

58 S. Charnovitz, op. cit. 47.

59 S. Gaines, 'The WTO's Reading of the GATT Article XX Chapeau: A Disguised Restriction on Environmental Measures', 22 *University of Philadelphia Journal of International Economic Law*, 2001, 739.

60 Article 8 of the Dispute Settlement Understanding lays down the procedures for the composition of panels. The Secretariat puts forward the nominations for the panel for approval by the disputing parties. See 'Understanding on Rules and Procedures Governing the Settlement of Disputes', in *The Legal Texts: The Results of the Uruguay Round of Multilateral Trade Negotiations*, Cambridge University Press, Cambridge, 2004, p. 360.

The panel in its deliberations can call for expert reports or witnesses at their discretion.[61] There is no requirement to have an environmental expert on the panel. However, in certain circumstances the WTO stipulates that certain expertise should be present on a panel.[62] It is therefore not beyond the concept of the WTO to have specific rules for dispute settlement depending upon the nature of the dispute under consideration. This is elaborated further below.

Under Article 8 of the DSU, the procedure for the composition of panels is explained. Normally the ad hoc panels consist of three members, though a maximum of five can be appointed.[63] This extension can only be granted if both parties of the dispute agree to a five-person panel. As the process currently stands the secretariat propose nominations for the panel to the parties involved in the dispute.[64] Each candidate must have met certain requirements of expertise and independence, for example a panellist may not come from a member who has a third-party interest in a dispute,[65] though if the disputing parties agree it can be possible for such an individual to be appointed.[66]

Interestingly, when a dispute involves a developed and a developing country member, the panel must on request of the developing country include at least one panel member from a developing country.[67] This process suggests a 'precedent' of activity by the DSU. If a developing country can demand an expert on developing countries' needs, it would seem reasonable that a member state defending an environmental protection measure could request that an environmental expert be a panellist. There appears to be logic behind such a measure: if the DSU is willing to accept that developing countries can be distinguished, it should be able to see that environmental protection issues are different and need better consideration than disputes of a one-dimensional trade element.

The WTO acknowledges that 'many panellists are trade delegates of WTO members or capital-based trade officials'.[68] A wider base of WTO panellists' expertise could be suggested, given the growing involvement of the WTO in fields such as the environment. The activity of the WTO supports such

61 Article 13, 'Understanding on Rules and Procedures Governing the Settlement of Disputes', in *The Legal Texts: The Results of the Uruguay Round of Multilateral Trade Negotiations*, Cambridge University Press, Cambridge, 2004, p. 364.

62 ibid., Article 8.10, p. 361.

63 ibid., Article 8.5, p. 361.

64 ibid., Article 8.6, p. 361.

65 ibid., Article 8.3, p. 360.

66 ibid.

67 WTO, *The Legal Texts*, op. cit. 60, Article 8.10, p. 361.

68 WTO Training Module, '3.3 Panels: Functions and Composition of Panels', WTO website, http://www.wto.org/english/tratop_e/dispu_e/disp_settlement_cbt_e/c3s3p1_e.htm (accessed 24 January 2010).

a proposition: under GATS paragraph 4 of the Annex on Financial Services, it expressly provides for the selection of panellists to ensure that panels have the relevant specific expertise.[69] This is an example of the operation of the WTO recognising that experts are needed in certain dispute areas. Another area where specific expertise is required for panellists is under the Subsidies and Countervailing Measures (SCM) agreement. Again, Article 4 recognises that specific panellists must be appointed with the necessary skill and expertise to adjudicate a dispute.[70]

This could be extended, formally, to environmental disputes, especially where disputes under Article XX (b) and (g) are convened. Given the already existing rules of recognising different needs in panels under the WTO, it seems highly plausible that such a system could be extended to environmental cases. This would reduce the ability of critics to easily castigate the WTO DSU for its decisions, whilst also serving the purpose of improving the quality of decisions in such cases. Evolution of judicial competence demands evolving rules to support improved decision making. The WTO is no different – and indeed the resolution of cases may take different forms and lead to different outcomes.

The resolution of cases relating to the environment may be handled better and therefore reduce the level of controversy surrounding WTO decisions that impact the environment. Of course, it is also worth noting that in the opinion of many commentators the current decisions of the DSB/AB in relation to the environment have not been decided beyond the competence of the panellists, and that in fact the norms of international law have been upheld.[71] Irrespective of this, general criticism needs to be answered and such modifications, as expressed above, could reinforce the high standard of decision making under the WTO DSU. In this context, cases with environmental concerns falling under Articles XX (b) and XX (g) will be examined later in the chapter and the legal practice in relation to these articles will be analysed.

7.5 The interpretation of Article XX (g) through the DSU process

As referred to previously the AB has developed a mechanism for considering the application of implemented measures that are defended under Article XX, by firstly reviewing the paragraph that is sought to cover

69 'GATS', in *The Legal Texts: The Results of the Uruguay Round of Multilateral Trade Negotiations*, Cambridge University Press, Cambridge, 2004, p. 312.

70 'Article 4.5 Agreement on Subsidies and Countervailing Measures', in *The Legal Texts: The Results of the Uruguay Round of Multilateral Trade Negotiations*, Cambridge University Press, Cambridge, 2004, p. 233.

71 S. Charnovitz, op. cit. 47.

the measure.[72] In the context of the environment and trade-related environmental measures, Article XX (b) and (g) are the main points of review in the context of this discussion. The work of the AB has resulted in the creation of a number of rules and procedures with relevance for states considering implementing a measure to protect the environment.[73] To recall, Article XX (g) is concerned with the conservation of exhaustible natural resources and the implementation of domestic restrictions in parallel.

Under Article XX (g), the AB has deemed that a *resource* can be living or non-living and it does not need to be rare or endangered to be potentially exhaustible.[74] Thus, a wide interpretation has been given for commodities that could qualify as exemptions under Article XX (g).

In relation to current thinking within the EC, the application of a border adjustment mechanism as a means to protect the global commons from climate change could be sought to be defended under Article XX (g), given that the main aim is to protect the global commons from irreparable damage.[75] The global commons could be broadly interpreted as a 'resource'.[76] It is important that the meaning of the term 'resource' has been given a broad interpretation as it can therefore be seen to cover more of the elements of the natural environment that may be protected by states against degradation. This provides more leeway for the protection of the environment through trade-related measures. However, this is just one of the parts of the overall decision of the panel in determining cases under Article XX (g).

The AB also ruled in the *Shrimp-Turtle* case that previous GATT interpretations of Article XX (g) regarding the phrase *relating to* as synonymous with *primarily aimed at* was erroneous.[77] Under the *Reformulated Gasoline* case the AB had ruled in accordance with the standing interpretation of the phrase 'relating to', which had been based on the 1988 GATT judgment of the *Canada – Herring and Salmon* case. This ruling had given the meaning to the phrase 'relating to' the somewhat narrow interpretation that a measure must be 'primarily aimed at' the objective under consideration.[78] This would therefore limit the application of measures unless it was easily provable that the measure was primarily aimed at the environmental objective stated.

72 S. Gaines, op. cit. 59.

73 See S. Gaines, op. cit. 59 for a detailed discussion of the approach of the AB.

74 WTO, *United States – Import Prohibition of Certain Shrimp and Shrimp Products*, Report of the Appellate Body, WT/DS58/AB/R, 12 October 1998, para. 127.

75 See T. Manders & P. Veenendaal, 'Border Tax Adjustments and the EU-ETS: A Quantitative Assessment', CPB Netherlands Bureau for Economic Policy Analysis, Netherlands Environment Agency, No. 171, October 2008.

76 See S.J. Buck, *The Global Commons: an Introduction*, The Centre for Resource Economics, Washington, DC, 1998, p. 5.

77 WTO, *The Legal Texts*, op. cit. 60, p. 453.

78 E.-U. Petersmann, *The GATT/WTO Dispute Settlement System: International Law, International Organisations and Dispute Settlement*, Kluwer Law, London, 1997, p. 99.

Under the *US Reformulated Gasoline* case, the measure had been found to be primarily aimed at the maintenance of air quality. The AB had also stated: '... the phrase primarily aimed at is not, itself, treaty language and was not designed as a simple litmus test for Article XX'.[79] This may have given the opportunity for the potential revision of the meaning in subsequent cases. Indeed, the definition was not deemed satisfactory by the AB in the *US Shrimp-Turtle* case.[80] Instead, the AB in the *Shrimp-Turtle* case found that the measure at issue could be relied on if it were to 'reasonably relate' to the ends intended regarding the conservation of exhaustible natural resources.[81] A measure that reasonably relates to an objective does not have to be primarily aimed at the subject; this again broadens the application of measures to protect the environment under the Article XX (g) exemption.

The 'in conjunction with restrictions on domestic production and consumption' provision of Article XX (g) has also been given a wide definition.[82] The AB has stated that it would expect a fair degree of even-handedness and that restrictions on either domestic production or consumption would be satisfactory.[83] Under these terms it can be argued that the 1994 GATT *Tuna-Dolphin* case would now result in the measures passing the test as applied to Article XX (g), and would result in the environmental protection measure being upheld.[84] This would of course depend upon the US being able to prove that it did indeed apply the measures under dispute in its own fleets, and would be only one aspect of the larger concern. Nevertheless, such interpretations do widen the scope for environmental protection measures under the WTO and their defence relying on Article XX (g).

As mentioned earlier, the application of environmental protection measures extra-territorially is an important principle for international environmental agreements and environmentalists, as a necessary principle to ensure global protection – animals such as turtles are highly migratory and therefore global rules are needed to protect them.[85] In the ruling on the *Shrimp-Turtle* case the AB also gave the opportunity for the use of the Article XX (g) exceptions extra-territorially by recognising the means applied by the US beyond its national jurisdiction as having merit, and accepting that they met the

79 WTO, *United States – Standards for Reformulated and Conventional Gasoline*, Appellate Body Report and Panel Report, WT/DS2/9, 20 May 1996, p. 19.

80 WTO, *United States – Import Prohibition of Certain Shrimp and Shrimp Products*, Report of the Appellate Body, WT/DS58/AB/R, 12 October 1998, p. 53.

81 ibid.

82 ibid., p. 54.

83 ibid., p. 55.

84 M. Matsushita, T.J. Schoenbaum & P.C. Mavroidis, *The World Trade Organization: Law, Practice and Policy*, Oxford University Press, Oxford, 2004, p. 453.

85 See J.H. Epstein et al., 'Pteropus Vampyrus, a Hunted Migratory Species with a Multinational Home-Range and a Need for Regional Management', *Journal of Applied Ecology*, 2009.

purpose proposed.[86] The interpretation of the AB appears to be giving greater power to rely on the exceptions of Article XX (g). This should be welcomed by environmentalists, as the interpretations of critical aspects of the Article XX (g) exemption have been favourable from their point of view.

7.6 The interpretation of Article XX (b) through the DSU process

Article XX (b) also has some relevance for trade-related environmental measures, although the wording looks more at health rather than conservation of natural resources.[87] Article XX (b) allows exemptions to the general rules of the WTO on the grounds that measures are necessary for the protection of human, animal or plant life or health. As discussed previously, Article XX (b) relies on scientific evidence, and where this cannot immediately be provided a provisional trade embargo is allowed, reflecting the ideas of the precautionary principle. Article XX (b) is, however, more related to the SPS agreement, and the activation of this defence usually involves health and safety issues rather than environmental concepts of a broader nature.[88] Yet it does contain useful elements that impact on the defence of environmental measures under the WTO DSU.

Article XX (b) has also been reviewed by the AB to create a current interpretation of its remit and meaning.[89] One of the most important cases to have been considered under the Article XX (b) exemptions related to the importation of asbestos into France and therefore the wider EU.[90] The case is important as the panel and AB addressed the meaning of the term 'necessary' under Article XX and also the application of the principle of 'like' products under Article XX (b).[91] The decision also examined the use of different levels of risk being applied in different WTO member states.

The case related to the French who had acted to ban asbestos use, production and trade, and only allow the use of asbestos where less harmful

86 *United States – Import Prohibition of Certain Shrimp and Shrimp Products*, op. cit. 80, para. 133.

87 WTO, *The Legal Texts: The Results of the Uruguay Round of Multilateral Trade Negotiations*, Cambridge University Press, Cambridge, 2004, p. 455.

88 Policies such as encouraging the reduction of smoking, the dangers associated with asbestos, or health hazards from waste tyres have tended to be covered under Article XX (b): see 'WTO Rules and Environmental Policies: GATT Exceptions', WTO website, http://www.wto.org/english/tratop_E/envir_e/envt_rules_exceptions_e.htm (accessed 24 January 2010).

89 See B.J. Condon, 'GATT Article XX and Proximity of Interest: Determining the Subject Matter of Paragraphs b and g', 9 *UCLA Journal of International Law & Foreign Affairs*, 137–62, 15 December 2004, p. 11.

90 WTO, *European Communities – Measures Affecting Asbestos and Asbestos Containing Products*, Report of the Appellate Body, WT/DS135/AB/R, 12 March 2001.

91 ibid.

substances were not available for use.[92] Canada had instigated DSU procedures against the ban as they argued that imported asbestos products were treated less favourably than the domestically produced 'like' non-asbestos products, and therefore the fundamental principle of non-discrimination had been breached. Canada also argued that asbestos did not pose a health and safety risk if it was used in a safe way by trained individuals, and that exposure of low doses did not pose a risk to health. The AB in adjudicating the case found in favour of the ban used by the EC and held that under Article XX (b) the ban was in accordance with the necessity to protect human life or health.[93] The panel did recognise that the controlled use of asbestos could reduce risks to health, but this was not material if the risks did not reduce to the levels acceptable in France.[94] The AB agreed and recalled the right of member states to set their own risk limits.[95]

In the *EC-Asbestos* case the AB also stated that consumers' behaviour in relation to a product can be used to determine whether a product is a 'like product' for the purposes of applying the national standard under Article III of the GATT.[96] Thus, a product that entails health or environmental risks may justify different treatment if consumers' behaviour is influenced by the health or environmental risk associated with a product. This is qualified with the requirement that there must also be a domestic ban on the product.[97] The AB also believed that there were scientific differences between the asbestos and non-asbestos based equivalents that could make the products different as opposed to 'like'.[98] In this respect the AB agreed that although there is not scientific 'certainty' that asbestos is more harmful than other substitutes, the product could be banned to support reducing risk to human life or health, given that the scientific evidence they had received suggested that its use was not without risk.[99]

92 M. Footer & S. Zia-Zarifi, 'Case Notes European Communities – Measures Affecting Asbestos and Asbestos Containing Products, The World Trade Organisation on Trial for its Handling of Occupational Health and Safety Issues', 3 *Melbourne Journal of International Law*, 2002.

93 *European Communities – Measures Affecting Asbestos and Asbestos Containing Products*, op. cit. 90, para. 193.

94 *European Communities – Measures Affecting Asbestos and Asbestos Containing Products*, op. cit. 90, para. 168.

95 ibid.

96 *European Communities – Measures Affecting Asbestos and Asbestos Containing Products*, op. cit. 90, para. 122.

97 See G. Marceau & J.P. Trachtman, 'A Map of the World Trade Organisation Law of Domestic Regulation of Goods', in G.A. Bermann & P.C. Mavroidis, *Trade and Human Health and Safety*, Cambridge University Press, Cambridge, 2006, p. 18.

98 *European Communities – Measures Affecting Asbestos and Asbestos Containing Products*, op. cit. 90, para. 114.

99 *European Communities – Measures Affecting Asbestos and Asbestos Containing Products*, op. cit. 90, para. 168.

The interesting aspect of this ruling is that the burden of proof is firmly put on the exporting party to prove that their products are 'safe'.[100] The importing party is not under the pressure of proving that the imports are unsafe. This could again be interpreted as supporting the notion of the precautionary principle, stopping the flow of trade even when no threat has definitively been proved. This is unusual in the nature of the WTO, which would normally be considered to be more favourable towards unimpeded trade flows. With the burden of proof being put on the exporter, the AB has in effect given a greater emphasis for exemptions to the fundamental WTO rules under Article XX. Where there is scientific uncertainty the burden of proof will still remain with the importing party, putting the emphasis less on certainty and more on preferences and speculations as to the impact on a population or the environment.

This should be interpretable in the way that environment-related defences based on Article XX (b) will be judged on the basis of the needs of the population into which the good is being imported. Taking the outcome of the case and the ruling of the AB it is possible to state that the concept of like products was given a wide interpretation under the WTO, but if there is a distinguishing aspect of the product that is relevant to the protection of health or the environment (through plant and animal health) it can be differentiated and considered not 'like'. This is very important as a concept for the consideration of environmental issues under the WTO DSU. This decision should give national governments more flexibility when dealing with concerns over environmental protection and public health. This represents a considerable benefit for environmental health concerns in the WTO: the AB has shown through this decision that it will apply flexibility with regard to environmental issues in the dispute process under Article XX (b).

Article XX (b) also has a requirement that the measure is *necessary* to protect human, animal and plant life/health.[101] The use of the word 'necessary' is only found in three of the tests under Article XX (out of the ten exemptions that currently exist). Its use has been considered problematic as it is a relatively subjective concept.[102] Under GATT the necessity criterion had been interpreted very narrowly.[103]

In the US *Tuna-Dolphin* case the term had been defined to mean that a measure must be a measure that was reasonably available to a party and that

100 WTO, *WTO Analytical Index Guide to WTO Law and Practice*, 2nd edn, Vol. 1, Cambridge University Press, Cambridge, 2007, p. 284.

101 WTO, *The Legal Texts*, op. cit. 87.

102 B.J. Condon, op. cit. 89, pp. 9, 10 & 11.

103 M. Matsushita, T.J. Schoenbaum & P.C. Mavroidis, *The World Trade Organization: Law, Practice and Policy*, Oxford University Press, Oxford, 2004, p. 454; also see B.J. Condon, op. cit. 89, p. 11.

it was the least inconsistent with other GATT provisions.[104] This interpretation had previously been given in the consideration of a case under Article XX (d), which also utilises the term 'necessary'.[105] The interpretation of necessary under the *Tuna-Dolphin* case had been controversial – the panel stated that in finding against the measure adopted by the US 'the USA had not demonstrated that it had exhausted all options reasonably available to it to pursue its dolphin protection objectives, in particular through not negotiating international cooperative agreements'.[106]

This judgment therefore required an international negotiation element to ensure that a measure was necessary for the protection of animal life. This means that the GATT would require a negotiation to determine whether a measure was necessary. Clearly, this shows that the GATT has a narrow and complex formulation for determining the necessity of measures under Article XX (b).

The WTO AB has since interpreted *necessary* to mean *reasonably available*.[107] In the *EC-Asbestos* case the AB re-evaluated the interpretation that had been used, and gave it a less narrow and less trade-focused interpretation. This would be more consistent with the meaning of the words given their intended meaning in line with the Vienna Convention on the Law of Treaties, which requires words to be given their natural meaning in the context of the meaning and effect of the Treaty.[108]

The AB therefore essentially reversed the previous decisions and gave the opportunity for national governments to again consider relying on Article XX (b) for derogations from the fundamental principles of the WTO. The AB went on to state that WTO members have the right to determine the level of protection they feel is right for their domestic populations.[109] This would be based on qualitative (as explained above in relation to how socially acceptable a risk is) and quantitative judgments of the risk to health. When a member can demonstrate a common interest or value strongly linked to a product, a measure will be more likely to be considered 'necessary'.[110] In essence the AB simply applied the proportionality test that is widely

104 WTO, *United States – Restrictions on Imports of Tuna, Report of the Panel*, DS21/R – 39S/155, para. 4.4, p. 21, 3 September 1991.

105 WTO, *United States – Section 337 of the Tariff Act of 1930*, 7 November 1989, GATT BISD (36th Supp) 345, para. 5.26, 1990.

106 WTO, *United States – Restrictions on Imports of Tuna*, 30 *I.L.M.* 1598 (1992), para.5.28; see S. Cho, 'A Quest for WTO's Legitimacy', *World Trade Review*, Cambridge University Press, Cambridge, 4:3, 391–9, 2005, p. 396.

107 WTO, *Korea – Measures Affecting Imports of Fresh, Chilled and Frozen Beef*, Report of the Appellate Body, WT/DS169/AB/R, 11 December 2000, paras 159–85.

108 UN, Vienna Convention on the Law of Treaties, Treaty Series, Vol. 1155, 2005, p. 331: see Article 31.

109 *European Communities – Measures Affecting Asbestos and Asbestos Containing Products*, op. cit. 90, para. 168.

110 ibid.

considered in the jurisdictions of nations/regions such as the USA and the EU, especially in trade and environment disputes in those entities.[111]

Thus, the panel will now have the discretion to determine what a 'reasonably available' alternative is to the measure proposed by a member state. In the *EC-Asbestos* case, controlled use of asbestos was not a reasonable alternative as tested against the criterion laid down above. Again this tends to show that under Article XX (b) a wider interpretation will now be given to the measures that are being held as exceptions to the general WTO principles.

This assertion can be further supported by briefly assessing the ruling in the *Brazil-Tyres* case of 2007.[112] In this case the Brazilian government operated a ban on imported retreaded tyres on the basis that such tyres rapidly became waste and a fertile breeding ground for mosquitos which posed a public health threat. Brazil also claimed that disposing of so many waste tyres had environmental consequences. The EU objected to the ban as it is an exporter of retreaded tyres, claiming that the measure was simply a disguised restriction on trade – aimed at protecting the Brazilian domestic retreading industry. Brazil sought to rely on Article XX (b) as the grounds for the ban – on the basis of being necessary for protecting human, animal or plant life and health.

The panel and Appellate Body in reviewing the case agreed with Brazil that under Article XX (b) its ban was necessary to protect human health. The EU had contended that the measures were not 'necessary', instead the Appellate Body accepted the Panel's earlier ruling that the correct approach had been to weigh and balance factors and that as no reasonably available alternatives had been identified as suitable the ban was justifiable under Article XX (b).[113] Under Article XX (b) case law, a measure (in this case the ban) is 'necessary' only if there is no less trade-restrictive alternative reasonably available. This was the situation in this case. This ruling demonstrates that under Article XX (b) contracting parties may now have wider leeway to determine policies that are WTO compatible.

7.7 The chapeau of Article XX: tests for compliance

Once a measure satisfies the conditions set by paragraph (b) or (g) (or any other of the exceptions under Article XX), the chapeau is then considered by the panel or AB. This is the way in which the panels and the AB have developed their methodological approach to addressing disputes falling under the

111 That is put simply that the object should be pursued with proportional aims to the outcome. In criminal law this can be that the punishment should fit the crime.

112 WTO, *Brazil – Measures Affecting Imports of Retreaded Tyres*, WT/DS332/AB/R, 3 December 2007.

113 ibid.

exemptions of Article XX (b) and (g).[114] The chapeau contains three distinct 'tests' that also have to be applied to determine whether a measure can be legitimately based on Article XX.[115] The panel or AB will determine whether the measure is arbitrary discrimination, unjustifiable discrimination (these could be considered as one test) and whether the measure is a disguised restriction on international trade.[116]

The AB has put a great deal of emphasis on the tests of the chapeau and has described the chapeau as the test to equate the rights of member states to pursue their own national policies and maintain their obligations under the international trade regime to other countries.[117] In the *US Shrimp-Turtle* case, the AB made a number of references to the ultimate importance of the chapeau of Article XX when considering exemptions – as in the words of the AB, the chapeau protects the 'substantive and procedural requirements' of the WTO.[118] This means that the chapeau has a great significance attached to it by the AB in the application of the exemptions, and that even if a measure can pass the tests applied to the individual exemption clauses, it must also pass the ultimate test of the chapeau.

In that important case the AB also laid down other principles that the chapeau should be considered as protecting: that the chapeau qualifies the exemptions so that they are limited and conditional; that the chapeau is an expression of the principle of good faith in international law; and that ensures that the exemptions are reasonably applied by the member states.[119] This ruling can leave no doubt in the observer's mind that the chapeau is the major test for exemptions under Article XX.

It is arguable as to whether this is the correct application of the article – as demonstrated later in the section on *Environmental Criticisms of the Article XX Chapeau Tests* there are many commentators who do not agree with this reasoning.[120] However, from the perspective of trade professionals it can be seen that this is a reasonable approach balancing the principles of free trade against national differences. In the following paragraphs the three main tests will be examined in detail. (For the purposes of this chapter the issue of arbitrary or unjustifiable discrimination will be considered as one issue.)

114 See S.E. Gaines, 'The WTO's Reading of the GATT Article XX Chapeau: A Disguised Restriction on Environmental Measures', 22 *University of Pennsylvania Journal of International Economic Law*, 4, Winter 2001.

115 ibid., p. 824.

116 See *WTO Analytical Index Guide to WTO Law and Practice*, op. cit. 100; and 'General Agreement on Tariffs and Trade 1994', WTO website, http://www.wto.org/english/res_e/booksp_e/analytic_index_e/gatt1994_e.htm (accessed 24 January 2010).

117 *United States – Import Prohibition of Certain Shrimp and Shrimp Products*, op. cit. 80, para. 157.

118 ibid., para. 160.

119 ibid., see paras 157, 158 and 160.

120 S.E. Gaines, op. cit. 114.

7.7.1 *Tests to determine compliance of a measure with the WTO under the chapeau of Article XX*

Firstly, the issue of arbitrary or unjustifiable discrimination can be considered. The AB has deemed that it is not the measure or its specific contents that are questionable, but rather the manner in which it is applied.[121] To determine whether the measure is applied in an unjustifiable manner, two requirements have been identified by the panel and AB:[122] first, whether there has been a serious effort to negotiate the implementation of the measure with other members who may be affected; secondly, whether the measure is flexible – can similar measures be used as the measure being defended under Article XX exemptions? In the *US Shrimp-Turtle* case, the AB applied its tests to the US measure (requiring the use of TEDs for shrimp fishing) that had been enacted.

In assessing whether the US measure was consistent with the Article XX chapeau, the AB approved of the panel's approach of determining whether the US had undertaken any serious efforts to negotiate an international agreement for protecting sea turtles.[123] In this case the panel stated that the US would have been justified in its position if it had made such effort, therefore passing the test of avoiding application of a measure that unjustifiably discriminated against other member states. As it happened the US in this case had not made such efforts and the AB found that the measures did violate the criteria of the chapeau and were unjustifiable.

In paragraph 5.103 of the panel report on the *US Shrimp-Turtle* case it was concluded that members can use measures that limit access to their markets depending on whether the other member state in question has similar legislation in place.[124] This was qualified with the need to conduct good faith negotiations.[125] The approach of the US government in the *US Shrimp-Turtle* case was so displeasing to many governments because it was telling them what policy to pursue to export to the US market.[126] This also seemed to be the position of the panel – a member must justify policy choices by ensuring that good faith negotiations had taken place. Instead of this approach it has been contended that the panel infer that the US should have applied a condition that all shrimp products sold in the US meet certain standards – and this standard applies to the producers of the products rather

121 See WTO CTE, GATT/WTO Dispute Settlement Practice Relating to GATT Article XX, Paragraphs (b), (d) and (g), WT/CTE/W/203, 8 March 2002, pp. 23 and 24.

122 ibid.

123 *United States – Import Prohibition of Certain Shrimp and Shrimp Products*, op. cit. 80, para. 172.

124 WTO, *United States – Import Prohibition of Certain Shrimp and Shrimp Products*, Recourse to Article 21.5, Report of the Panel, WT/DS58/RW, 15 June 2001.

125 ibid.

126 See J.P. Kelly, op. cit. 57.

than the government.[127] These would be a product standard rather than a policy standard. However, there is always the danger these could be interpreted as a disguised restriction on trade.

The conditions would therefore be imposed on the producers and the government would not be in the position of being told what to do to enter the US market. It is possible that this approach may have upset the respective complainant governments less. This would of course be dependent on the relationship between the shrimp industry of the affected member state with its government, and the likelihood is that most governments would act to protect their own industries from any perceived disadvantage anyway. A further criticism of this argument would be that it also fails to protect all turtles, as it would only affect shrimp catching practices for the US market. Taking into account that the US is the largest consumer market for most products it is true that the practice of producers would be affected to a certain extent, but it is not necessarily the case that all shrimp catches would be in accordance with the US TED principle. Therefore, such an approach would not be an effective means to enact turtle protection globally.

Also it is a requirement that the member relying on Article XX discusses with other members to determine if they apply similar measures before acting in a discriminatory way.[128] This helps to determine if the exporting nation's government is applying a similar measure to that required by the importing country's regulations. If an exporting country claims to be applying a measure with the same policy goal, it is up to the importing country to demonstrate that the measure is in fact not equivalent to the domestic regulation.[129] This is the flexibility test that is applied to determine whether the measure is an unjustifiable or arbitrary discrimination taking place.

Therefore it is possible to determine through examining the *US Shrimp-Turtle* case, in relation to the tests for arbitrary or unjustifiable discrimination, that the AB applies a clear methodology in determining whether a measure is such a constraint. In the AB's opinion the measure in that case had been an arbitrary discrimination because the measure had been applied in a rigid and unbending manner.[130] This had been without consideration for the appropriateness of that measure in the exporting country. The manner in which the measure was applied in practice was also held to form part of the arbitrary discrimination, because the import authorities of the US in their certification for shrimp products did not comply with the standards of fairness and due process in a number of ways (including giving notice,

127 ibid.

128 *United States – Import Prohibition of Certain Shrimp and Shrimp Products*, op. cit. 80.

129 See WTO, *United States – Measure Affecting Imports of Woven Wool Shirts and Blouses from India*, Appellate Body Report, WT/DS/33/AB/R, 23 May 1997.

130 *United States – Import Prohibition of Certain Shrimp and Shrimp Products*, op. cit. 80, para. 177.

gathering necessary evidence and allowing importers the right to voice or raise concerns).[131]

In this regard the AB also noted that the application of exemptions should be conducted in compliance with the requirements of due process.[132] In determining the unjustifiable nature of the measure the AB had cited the requirement that the US programme be applied in the same manner in the third countries, irrespective of their situations.[133] The measure had also been required to be phased in by the third parties over different timescales, which would put more of a burden on some exporters than others (unnecessarily in the AB's opinion).[134] The failure to negotiate on global protection of turtles was the final fault of the US which allowed the AB to determine that the measure was unjustifiable.[135]

After this initial AB report, the US maintained its ban on shrimp products from some of the applicant countries, but revised its regulations to allow importation of shrimp products that were fished using other means to TEDs that did not harm turtles.[136] The US also entered into negotiations with the applicant countries on the preservation of marine turtles, and offered technical and financial assistance to support measures in those countries to sustain turtle populations.[137] When the US policy was tested at the WTO in 2001, the AB found that the newly enacted measures by the US had satisfied its original ruling and now with the above measures in force the measure was not considered to be an arbitrary or unjustifiable restriction on trade.[138]

Therefore the environmental measure will only pass the test of non-arbitrary or justifiable discrimination under Article XX if the above tests are met and proved.

Once these issues have been considered under the chapeau, the second issue to be reviewed is that of disguised restrictions on trade. Three criteria have been introduced in the workings of panels and the AB in the interpretation

131 *United States – Import Prohibition of Certain Shrimp and Shrimp Products*, op. cit. 80, para. 180.
132 ibid., para. 182.
133 ibid., para. 177.
134 ibid., para. 175.
135 *United States – Import Prohibition of Certain Shrimp and Shrimp Products*, op. cit. 80, para. 185.
136 WTO, *United States – Import Prohibition of Certain Shrimp and Shrimp Products*, Recourse to Article 21.5 of the DSU by Malaysia, WT/DS58/AB/RW, 22 October 2001, paras 146 and 147.
137 ibid., para. 134.
138 ibid., para. 152.

of Article XX with regard to the test for disguised restrictions on trade.[139] These are:

1. Has the measure been publicly announced?
2. Does the measure also amount to an arbitrary or unjustifiable discrimination?
3. An examination of the design, architecture and revealing structure of the measure at issue.[140]

These tests have been devised and developed by the WTO panels and the AB over a period of time.[141] Again, if these three tests in this context have not been met the measure at issue will be held to have failed the applicability tests of Article XX and the chapeau. Each panel and AB now reviews these tests to determine the applicability of the measure; this has developed into a formal process. The *EC-Asbestos* case paid particular attention to this issue in the field of trade–environment disputes.

At the time of the case the scope of the meaning of the term 'disguised restriction on trade' had not been clearly defined. Under the GATT 1947 the definition had been given some attention, and in the *US Spring Assemblies* case the following issues had been highlighted to determine what a disguised restriction was: it is a restriction that has not been taken in the form of a trade measure, and that had not been publicised before the measure took effect and had not been subject to an investigation.[142] In the *EC-Asbestos* case the panel made a detailed explanation of what they believed the phrase to mean:

> Referring also to the remark made by the Appellate Body in the same case [reference to *US-Gasoline*] according to which 'the provisions of the chapeau [of Article XX] cannot logically refer to the same standard(s) by which a violation of the substantive rule has been determined to have occurred', we consider that the key to understanding what is covered by 'disguised restriction on international trade' is not so much the word 'restriction', inasmuch as, in essence, any measure falling within Article XX is a restriction on international trade, but the word 'disguised'. In accordance with the approach defined in Article 31 of the Vienna Convention, we note that, as ordinarily understood, the verb 'to disguise' implies an *intention*. Thus, 'to disguise' means, in particular, 'conceal beneath deceptive appearances, counterfeit', 'alter so as to

139 WTO, *European Communities – Measures Affecting Asbestos and Asbestos-Containing Products*, Panel Report, WT/DS135/ R, 18 September 2000, paras 8.233–8.238.

140 ibid.

141 Both the *US-Gasoline* and *EC-Asbestos* cases considered these tests.

142 *European Communities – Measures Affecting Asbestos and Asbestos-Containing Products*, op. cit. 139, para. 8.233.

> deceive', 'misrepresent', 'dissimulate'. Accordingly, a restriction which formally meets the requirements of Article XX(b) will constitute an abuse if such compliance is in fact only a disguise to conceal the pursuit of trade-restrictive objectives.[143]

Therefore the phrase is to be given its literal meaning under the GATT and in that context it should be the case that only measures whose primary purpose is to restrict trade could be considered to be disguised restrictions.

As noted above, the test for a disguised restriction on international trade has evolved into three separate issues. The first of these is the determination as to whether any publicity had been made of the measure in the member state. In the *US-Canadian Tuna* case the panel looked at the literal implication of the publicity of a measure and determined in that case that as the US had stated that they were taking a measure against the import of Canadian tuna they had publicly announced such a measure.[144]

It is therefore a prima facie test. Thus, the first part of the test is a simple standard as to whether there has been a notification that was publicly available. Subsequently, in the *US-Gasoline* case, the AB stated that a concealed or unannounced restriction was not enough to simply determine whether a measure was a disguised restriction on trade under Article XX.[145] The AB believed that there were other elements to consider.[146] Further, in the *EC-Asbestos* case, the panel noted that (in reference to the *US-Gasoline* case), despite the fact that the French decree banning asbestos imports and exports had been publicly made, this was insufficient to determine whether the measure was indeed a disguised restriction on trade.[147]

The panel noted that if the simple publicity test were to be applied, the measure would already pass the test of the disguised restriction on trade.[148] The panel also noted that more than publicity was needed to determine the intention of the measure applied.

In the *US-Gasoline* case the AB had decided that there were other pertinent tests to take into account when considering whether a measure was a disguised restriction on trade. They stated that the test should also be to determine

143 ibid., para. 8.236.

144 GATT, *United States – Prohibition of Imports of Tuna and Tuna Products from Canada*, Panel Report, L/5198 – 29S/91, 22 February 1982, para. 4.8. It is worth noting that the Canadians rejected this interpretation of a disguised restriction to trade, considering that it was insufficient to suggest that simply by stating that a measure was being taken it was not 'disguised'.

145 WTO, *United States – Standards for Reformulated and Conventional Gasoline*, Appellate Body and Panel Report, WT/DS2/9, 20 May 1996, p. 25.

146 ibid. These were not formally elaborated, but the relationship with arbitrary or unjustifiable discrimination was referred to.

147 *European Communities – Measures Affecting Asbestos and Asbestos-Containing Products*, op. cit. 139, para. 8.235.

148 ibid., para. 8.234.

whether the application of a particular measure also amounts to an arbitrary or unjustifiable discrimination. The AB stated:

> 'Arbitrary discrimination', 'unjustifiable discrimination' and 'disguised restriction' on international trade may, accordingly, be read side-by-side; they impart meaning to one another. It is clear to us that 'disguised restriction' includes disguised *discrimination* in international trade (...). We consider that 'disguised restriction', whatever else it covers, may properly be read as embracing restrictions amounting to arbitrary or unjustifiable discrimination in international trade taken under the guise of a measure formally within the terms of an exception listed in Article XX.[149]

The AB equated the meaning of disguised restriction with the terms arbitrary and unjustifiable discrimination, stating that they give meaning to one another.[150] Therefore the term would be considered in a more broad sense and not simply as disguised restrictive practices, but also whether the measure is unjustifiable discriminatory practice.

This makes the test more stringent, as the need is to show not only that the measure has been published, but also that the measure is not a discrimination against other members' imports. This significantly tightens the definition. The panel in the *EC-Asbestos* case followed the ruling and logic of the AB in the *US-Gasoline* case:

> We recall that in *United States-Gasoline*, the Appellate Body considered that the kinds of considerations pertinent in deciding whether the application of a particular measure amounts to 'arbitrary or unjustifiable discrimination' may also be taken into account in determining the presence of a 'disguised restriction' on international trade.[151]

The panels and AB will now apply the same test to determine whether the disguised restriction is also an unjustifiable discrimination. This is also covered in the context of the overall chapeau requirements, but the application is the same.

Finally, the third test that has been included to determine whether the measure is a disguised restriction on international trade is that of whether the measure in its design, architecture or revealing structure has a

149 *United States – Standards for Reformulated and Conventional Gasoline*, op. cit. 145.

150 ibid.

151 *European Communities – Measures Affecting Asbestos and Asbestos-Containing Products*, op. cit. 139, para. 8.237.

protectionist aim.[152] This had first been introduced as a consideration in the *Japan Alcoholic Beverages* case.[153] The decision was taken into account in both the *US Shrimp-Turtle* case and the *EC-Asbestos* case. Indeed, in the *EC-Asbestos* case the panel referred to the methodology that had been employed by the AB in the *Japan Alcoholic Beverages* case, and recognised that it is difficult to assess the intention of a measure unless it is determined from its design, architecture or revealing structure.[154]

In that case the panel determined that from the design, architecture or revealing nature of the French Decree, there was nothing to suggest that it was a protectionist measure.[155] Likewise, in the *US Shrimp-Turtle* case the panel also examined the design, architecture and revealing nature of the measure and concluded that it was not a disguised restriction on trade.[156]

So, to pass the test of the chapeau the measure at stake must not be a disguised restriction on trade, nor should it be arbitrary or unjustifiable discrimination. Discrimination has a large part to play in the chapeau as it is also one of the criteria to determine the test of disguised restrictions. In relation to the environment the application of the tests has not been unfavourable, and there is now a great deal of transparency involved in the application of the chapeau, provided by the interpretations and tests set in place by panels and AB decisions since the inception of the WTO. This can only be a good development, as nations have a better idea of what they should do to ensure that their environment-related measures are in accordance with the requirements of the WTO agreement.

In the *Brazil-Tyres* case the AB also applied the tests of the chapeau of Article XX to the original decision that the ban on imported tyres from the EC was justified under Article XX (b).[157] For this the measure must not be an arbitrary or unjustifiable discrimination between countries or a disguised restriction on trade. In this case the AB found that the fact that Brazil was allowing imports from Mercosur countries whilst denying imports from the EC to constitute arbitrary and unjustifiable discrimination. This was because the imports were not coherent with the stated policy aim defended under Article XX (b). Brazil's defence was based on the ruling of the Mercosur tribunals, and the AB did not agree that this should lead to the imports being allowed. The WTO effectively overruled the Mercosur tribunal – though it

152 *European Communities – Measures Affecting Asbestos and Asbestos-Containing Products*, op. cit. 139.

153 WTO, *Japan – Taxes on Alcoholic Beverages*, Appellate Body Report, WT/DS8, 10, 11/AB/R, 4 October 1996, p. 31.

154 *European Communities – Measures Affecting Asbestos and Asbestos-Containing Products*, op. cit. 139, para. 8.236.

155 ibid., para. 8.238.

156 WTO, *United States – Import Prohibition of Certain Shrimp and Shrimp Products*, Recourse to Article 21.5 by Malaysia, Panel Report, WT/DS58/RW, 15 June 2001, para. 5.142.

157 *Brazil-Tyres*, op. cit. 112.

is not clear it would have done so if this had been a decision of an environmental treaty. The message coming through from this case has been clear – environmental and health policies will be protected, but not if they are applied in a discriminatory way. The result of the AB process has been hailed in environmental corners as balancing the interests of trade and environmental protection.[158]

It has been demonstrated that the WTO DSU interpretation of Article XX, both through the meanings attributed to the chapeau and the subsequent sub-paragraphs, has been developed by the panel/AB decisions into a more even-handed approach with regard to trade and environmental issues. Not only this, it also has been shown that there is a much more transparent approach to the interpretation of Article XX. Member states are now more certain as to the approach to take to adopt an environment-related measure that needs to be relied on as an exemption to the general WTO rules. Tests have been set and rulings explained so that future cases can have some certainty as to whether a measure may be allowed under Article XX. This is part of the process of the WTO enhancing its judicial competence and its involvement in national and international environment–trade-related measures.

The *US Shrimp-Turtle* case is a case of great importance for the trade–environment debate and it is arguably a well-reasoned case that has balanced the interests of national policies with the requirements of global trade.[159] The AB did not declare the unilateral action of the US illegal per se; they instead suggested ways in which making such a policy in a national context could be given life under the international legal regime.[160] In a way this could be interpreted as a guide by the WTO AB to the US administration on how to conduct their environmental policy.[161]

This raises questions of the jurisdiction of the AB and its competence to determine the best way to implement an environmental policy. The make-up of the AB would be crucial in deciding whether the AB has the necessary skills to make such decisions. Nevertheless, returning to the decision of the *US Shrimp-Turtle* case, the decision has allowed policy space for governments to enact environmental legislation that has an extra-territorial impact. To turn the original argument of the AB around, it would be possible to say that had due process been followed, and the US measure had taken into account

158 ICTSD, 'Brazil Tyres: Policy Space Confirmed under GATT Article XX', *WTO Cases*, Vol. 12, No. 1, February 2008.

159 See E.R. Desombre & J.S. Barkin, 'Turtles and Trade: The WTO's Acceptance of Environmental Trade Restrictions', 2 *Global Environmental Politics*, 12–18, 2002, p. 13.

160 For example, by suggesting that the regulations be applied in a uniform manner and that good faith international negotiations should take place.

161 The ruling has essentially given direction as to how to conduct environmental policy that is applied extra-territorially. The US taking this advice was then protected from further complaints from Malaysia in the Article 21.5 proceeding.

conditions in other countries, and if those countries had not been willing to negotiate in good faith on the issue of turtle preservation, the AB would have found that the US had done all that could reasonably have been expected of it, and therefore upheld the unilateral measures enacted by the US.[162]

This has been seen by some commentators as a heightening of the importance of the issue of 'good faith' and the AB's insistence that it is a fundamental principle of international law – suggesting that if a country refuses to enter into discussions about the depletion of resources beyond its national jurisdiction it would be in breach of 'good faith' allowing the adoption of unilateral measures by the other party.[163]

However, not all parties have been pleased with the development of the interpretation of Article XX by the AB in the *US Shrimp-Turtle* case.[164] In fact the AB interpretation has opened up schisms in a number of fields – some environmentalists are pleased with the new rulings, while others are concerned about the weight that has been placed on the interpretation of the chapeaux.[165] In this context the role of the chapeau is arguably of greater significance than the tests to be applied to the sub-paragraphs that are being relied on by parties, as this is the trade-oriented aspect of the Article. It is in many ways unsurprising that some environmentalists still attack this process of determination as inadequate protection for environmental-related measures.[166] But it should be considered that the result of the *US Shrimp-Turtle* case seems to balance the competing concerns in a reasonable manner.

Not only in the environmentalist interest group have there been divisions. Trade policy analysts have expressed some concern – and more importantly a number of developing country member states involved in the *Shrimp-Turtle* case expressed deep concerns – about the interpretation of the meaning of Article XX, and the potential for extra-territorial application of national environment–trade impacting measures resulting from that decision.[167] So, despite their victory, and in the case of Thailand a third party to the case whose practices were accepted by the USA, the developing countries felt that

162 A.H. Qureshi, 'Extraterritorial Shrimps, NGOs and the WTO Appellate Body', 48 *International and Comparative Law Quarterly*, 1, 1999, pp. 199–206, p. 205; and M. Matsushita, T.J. Schoenbaum & P.C. Mavroidis, op. cit. 84.

163 ibid., p. 459.

164 See S. Pyatt, 'The WTO Sea Turtle Decision', 26 *Ecology Law Quarterly* 815, 813 (1999); and S.E. Gaines, op. cit. 114.

165 ibid.

166 Many environmentalists are simply opposed to the notion of free trade and believe that global trade intrinsically harms people and the environment: see Friends of the Earth, 'What's Wrong With World Trade? An Introduction to the Trade and Sustainability Debate', Briefing, September 2005, http://www.foe.co.uk/resource/briefings/wrong_with_world_trade.pdf (accessed 24 January 2010).

167 J.P. Kelly, op. cit. 57; see also the comments of A. Mukerji, 'Developing Countries and the WTO: Issues of Implementation', 34 *Journal of World Trade*, 33, 2000, 51–3.

the AB had gone too far in its reasoning.[168] This can be seen in the light of the judicialisation of the dispute process in the WTO and the increased amount of weight that member states put on the outcomes of cases.

The devised rules as expounded by the AB do allow national environmental laws to take precedence over trade, and that will concern the member states who still value economic development as the main goal of their national policies. Given that the judicialisation of the WTO dispute process also implies a form of informal precedent, the concerns over the judgment for developing countries should be taken seriously. The effective interpretation of the Article XX tests, as demonstrated in the sections above, suggests that their policy space will be reduced in relation to third countries' environmental policies – as long as such countries pursue their environmental policies in accordance with the AB ruling. The position of the developing countries in relation to the AB decision in the case can be seen in contrast to the supposedly vanquished USA, who welcomed the report.[169]

Interestingly the new AB interpretation led Jackson to state that: 'Environmental interests have lost some battles, but have won the war in the WTO.'[170] This is supported in the sense that Article XX has been argued to have been given a transformation into an adequate tool for a balanced approach to the trade and environment controversy.[171] The concerns of the 'victorious' Asian countries should not be taken lightly. After all, the proper functioning of international agreements such as the WTO and MEAs depends upon the willing participation of all nations.

Malaysia was so indignant at the decision that it expressed its dissatisfaction in a formal recourse proceeding under Article 21.5 of the DSU.[172] This action stated, inter alia, that the import prohibition should have been removed entirely, not applied in a different manner.[173] This was supported by Thailand who officially stated: 'This decision permitted members to discriminate against products based on non-product related processes and production

168 See N.L. Perkins, 'Introductory Note: World Trade Organization: United States – Import Prohibition of Certain Shrimp and Shrimp Products', 38 *I.L.M.*, 1999, at 120 (citing D. Pruzin, 'Environment: WTO Formally Adopts Shrimp-Turtle Ruling as Thailand Fears Victory May Be Pyrrhic', 15 *International Trade Rep.* 1884 (BNA) (11 November 1998)). See also V. Ramangkura, 'Thai Shrimp, Sea Turtles, Mangrove Forests and the WTO: Innovative Environmental Protection under the International Trade Regime', 15 *Georgetown International Environmental Law Review*, 4, 2003, pp. 677–708.

169 WTO DSB, minutes of meeting, November 1998, WT/DSB/M/SO (14 December 1998).

170 M.W. Weinstein, 'Greens and Globalisation: Declaring Defeat in the Face of Victory', *NY Times*, 22 April 2001, S4, p. 18.

171 See A.H. Qureshi, op. cit. 162, p. 204; and M. Matsushita, T.J. Schoenbaum & P.C. Mavroidis, op. cit. 84, p. 456.

172 *United States – Import Prohibition of Certain Shrimp and Shrimp Products*, op. cit. 156.

173 *United States – Import Prohibition of Certain Shrimp and Shrimp Products*, op. cit. 156, paras 3.35–3.37 and 3.55–3.60.

methods (PPMs).' The statement went on to point out: 'This is a fundamental and impermissible alteration to the present balance of the rights and obligations of Members under the WTO Agreement.' And further: 'The Appellate Body under its own will, had altered the balance of rights and obligations under the WTO Agreement.'[174] India also stated: 'If the present decision of the Appellate Body were deemed applicable to future measures, then the door would be open to unilateral measures aimed at discrimination based on non-product related PPMs.'[175]

The recourse under Article 21.5 was also rejected by the AB who stated that the actions of the US were now in conformity with the ruling under the original AB decision.[176] This would further exacerbate the developing countries. These serious claims from the developing countries involved in the case show how fine the line is between differing interests of trade liberalisation and environmental protection and how it is handled under the auspices of the WTO and its DSU in particular, given the value attached to the decisions of the AB and to a lesser extent the panels.

The arguments around the outcome of the case also demonstrate the concern that can be raised by AB decisions, which are clearly felt (in a practical sense) to create a form of binding precedent and obligations on states. The statement made by India certainly reflects this mentality, raising concerns of the future application of the AB decision and its relationship to the previously sacrosanct principles around PPMs.[177] This recognises the power of an AB decision to set up a new interpretation of a principle that will be relied on in the future by member states.

7.7.2 *Environmental criticisms of the chapeau of Article XX tests*

It must also be remembered that not all commentators with an environmental interest are satisfied with the new interpretation of Article XX.[178] Gaines has produced detailed work on the issue of the new interpretation of Article XX, stating that the new generous interpretation of Article XX (b) and (g) has been thwarted by an '*eye of the needle*' test with regard to the chapeaux of Article XX.[179] He states: 'The environmental interests lost important battles that leave the war far from won.'[180] This position is supported by the

174 WTO DSB, op. cit. 169, p. 4.
175 ibid., p. 10.
176 WTO, *United States – Import Prohibition of Certain Shrimp and Shrimp Products*, Recourse to Article 21.5 of the DSU by Malaysia, Report of the Appellate Body, WT/DS58/AB/RW, 22 October 2001, paras 153 & 154.
177 WTO DSB, op. cit. 169, p. 10.
178 S. Gaines, op. cit. 59.
179 ibid.
180 ibid., p. 743.

contention that the flawed arguments of earlier cases condemning unilateral measures regarding environmental protection under Article XX (b) and (g) have been transferred from the interpretation of the sub clauses to the interpretation of the chapeau,[181] thus ensuring that environmental measures will still fall foul of the DSB rules (though the contention here remains that the tests have given a much greater transparency to the process).

However, on a close examination, in the *US Shrimp-Turtle* case the AB put a large amount of emphasis on the behaviour of the US in relation to finding a multilateral agreement on the protection of turtles.[182] The AB believed that the principles in the chapeau required that the US needed to do this, and therefore to meet the requirements of Article XX the US needed to act in this manner. This suggests that the AB recognised the value of protecting turtles, not just the value of trade for the affecting countries. This suggests a greater openness to the needs of the environment as understood by AB panel members.

Despite the high level of cynicism from some environmentally minded commentators and the criticism of some developing countries of the use of Article XX, particularly the chapeau and sub clauses (b) and (g), the position argued here is that the new AB rulings and processes, coupled with the stated environmental interests of the WTO, have enabled the DSB to take a meaningful role in serious discussions of environmental issues within the WTO. Even Gaines accepts that the recourse panel report 'takes some of the hard edges off the panels' conclusions ... that limits some of the damage to (the use of) Article XX'.[183] This is still tempered with criticism that the pre-conditions apparent before a member can apply Article XX for environmental measures are extraordinary, due to the role of the chapeau in the tests of a measure.[184]

Notwithstanding, this must be seen in the terms of the stated aims of the WTO and the primacy of Articles I and III (MFN and national treatment). These are the main focus of all WTO undertakings and member states are aware of this at the time they join the WTO; the actions of the AB in the *US Shrimp-Turtle* case are therefore all the more worthy of note in their appreciation of environmental protection necessities.

The WTO dispute settlement process seems to have improved the consideration of environmental matters in its dispute settlement process. The *US Shrimp-Turtle* case is a balanced decision and sets out tests just as any court would do. This helps national decision makers for future environmental interventions and introduces a degree of certainty in the process of undertaking such environmental measures. This can be seen to be the start of the

181 ibid.

182 *United States – Import Prohibition of Certain Shrimp and Shrimp Products*, op. cit. 168, paras 115–52.

183 S. Gaines, op. cit. 59, pp. 744–5.

184 ibid.

incorporation of environmental procedures and policies into the DSB forum: through its work, and the informal precedent effect, it is likely that more processes for dealing with trade–environmental measures will be developed in the WTO in the future as cases arise.

7.8 Conclusion

Given the far reaching nature of the areas brought to the DSB, the working of the DSB needs to be as effective as possible, and this is true for trade–environment disputes. The WTO system represents a highly evolved international dispute resolution system, with developed processes and reasoning that can be applied to create a level of certainty. Shortcomings of the system have been recognised – certainly with regard to environmental disputes – but with minor amendments to Article XX, and a review of the composition of the dispute panel, the WTO should become highly effective in dealing with all environmental disputes.

The aim of any alteration to the DSU would be to make the WTO more effective in addressing the disputes that arise in relation to international/national environmental protection and trade measures. This would have an impact on the larger international/national environmental policy decisions that are being made, given the influence of the WTO DSU.

This will create a forum for trade–environment disputes to be solved with far-reaching effect, given the reliance put by members on decisions. There is certainly hope that the DSB could evolve to this level of effective ruling given the outcome of the *Shrimp-Turtle* case.

Indeed, if the WTO is to develop further competence in environmental matters, one of the areas of potential reform could be under Article XX, giving greater status to the environment in general. This could mean that inherently there should be an environmental expert on panels considering issues relating to Article XX exemptions under (b) and (g), especially if the party defending its action is citing broad environmental concerns for the measure under dispute. At the present time such a requirement, or even an option, does not exist. Instead, the cases are determined by trade experts examining the measure in light of the relevant trade law under consideration.

If the WTO were to diffuse accusations of lack of environmental awareness and competence in decision making, it is in this area that reform could be proposed. A more balanced panel may make operations smoother and less controversial for the consideration and outcome of measures relating to the environment in the DSU. For example, a contention for Article XX (b) and (g) cases would be that the panel should automatically be five-person – comprising two relevant trade experts and two environmental science/policy experts, with an experienced diplomatic chair to oversee the dispute resolution process.

This could be a reform that could improve the operation of the panel when dealing with environmental protection issues, at least to provide a more balanced discussion of issues and ensure an outcome in line with both environmental and trade legal norms. The criticism that has been levelled at the WTO in relation to the environment usually concerns the failure of the panel to take into account environmental considerations. This argument would be seriously undermined with a simple reform as outlined above.

Every court of justice looks to improve the quality of its decisions, and the WTO DSU should be no different. With the WTO voluntarily, or involuntarily, extending its remit beyond trade and classic trade disputes, it is now necessary to examine the possibility of such a reform.

Conclusion

This work has outlined the impact of the judicialisation of WTO decision making on member states' behaviour, and has also echoed the commentators who recognise the existence of an informal precedent resulting from this judicialisation. Applying this to the field of trade and environment, it can be seen that the WTO influences environmental policy at both international and national levels.

This study reinforces the notion that the WTO has a powerful role to play in setting trade policy in the global context. The development of a judicialised dispute settlement body has had far-reaching effects in the international law and policy arena. Through the transition of the dispute system from the more arbitrational GATT format to the more court-like WTO process, the decisions and rules suggested and made in dispute resolution by the WTO panellists carry weight. This in turn has led to reliance being placed on the decisions of WTO panels by the member states, as to how they should act in policy fields to be in accordance with international trade law. Thus, the informal precedent of the decisions of the WTO AB has strong influence over the actions of member states.

This is not limited to trade policy, but has wider implications. The focus here has been on environmental concerns, but the WTO rulings impact fiscal policy, social policy, as well as other areas of political decisions.[1] This can be seen as an extension of the powers of the WTO beyond the traditional trade sphere and an unintended consequence of the active and intelligent rule making of the AB and the panels. The WTO has not developed formal methods for addressing these concerns within the text of the agreements, but through informed decision making at ministerial meetings and application of developed jurisprudence the WTO has come to gain competence in some

1 The WTO has made rulings in the *Foreign Sales Corporation Tax* case and the *Offshore Gambling* case that impact nations' abilities to use fiscal policy and influence social policy.

areas – notably the environment.[2] However, this competence needs to be enhanced to improve decision making and external perceptions.

The decisions of the AB under the DSU have come to stand as important indicators for member states to the WTO in their policy choices. The impacts of the decisions of the AB also go beyond the confines of trade issues and influence behaviour of member states in other areas, such as the environment. The *Shrimp-Turtle* case is a good example of how the AB decided how the US should approach its desire to conserve sea turtle populations.[3]

This poses serious questions as to whether the WTO AB is a place with sufficient competency to deal with environmental policy decisions. Indeed the WTO itself recognises the need to develop further jurisprudence in such areas.[4] Therefore it is important for the WTO and its member states to determine how best they should grow within these challenging areas. The interest in trade–environment cases remains great and the WTO has been criticised for its role by many commentators. The impact of a judicialised and active dispute resolution system has a major part to play in this discussion as the AB decisions are those that attract most attention from WTO commentators.

So how does this relate to the way the WTO DSU reviews cases with environmental protection issues involved? There have been long-standing concerns about the GATT and the way environmental issues have been dealt with. These, it appears, have been transferred to the WTO.[5] In fact the relative success of the WTO DSU in creating a more effective/efficient process has caused criticism by environmentalists.[6] The fact that there is no opportunity to block the creation of a panel, a panel report, an AB report and retaliation by a disagreeing member, means that the decision of an AB becomes 'law' in international trade. This is especially true given that informal precedent is in existence at the WTO.

As panel reports can no longer be blocked by a losing member, national laws cannot be protected from WTO DSB scrutiny, and therefore national environmental laws that impact international trade are open to international scrutiny through the WTO DSB. The negative consensus rules do have an effect on trade–environmental protection cases as it is more likely the outcomes of disputes will be adopted by the member states. The effect on both international and national environmental law is potentially far-reaching

2 The creation of the CTE and the development of an understanding of the interaction of trade and environment in AB decisions can be seen as examples of this.

3 P. Sutherland et al., *The Future of the WTO: Addressing Institutional Challenges in the New Millennium*, WTO Publications, Geneva, 2005, p. 53.

4 ibid.

5 See *Dispute Settlement in the WTO: A Crisis for Sustainable Development*, WWF, Switzerland, 1998.

6 ibid.

and has generated the fear that conflict could arise between environmental and trade agreements at global level.

As of yet there has been no conflict between the WTO DSB and an MEA, but it is possible such a situation could arise. The WTO could be described as making a concerted effort to avoid such a situation.[7] Nevertheless fears exist that the WTO DSB, backed by the application of powerful enforcement mechanisms in the case of non-compliance, could eventually rule on an MEA that uses trade restrictions for effectiveness. Certainly the GATT made decisions on cases relating to the environment to unpopular effect, but few of these were adopted by the parties. Therefore these decisions did not enter the acquis of the WTO.

The WTO, with its recognition of environmental protection and sustainable development, appears to be trying to avoid such repeats. However, with just slight reforms of the WTO DSU the potential for such WTO–MEA conflicts could be significantly reduced. The issue could be addressed through the interpretation of Article XX of the GATT.

This is important in the context of the notion of judicialised decision making under the DSU, as the WTO dispute results carry the weight of future expectation of the member states, the wording expressed therein being relied on through informal precedent in the actions of member states. WTO practice has expanded the scope of the operations of the WTO beyond simple trade activities. Outlined below are some of the key findings of this study and the accompanying recommendations for potential institutional change that can engender a better sense of WTO competency in areas beyond trade that come into contact with the global trading system.

Reforms of the WTO system

There have been many articles, theses and books written about the WTO dispute settlement system and the need for reform, but there has been little attention paid to reviewing how the current set-up of certain aspects of the agreements under the WTO framework can be re-applied to other agreements to make a more consistent whole within the WTO. Indeed, the WTO agreements may hold the keys themselves to addressing some of the challenges that arise with conflicts between policy needs in the trade and environmental fields. It appears that the WTO and its constituent member states are aware of the fact that trade cannot be taken in isolation, so it must therefore take account of other policy areas such as the environment.[8]

7 N. Singh, 'Trade Related Environmental Measures in Multilateral Environmental Agreements and the WTO: Irreconcilable Differences?', *American Journal of Economics and Business Administration*, 2009, 1(3), 249–54.

8 The creation of the CTE and the granting of its permanent status in the Doha Round of negotiations confirm this view.

As argued in this book, through the working of informal precedent the decisions taken by the panel/AB provide greater certainty that the cases relating to environmental protection, such as the *Shrimp-Turtle* case, will in the future be resolved with greater environmental awareness. Indeed the *Shrimp-Turtle* case can be seen to be the final evolution of a chain of decisions starting in *Tuna-Dolphin I*, with each case becoming more sensitive to the need to balance trade with environmental objectives.

However, the contention is tempered by the knowledge that certain reforms of the DSB would be a further guarantor of balancing trade and environmental concerns more effectively. There are reforms that would improve the DSB operation to better consider environmental disputes. As stated above, the WTO can use the provisions of its agreements to find solutions to some of the challenges it faces in the environmental field. The reforms suggested below would be a good start for the member states to consider when reviewing the functioning of the WTO and its dispute resolution processes:

1 Inclusion of environmental lawyers/scientists/experts on panels as a matter of course if environmental issues are to be addressed by a panel/AB. This is not yet expressly stated as a right of a member state to request such a person. Yet, in the case of developing countries' concerns being handled, there is a right for a panel member to contain a panellist from a developing country. Therefore, applying a similar principle with minimal need for reform could be a way of improving competency when panels address environmental issues.
2 A widening of GATT Article XX (b) and (g) so that environmental protection is expressly stated – as it is in the TBT agreement. However, this would be difficult as it would take a full re-writing of Article XX and approval by a ministerial conference. Though it should be noted that the WTO is capable of making such a radical move and does indeed occasionally amend its agreements.
3 Alternatively, the AB could expressly state that the environment is covered by the article in one of its decisions. A bold statement to recognise that environmental protection is covered by Articles XX (b) and (g) would be as effective as a change to the Agreement itself. This is due to the nature of the reliance by member states on AB decisions; this would then be accepted through the informal precedent system present in the WTO.
4 There could also be some consideration of including specific wording about the relationship between the WTO and MEAs. This could possibly take the form of a clear legal statement by WTO member states, that disputes arising from provisions in MEAs will be settled under the dispute resolution procedures of the MEA concerned first, before redress to the WTO. This could be made under the auspices of a recommendation from the CTE and this would also strengthen the perception of

the CTE as an authoritative body on trade and environmental issues. Of course, this would not solve the problem of a non-MEA WTO member bringing a dispute to the DSB in the WTO. Thus in such a circumstance there could be further exploration of the possibility for the WTO to look at working on such a dispute in co-operation with the secretariat of the MEA in question, should the MEA have a suitable functioning secretariat. Again, a statement from the workings of the CTE on this could enhance its own standing as a body for dealing with trade–environment issues. This would help to ensure a consistent outcome that would not undermine either trade or environmental international law. This may be a discussion that is further from being resolved, given the interest of many member states to see MEA provisions being kept separate from the WTO.

5 An increase in the role of the CTE in the DSB process when environmental cases are being considered under Article XX or the GATS, SPS or TBT agreements. The Secretariat could have a formal advisory role to panels as to who should be called for evidence purposes. There has been very little use of the CTE in the area of environmental disputes; only one member state has ever raised an environmental policy dispute in the CTE. It could be possible for the CTE to have a potential role by acting as an arbitration centre before a formal complaint is lodged. This would be highly informal, but would allow the CTE to gain more influence in dealing with trade and environment disputes. The CTE could also have a formal role of advising the panel and AB when environmental issues are being considered. This would need to be included in the rights and obligations of the CTE and would formally be recognised under its activities. At the present time it is up to the panellists to decide who should be called to give evidence; there is no formal role for the CTE Secretariat. The CTE would then play a proactive role in the advising of panels and the AB on environmental matters. This would be especially in relation to other international agreements so that MEAs would not be undermined, and co-ordination would be enhanced.

6 A strengthened role for the CTE in implementing committees would also give a greater consideration of environmental issues in the implementation of the WTO. Here the member states need to agree to give the CTE a greater role than its current largely political role. However, the CTE could also proactively increase its influence by making more recommendations to implementing committees. Now that the Doha agenda has given particular powers to the CTE it should be looking to improve its own standing.

7 Another reform of potential benefit for the WTO would be to consider access for third parties in the style of that offered by NAFTA under the North American Agreement on Environmental Cooperation (NAAEC). This would possibly lead to an improved perception of the operations of the WTO dispute settlement procedure; from a point of view of law

making it could also enhance decision making. The NAAEC allows individual redress through Articles 14 and 15 for states' environmental behaviour, and whilst this is unlikely to be entirely possible through the WTO dispute resolution process a similar system could be explored. It could be possible for citizens' groups to be given standing to present cases where trade rules are having negative impacts on the environment in member states. Criteria and rules would need to be examined, but even the discussion of such an idea would offer the WTO a chance to enhance its environmental credentials.

8 An interesting call could also be to alter the remit of Article XX (b) by changing the wording from 'necessary to' protection of plant life, etc. Replacing the 'necessary to' with 'relating to' would improve the scope of the application of the Article, as it is accepted that these phrases imply different standards of rigour.[9] Whilst this could be said to have been achieved to some extent (a wider understanding of 'necessary' through the *EC-Asbestos* case), actually making the formal change could stop some of the ill-judged litigation and disappointment from parties who have legitimately disagreed with such an interpretation. In fact in Article XX (g) the term used is 'relating to', so there is a precedent for using this terminology in Article XX. Together with the inclusion of an explicit mention of the environment in Article XX, much of the confusion could be cleared. These are relatively low-hanging fruit for the WTO to consider, and would require a relatively limited amount of political will.

9 Related to point 7 above, general inclusion of reference to the term 'environment' in GATT Article XX, the SPS Agreement and GATS Article XIV could be a means to allow greater consideration of general environmental protection issues in the WTO dispute resolution system.

10 The member states could also consider the possibility of a trade-related environmental measures agreement being concluded under the WTO. This would encompass the issues above, but provide a clear recognition of how the WTO would interact with environmental concerns, including MEAs. This may be more difficult to assure than some of the other options outlined above, as political will among the member states may not yet favour clear environmental rules in the umbrella of the WTO agreements.[10]

9 B.J. Condon, 'GATT Article XX and Proximity-of-Interest: Determining the Subject Matter of Paragraphs (b) and (g)', *UCLA Journal of International Law and Foreign Affairs*, Vol. 9, 2004, pp. 137–62.

10 R. Rajesh Babu, 'Trade and Environment Interface: Implications on Developing Country's Trade', Essays on Contemporary Issues in International Law, Centre for Research and Training, AALCO, New Delhi, 2009.

These suggestions would enhance the operation of the WTO, through the CTE, TBT, SPS, GATS and Article XX, with regard to the environment, and would further address remaining concerns of environmentalists regarding the operation of the AB and panels when considering trade–environment disputes.

Indeed, the changes proposed could be made wider and include more fields – if the political will were available. For example, calls for the introduction of labour standards into the WTO could be included in the exemptions of Article XX through this method of using practice and language from one WTO agreement and placing it in another. Related to the environmental field, calls have been made to include animal welfare as another category under Article XX (b).[11]

Other options for redressing the dangers of potential conflict between the environment and trade have been put forward. Esty has called for a Global Environmental Organisation and there is a movement for an International Environmental Court.[12] It is contended that these organs would promote the protection of the global commons and realign international interests in trade to provide protection for MEAs. It is important to consider that these options such as an International Environmental Court or a Global Environmental Organisation would require huge amounts of political will and money to create, and could risk locking global institutions in long-running disputes with one another. In the present global economic situation it seems unlikely that the will to provide the required support exists.

Therefore, these options are not necessarily models for success in terms of improving the progression of global rule making. Efficiency of the existing institutions is a much more cost-effective means of achieving equally desirable outcomes. It is also contended here that the political will and capital to finance such projects is not likely to be forthcoming at any point in the near future. Therefore, in practical terms it is better to consider the reforms of existing institutions, such as the WTO, that could be achieved, which would improve the operation of the global decision-making process on trade and the environment. These are outlined above for the WTO.

Returning to the WTO and its agreements, it is important to assess where the agreements have something to offer for environmental protection. This is challenging given that the main tool utilised and focused on in the trade–environment debate has been Article XX of the GATT. The exceptions rule

11 P. Stevenson, 'The World Trade Organisation Rules: A Legal Analysis of Their Adverse Impact on Animal Welfare', Compassion in World Farming, available on the EC Trade website, http://trade.ec.europa.eu/doclib/docs/2005/april/tradoc_122188.pdf (last accessed 7 February 2010).

12 D.C. Esty, 'From Local to Global: The Changing Face of the Environmental Challenge', *SAIS Review* 26, No. 2, Johns Hopkins University Press, Washington D.C., 2006, pp. 191–197; and see the Coalition for an International Court for the Environment campaign website, http://www.environmentcourt.com/welcome.php (accessed 7 February 2010).

under the SPS and GATS agreements are as of yet untested in relation to environmental issues. The *EC-Hormones* case is as close to an 'environmental' dispute considered under the SPS agreement. In this case the AB did rule in favour of the measure taken as it was not a disguised restriction on international trade nor did it result in discrimination.[13]

It is likely that if cases were to be raised under these particular WTO agreements the definition applied to Article XX (b) and (g) would be cited. It can only be hoped that if and when such cases do arise the principles of informal precedent relating to the interpretation of Article XX will be applied to these agreements. Again it would be beneficial to see the term 'environment' inserted into the SPS agreement and GATS Article XIV.

Issues for the future

This study contributes to the well of knowledge that is being built on the subject, but does not complete the search for solutions to resolving the potential abrasion between trade and environment. Concrete ideas are offered here for improving the current status quo, but the need for more work in the area remains.

One such issue that would lend itself to further research is an empirical study into the workings of precedent in the WTO. Identifying the number of cases that have been distinguished or departed from would be a good point to reinforce the notion of precedent in the WTO's DSB decisions. To date this study does not appear to have been completed. This is something that has broader application than the trade and environment debate, but one in which, nevertheless, the outcomes would have strong implications for trade and environmental policy in the international arena. Many commentators have discussed whether precedent exists or not in the actions of the WTO, with many agreeing that some form does exist, but an empirical study of the cases since 1995 would shed further light on this vital phenomenon.

In the trade–environment debate particularly, the work on the trade–MEA dispute scenario also needs to be complemented with further research on the likelihood of specific mention of MEAs being made in the WTO Agreement. This in turn could play a part in a bigger debate about the institutional change that can occur in the WTO, and the difficulties associated with making changes to the WTO agreements. Equally the research could also be included within a study on the possibility of a formal WTO Environmental Related Aspects of Trade Agreement being agreed by the member states. This would seem also to be a way to avoid the need for a Global Environmental Organisation or an International Environmental Court to resolve trade-related disputes in environmental fields.

13 WTO, Appellate Body report, *EC Measures Concerning Meat and Meat Products (Hormones)*, WT/DS48/AB/R, 1998, para. 246.

This work offers solutions for immediate problems in a pragmatic way, with the intention of remaining realistic in assessment of what is possible now. However, there are aspects around this work that can be explored further to develop the ideas espoused here.

To sum up, the evidence is clearly outlining that the WTO possesses a strong dispute resolution system that is effective and seen by member states as an indication of policy options and opportunities. It is a reliable forum for trade disputes to be resolved. It has also grown in competence to deal with other issues, such as the environment, but this is just the beginning. Further actions need to be taken and decisions made by the member states. Enhancements to the DSU and Article XX would drive this competence further forward – this is entirely plausible and a more realistic option in the current global scenario than other alternatives calling for separate and new institutions. This proposition is supported by institutional development theory that takes account of the fact that institutions develop and adapt to the environment within which they operate.[14]

The current social value that is put on the environment makes it more likely that such changes should occur. Therefore, the WTO can be seen to be developing and adapting to its global situation and, indeed, over time, its decisions and attitude towards the environment has changed. The further amendments proposed here would be the next steps in the incorporation of environmental competence in the WTO. It is clear that the WTO is developing its competence beyond trade and that in time it will be able to improve its dealing with such issues, provided that further institutional reforms are undertaken as suggested here.

14 See W.R. Scott, 'Institutional Theory: Contributing to a Theoretical Research Programme', in K.G. Smith & M.A. Hitt, *Great Minds in Management: The Process of Theory Development*, Oxford University Press, Oxford, 2005.

Index

Page numbers in **Bold** represent figures.